1794: Janie Miller's Whiskey Rebellion Saga

by
Anna T. Connor
and
Laura Connor Zajdel

Illustrated by Laura Connor Zajdel

First Edition

Published by Laura Connor Zajdel
203 Old Oak Road
McMurray, PA 15317

Printed in the United States of America
March 1994

Under an arrangement with:

Mathews Printing
2202 Liberty Avenue
Pittsburgh, PA 15222

ISBN 0-9640994-0-3

To the Oliver Miller Homestead Associates—
a unique organization of volunteers who adhere to
the frontier philosophy of working together and who
keep the heritage of the old stone house alive.

And,
to our husbands—
John C. Connor and Daniel Zajdel—
your vision, support and encouragement
made this project possible.

ACKNOWLEDGMENTS

The authors would like to thank the following people for their assistance and help in compiling research:

Mr. Harold R. Philips
Mr. Noah Thompson
Mrs. Alice Balliard
Mr. A.D. White
Mrs. Jo McCully
Miss Margaret Gilfillan
Miller Family Descendants of Oliver and Mary Miller:
    Mrs. Edna Miller Maits
    Mr. Elmer Aggers
    Mr. Preston Wolfe
    Miss Nancy Carmichaels
    Mr. William Barton
    Mr. Harold Wright
Mrs. Martha Hile
Mrs. Ruth Valentine
Miss Sally Lickovich and Mrs. Dorothy Lickovich
Mrs. Warren Shuck
Miss Amy Connor
Mr. John C. Connor
Mr. Daniel J. Zajdel

CONTENTS

PREFACE

It was the Summer of 1933 that I first remember seeing the old stone house. I was ten years old the day my mother packed a picnic lunch and took my sisters and I by streetcar to South Park. We walked from the car stop for what seemed many miles to a lovely grove with two large ponds surrounded by rocks. In the midst of our swim, I glanced down through the trees, then stopped to look again. There in the distance was a very old house. I felt drawn to the place—as if I were momentarily living in the past. I wondered who lived in such an old, old house.

Mother took me by the hand and we walked down the path to get a closer look, but the doors were locked and the house appeared empty. Mother stooped down to pick a snippet of mint near the door. "Ann, I'm sure this house has stood here for a long, long time. If only these stones could speak, what a wonderful story they could tell." She crushed the mint leaves in her fingers and shared the fragrance with me. "Maybe some day you'll learn the history of the people who lived here. Maybe some day . . ."

Years passed. After college, after teaching, I moved to Bethel Park and began a family life with my husband John and daughter Laura. We were not too far from the old stone house which was called the 'Stone Manse,' according to a sign placed by Allegheny County. It was indeed an old house, I learned. One stone section dated back to 1808, the other to 1830. The stone dwelling was on the original site of Oliver Miller's two-story, split-shingle log house.

I began to assemble a patchwork of family histories, stories, and events which gave new meaning to my personal understanding of frontier history. Membership at Bethel Church, work on church history, and formation of a church historical room led to hours of research and contact with people interested in Western Pennsylvania history. Many of them were descendants of the early settlers of the area. I admired the stern dignity, religious faith, and hard work that characterized the day to day life of these pioneers.

After three years of working with some dedicated volunteers, it was obvious that the 'Stone Manse' was falling into disrepair. The building, part of the Allegheny County park system, was being used as a stop-over by county maintenance workers. We were concerned about the misuse of the historical house and also came to realize that the title 'Stone Manse' was a misnomer. (During November, 1775, long before there was any permanent meetinghouse in the vicinity, Rev. John McMillan visited the Millers and conducted one of the earliest recorded religious services on the frontier. He also baptized several children.) So although the gathering was considered to be the roots of the local Presbyterian church, the building had never been a minister's home, or 'manse.' It was the home of the Oliver Miller family who had followed a tributary of Peter's Creek up from the Monongahela River, claimed the land, and lived there through five generations.

vii

We felt strongly that preserving the history of the Miller family had much to do with preserving the heritage of the area. A letter was written to the county requesting permission to change the name Stone Manse to the Oliver Miller Homestead and to organize a group which would write a correct history of events there and provide care and programming for the homestead.

On January 22, 1973, a miracle happened. With the permission of Allegheny County, a volunteer group of especially talented people was officially formed. The old doors were unlocked, the floors were scrubbed, and the cobwebs pushed away. When the first of many visitors arrived, they were greeted by volunteer guides dressed in authentic frontier garb. Soon a complete inventory of the furnishings was made. Items inappropriate to the early history of the family were weeded out and a new historical brochure was published about the Millers. We were delighted the day the park replaced the 'Stone Manse' sign with a new one marked 'Oliver Miller Homestead.'

Each year our organization has grown in knowledge, research, and further contacts. Presently we have members who are experts on antiques, period dress, lace, weaving, leatherworking, country fiddling, open hearth cooking, etc. We have learned from each other, from fellow historical buffs, and from the many guests who have visited the old homestead.

In 1974, when my daughter and I formed a partnership to write a book on historical cornhusk craft, we became more and more involved in Western Pennsylvania history. During our research, we read through many dry, out-of-print tomes about the "Whiskey Insurrection." Doddridge, Brackenridge, Neville's proponents, even George Washington, left detailed written accounts of the time. Since it was all in black and white, we tended to accept the information as fact - and much of it was true. However, under close comparison, widely diverging opinions emerged from these books, depending on the politics of the author. Very little was written to explain the dilemma of the farmers.

Further research into county courthouses, diaries, wills, surviving relatives of the Oliver Miller family, deeds, ledgers, and other existing legal papers showed some errors and fact twisting on the part of these early authors. For example, several accounts have Oliver Miller, Senior (actually deceased twelve years before the 'rebellion') getting killed during the first gunfire on Bower Hill. Other accounts name the victim as his son Oliver. Recent research has proven that the slain Oliver Miller was actually Oliver Senior's grandson.

After much cross-checking of written texts with existing documents, many taped interviews with elderly citizens of the area, and considerable research into non-political books on frontier life, we began to glean out the color in a rugged, but dramatic time in our history.

This book is written to share with all—now and in future years, the heritage of the frontier families of Western Pennsylvania. Their willingness to make do, their dignity despite hardships, their sense of concern, and sharing of time and talent should inspire us all to meet the problems of today in similar spirit. We hope our care for historical detail and accuracy will be apparent in the real lives of these people. Now we will let the old house come alive to tell us the true happenings of the Miller family.

March 5, 1994   Anna T. Connor

I

MANSFIELD

Time is but the stream I go a-fishing in.
Its thin current slides away, but eternity remains.

—*Walden,*
Henry David Thoreau

From the top of our Orchard Hill, the green earth rises and falls gently in every visible direction. Why, hundreds of small streams must glide around these tree-infested mounts just like Mansfield Run. Strange how I've never considered them before. Then, my child thoughts were of the traces, runs, and haunts that were familiar territory. That was a big enough world for me and surely all streams must eventually wend their way to Catfish Run[1] and the wide valley bottom that was my home.

Even after all my years away, a quick look around stirs up vivid reminders of the plain and extraordinary happenings of my young life. To my back, the ground rolls on and on to a huge hill—rounded off at the crest. Jutting up from this plateau are some fallen log timbers and parts of an old chimney. These remnants of Uncle William's old house, *Milville,* will soon be completely hidden by lush spring foliage.

My poor father would be amazed to see the number of open fields that now quilt the landscape. Back then, every plantation was a thick tangle of lofty oaks, sugar maples and hickories which formed an impenetrable screen of

---

[1] Catfish Run is a stream which flows into Peters Creek. It was named for Chief Catfish, a Delaware Indian who had a hunting and fishing camp in the area of Washington, Pennsylvania.

branches. In the early days there was only a small clearing around the homestead, but Father's sons and nephews, and their children and our neighbors, were of Scotch-Irish blood and not often found idling. Gradually, they tamed the wilderness and claimed the sunlight from the stubborn trees.

Orchard Hill was always a breath-wrenching hike, but its summit used to be my secret spot. And where was my chestnut tree now? Its gnarled curves were so easy for my child-feet to climb. From the uppermost boughs I kept my private thoughts, posted a lookout, and sometimes even saw as far as Uncle William and Aunt Rachel's. How could my tree-top haven ever be this rotted-out stump?

Why, one morning from this same perch I saw columns of smoke rising from Elder Kiddoo's plantation, *Liberty*. That was the morning after Tom the Tinker's visit. The razed Kiddoo grist mill smoldered on for hours.

The horse path between the Miller farms seems wider now and the trace branching off along the run looks well traveled, but those same spring rivulets still escape Mansfield Run. They creep thinly over the ground, creating a cool, brown ooze that delights the toes.

Further down, the trace angles around to the point where Mansfield Run joins its mainstream, Catfish Run. To the best of my knowledge, there never was a catfish to be found there! In its leisurely, meandering course through this wilderness, the run yields nice fat chub, an occasional sunfish, and is full of slim, timid water snakes.

My brothers and cousins loved to play there; called the junction Fort Pitt, after Pittsburgh-town, where the Monongahela and Allegheny rivers join to form the Ohio. They pretended to be great adventurers—Indians, flat-boaters, soldiers—or any other characters who caught their fancy.

Closer to the improvement, a new log bridge connects the horse path across the run. For as many years as I could remember there were only a few split logs to do the job. At least the old swimming hole's the same—right beyond the crossing and before the sheep pens.

When I think of all the Sunday mornings we traipsed out that very path—past the old Boyer Farm where my Grandpa Miller lay buried—and up to Bethel Church Road. Worship would last all day, making the long walk home a welcome change for our pew-stiffened frames. If we got back before dusk, we'd plead with Mother to let us cool our feet down in the swimming hole. Outright swimming was considered frivolity—and such play was strictly forbidden on the Sabbath.

A chippermunk squealed from underfoot and scurried up the bank of the run. My eye traveled with it to the outdoor bake oven just off that fancy kitchen area of the new grey stone house. How Grandma would've loved it after all those years of struggling over the open fireplace in the old log house. I can see her right up there, minding her breads and pies a-baking—her hands jiggling all the while in a flurry of quilt stitches or apple peelings or pea shells. She kept me busy close by and just to prove her thinking that hand, mind, and heart should seek useful service, she started a Bible story. It was never long before a Grandma Tale crept into the telling. Just listening to Grandma's talk about her kin across the sea, her trek here to the wilderness of Peters Creek, and her flights to escape Indians at the fort beyond the Monongahela—made me proud to be sitting at her feet a-working at some small task.

The familiar faces are gone now. It's a holy puzzlement how it has all changed, ever so slowly. And how can I be old Aunt Jane, family storyteller, when I still carry my girl's heart inside? Seems like every well-known sight is real enough to jar the memory, erase the wrinkles, and raise the dead—making it impossible to sort out *now* from *then*. Why, one glance toward that old springhouse and I could step right back into a world long gone. . . .

Winter 1794

Thwack! Snap! I cracked my heel through the icy sheet then pulled back sharply to keep the frigid water off my shoe-pack. Bitter night air frosted the inside of my nose till it stung, so I worked quickly to dip each bucket half full. My short legs strained under the weight of the shoulder-yoke and I turned to follow the dim path cut by the taper dip from the cabin window.

The month-old snow was crusty. Often, I could walk without breaking through, but tonight my heavy yoke made each step crunch down deep. I squinted to block out the cold and with a pull of the latch string, delivered the wash water to my Grandma Miller.

"There's a strong girl, Janie," she praised, "off to the table with ye."

Grandma's face was leathery red as she turned from the cook fire and handed me a noggin of warm milk and a trencher of squirrel stew. I plopped down on my block chair and studied her carefully over the rim of my steaming drink. Deep-down kindness welled up from her grey eyes; their warmth was better than the mug in my hands. Grandma's eyebrows twittered and danced as she patted tomorrow's rye loaf into shape. "Poor man's loaf," she called it.

"Sarie, watch what yer doin' with that pumpkin! I just fetched it out of the loft. It's no toy down here, ye know."

My attention had wandered back to the small table where my brother, sister Sara, and I were eating by the fire. Supper was not the time to be afoot with one's elders. They would eat later at the big puncheon table.

"Sarie want a pun-kin seat. Tomorrow's pun-kin day!" The four-year-old beamed through a mouthful of stew. Her curly brown moppet glistened in the firelight as she propped herself up on her favorite attic play-pretty. Even three-year-old Ollie cooed at the prospect of stewed pumpkin—not to mention roasted pumpkin seeds.

"Sara Miller, Jane is right. Find yer proper chair afore ye bruise tomorrow's vittles. . . . An' don't talk until yer mouth is empty." Our mother's words took Sarie by surprise, causing one last bite of supper to lodge in her throat.

"There, there . . . no great shucks," soothed Grandma. She whisked the pumpkin into a basket and tapped the little girl firmly on the back. After calming Sarie, Grandma scoured out the cookpot and trenchers, humming contentedly to herself.

Only I noticed Mother's light blue eye-winkers casting a hard look on the scene. She creaked the rocker-chair faster and faster, till Baby John began his husky squall in her arms.

Grandma had great affection for the rocker-chair because Grandpa Miller had cut it out of a maple tree she'd been eyeing long before I was born. It had started as a chair, but Grandpa added the oak rockers just before he died.

The children of the house—not counting John, that is, as a babe-in-arms—were forbidden to use it. I'd sneak a ride

in it, though, when the house emptied out. It comforted me
so to rock away the day's chores; rock away the aching
tiredness; rock, rock, rock.

"Gather 'round, children."

Mother'd caught me in idle thought. My eyes jumped.
Strange how she could look right inside me. She could pick
out any impish notion that dallied in my head long before I
got up the gumption to try anything. If she'd read my mind
about the rocker, though, she didn't let on.

"Jane, ye've neglected yer catechism today. I fear
Reverend Clark will find ye unpracticed. . . . Let us pray,"
she continued, "Almighty God, who hast brought us safely
through the day and granted us to reach this holy hour in
peace, help us to remember that the Lord is mindful of
us . . . He will bless those who fear Him, both great and
small." She nestled John close. "God bless me folks in
Cross Creek."

"God bless Grandpa Miller, rest 'is soul," added Grandma.

"God bless Fawder—hope he nabs a bear!" Sarie piped.

"And God bless Cousin Oliver—wherever he may be.
Amen," I concluded.

Quickly, I looked up for a reaction. Mother didn't share
my affection for our Cousin Oliver, but she gave no hint of
this now as she rose to bid us off to bed.

The job of bedding down Sarie and Ollie had fallen to me
lately. Being the eldest, it was one of many tasks I'd taken
on at an early age. Grandma was a perky lady, but at
seventy-one, the climb to the second floor and on up the foot
ladder to the attic was too much for her. She preferred the
bedstead near the kitchen hearth and liked to call me "her
legs."

Mother expected a new babe come late summer and
depended on me to do her running. "Come back directly,
Jane. I want to hear yer scripture," she ordered.

"An' bring yer sampler," Grandma winked.

We clattered up the wooden stairs. First up the foot ladder was Sarie. She was nimble as a grey squirrel hunting for acorns, but Ollie's pudgy legs left him dawdling on every rung. I gave him a boost on the behind and plop— he went sprawling on all fours. He twisted up his face as if to cry, but with all his natural padding, I doubt whether he felt the tumble much. Chill night air hurried them into their linsey-woolsey bed gowns before I could even get their discarded clothing onto the wall pegs. They snuggled down between the feather ticking and mattress. I tucked the bed quilts up to their chins and dropped a kiss on Sarie's forehead.

Ollie pulled his bear skin up to his ears at the sight. "Go ahead an' kiss a bear. I don' care!"

I sped to the floor below. A homespun linen curtain divided the room in two. Mother, Father, and Baby John slept in a trundle bed near the fireplace, while Grandma had the other side near the stairs. Lately she'd moved down to the main floor, sometimes letting me sleep in her big bed. The beautiful, high-off-the-ground, four-poster had real goose down pillows and a shoo-fly quilt, but I still preferred the attic where I could press my feet against the chimney stones that took heat from the cook-fire below.

I stared at the sampler that hung above Grandma's bed. Though I couldn't read all the words yet, the contents were well ingrained in my young mind:

> There's not a sin that we commit
> Nor wicked word we say,
> But in Thy dreadful book is writ
> Against the judgment day.

—Mary Smith Miller, *Mansfield*, 1793

Mother'd presented Grandma with this handiwork on her last birthday. I often prayed there wouldn't be too much written about me in the "dreadful book." Sins—like not always remembering my scripture or interrupting my elders—had a way of piling up so quickly, and there was that rocker-chair—always so tempting, I shuddered.

"God is a spirit: infinite, eternal, and unchangeable in His being, wisdom, power . . . His being, power, wisdom . . . His being, power, holiness . . ." Now, how'd that line go? Bible talk got so tricky—like betwixt and behooved, or omnipresent and omnipotent.

Then there were the *-eths:* goeth and cometh, blesseth and praiseth. "The work of the faithless is dead work and so cannot 'pleaseth' a living God. An evil tree 'bringeth' forth ill fruit."

I gathered up my sewing pouch and glided down the stairs. My lips moved silently as I mulled over all the words by heart. Mother cradled my brother in her arms.

"I wish James'd get back soon, Mother Miller. It's frightful enough livin' this side o' the Monongahela without worryin' 'bout every huntin' trip takin' him further into that wild country beyond the Ohio."

"Jamie's got more on his mind than Injuns these days, Mary. With Tom the Tinker visitin' at our neighbor's door, I . . . Janie dear!"

She'd seen me for the first time. I wished I hadn't interrupted her. Mother told me often enough that it wasn't polite to join into grown-up talk uninvited, but just thinking about Indians was so exciting! And who was Tom the Tinker? I was aching to ask, but their conversation reached a dead halt as I mounted a high stool by the fire. I recited my new section of catechism. Even the part about preserveth and protecteth rolled right off my tongue. Oh, I'd be ready for the Reverend!

I looked up proudly, but was disappointed to see Mother still staring out that window pane. (Cousin Oliver had fetched the glass over the mountains on his last pack trip.) It's powerful strange to me how parents can make such a fuss about their children learning things, then take no note once it's learned. Maybe the Good Lord heard me anyway and scratched some of my wickedness out of his "dreadful book."

Grandma was bent over her diary scratching out one wiggle after another with a goose quill. I guess those slashes and curls were words. I couldn't read all of them yet, but I knew my alphabet and plenty of words, too! I'd fixed it in my head to write down some of Grandma's Tales one day. Just had to study up enough words to do it.

"Janie, yer stitches need to stand a mite straighter on this side, girl." She studied my sampler over my shoulder:

Jane Miller is my name,
America is my nation,
The woods of Mansfield is my home,
And Christ is my salvation.
Jane Miller, Mansfield, 1794

"Do ye think I'll finish in time, Grandma?"

"One letter every day, girlie, an' ye'll be done afore the white oak leaf is as big as a mouse's ear."

I hoped that meant before planting, when Cousin Oliver was due back. He told me once that the forest floor was his only pillow, so I aimed to stitch my sampler into a right fine headrest to surprise him.

The last line and my name were only sketched with a bit of charred wood, but the rest of the letters gleamed. My thread was dyed with goldenrod and each bright stitch had to be just so. They all started to blur together in the golden firelight. My first yawn gave me away, so I was sent off to bed.

I squirmed down beside Sarie and planted my stocking feet on the warm chimney, but my head wouldn't stop spinning. . . . Hope I finish my present for Cousin Oliver. Maybe he'd think to bring me a cut of silk ribbon from back East—like the one he promised Cousin Lizzie.

The wind wooshed in through that old chinking hole and rattled a loose split shingle—then silence. Shivering, I rolled into a ball trying to remember the last time I'd seen anyone besides my own kin. Winter's such a lonely time. I'd been no further than our iced-over swimming hole for months on end. Sure would be good to see someone my own age instead of babies like Sarie and Ollie and John. Why, Cousin Lizzie's probably thinking the same thing right this minute! She might know all about that Tom the Tinker fellow, too. . . . I'll bet there's a word or two writ about him in the "dreadful book" . . . somewhere. . . . I'll have to ask.

II

TALK IN THE BARN

*Children's children are the crown of old men;
and the glory of children are their fathers.*

—Proverbs 17:6

Father was home. He got back hours before dawn and already had half the stock tended. Bits of ice were dripping from his hair as he scooped up the last bite of his cornmeal with a hunk of rye loaf. His deerhide moccasins warmed on the hearth stone and his stocking feet were propped up on my block chair by the fire. Keeping a dry foot was a real trial for everyone. Moccasins were always seeping through, with the ground wet three-fourths of the year. Father claimed that people even died of chilblains.

My father was a mammoth sight to my young eyes. Timidly, I peered around his shoulder. Yessir, it was him all right!

"Janie!" he cried, hoisting me up in his big arms. His whiskers tickled my chin as I wrangled free. Neither of my parents were given much to outward signs of affection, but an old-fashioned bear-hug wasn't beyond Father once in a while.

"Yeah, Fawder! Did ye shoot a bear?"

"Bam! Bam!" hooted Ollie.

Sarie'd taken the last two stairs in one bound while her brother tumbled along behind. Ever since Ollie'd gotten that bearskin last winter, my sister'd been craving one of her own.

"Found me a two-horn bear, Sarie-babe!" He poked Sarie good-naturedly, then plummeted Ollie to his shoulders and grinned out at his womenfolk.

"Time's a-wastin', ladies.   There's two sides of venison waitin' to be dressed, an' a whole barnful o' hungry critters need tendin'."

"I'll help ye, Father."

"Later, Jane," Mother corrected, "You're needed in the house this mornin'."

It was still half dark as Father headed out across the farm yard. I sighed, wishing I'd been born a boy. A boy'd be expected to follow his father right out there. He'd get to do the outdoor work—like chopping wood or carving do-dads. Why did I have to get stuck with women's work? It seemed as if I had no choice in the matter.

"Save some extra grit fer Lady Tidball," Grandma called after him. She closed the heavy door with a thud, leaving the latch string on the outside. Shuffling back to the spit over the wood fire, she checked a wild turkey she was roasting.

Lady Tidball was Grandma's favorite goose. She looked like all the rest to me except she was bigger and meaner. Grandma claimed she'd plucked enough down off that goose to stuff a whole barn, and then some.

"That bird's already fat and spoilt," Mother complained. Grandma's brows wriggled uncontrollably. I knew she fretted over Mother's hankering to land Tidball in the cook-pot.

Three pairs of eyes were trained on Mother while she knotted her candle sticks. Each stick had six long strings dangling from it. Carefully, she plunged the wicks into a vat of tallow and hot beeswax, waited a few seconds, then

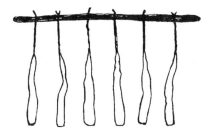

pulled them out to drip and harden. She balanced the unfinished candles on two wall pegs as a faint honey scent sweetened the air.

"Do it again, Mama, do it again," Sarie pleaded.

"Nay, let it dry awhile. 'Sides, I thought this was a special day 'round here." She smiled a bit, waiting.

"Pun-kins!" Sarie remembered.

"I've got a pot ready," chimed Grandma, hefting the pumpkin onto the cutting block. She sliced a neat ring around the stem with her kitchen knife and . . . th-thwomp! Ollie pulled off the lid. Eagerly, we reached in to sift the squishy inners for seeds. I sorted through a handful of little white tear-drops, saving the fattest seeds for a necklace. While Grandma readied the pulp for mashing, Sarie and Ollie placed fistfuls of seeds into a pan to dry roast. Later, the seeds would be eaten whole, or shelled and saved to flavor garden greens.

"Tell us a riddle, Grandma." It was our favorite pastime. Grandma had dozens of riddles tucked inside her head. She had a real knack for making them up, too.

Her eyes closed a minute, then she began, "Miss Nancy, dressed in white; the longer she sits, the shorter her height. Who is she, girls?"

"I don't know any Nancy."

We puzzled a while longer.

"We give up."

Grandma nodded toward Mother who was putting another layer on the candle dips.

"A lit candle," I shouted, picking up her clue. Sarie clapped her hands and Ollie jumped up and down, not understanding, but not wanting to be left out.

"But Mother Miller, these candles are still gettin' bigger," Mother pointed out.

"Horsefeathers! You're a smart one, Mary!"

Sarie and I giggled, but Mother turned back to her work. "Yer brother needs mindin' upstairs," she told me, changing the subject.

"Yes, ma'am."

I glanced out the window on my way to the stairs. New snow had fallen last night. The boughs on all the trees were weighted down with white. As the sun climbed higher, wisps of snow slipped off a branch or two. I smiled inside and hurried up to Baby John, knowing I'd get outdoors soon.

The barn door creaked shut with a push from my backside. I bent over, set down the pails, and climbed out of my shoulder-yoke. The barn was pitch black after the glare of sparkly snow outside. I squinted to see. The air was thick with a musty odor of sweet hay and farm animals. The scent clung to my senses like the bits of hay and dust I saw hovering mid-air in that slat of sunlight.

"Father?"

My voice sounded puny in this big chilly place. Maybe he'd gone off to the sheep shed. I didn't mind being alone, but the shadows in the barn crept over me. Hay rustled from somewhere. At least the animals were here. They chawed and sniggered and swooshed their tails. Their bells clanged noisily. I climbed the gate to the nearest stall to get a look at the new calves. All I could see were four very sad brown eyes. The rest was well-hid behind their mother,

Tessie, who bellered a warning. They were more afraid than me!

The horses on the other side of the barn began to frisk. Father didn't like me going near them—he said it was dangerous. Too many months of training could be lost by my tampering and many of these animals had what he called a "nervous temperament."

From out of nowhere, there was a solid boom on the barn floor. Father'd swung from a rope in the loft and dropped down right in front of me. He sure gave me a start!

"Thought I heard somethin' down here! Back off from those horses, Janie."

He let me help him make a bed of oat straw for the calves. The fine gold straw was as soft as the newborns. "Pile it high off the floor," he warned, "lest Tessie tramp on those totterin' young-uns by mistake." His look softened as he watched me bed down the wobbly calves.

"What's fer dinner?" he asked.

I'd almost forgotten! Quick as a firebug, I scrambled to fetch the pails. Walking back as lady-like as could be, I loosed the cloth wrapper and handed him a thick slab of rye loaf with lard drippings. There was smoked ham, too. While he munched, I found the cowhide skin in the other pail.

"What's this, girl?"

"Hot cider, flavored with whiskey."

I pulled out the stopper and passed over the skin. It felt real important to be sitting here with him. Father wiped his mouth with the cuff of his hunting shirt, handing it back.

"Take a sip, Janie. It's cold out here, lest yer up an' workin'." He unlaced his hunting knife from the side of his breeches and sliced me a wedge of bread and meat.

"Won't be much longer 'fore I'll have to feed these critters browse."

"What's that, sir?"

"Starvation food, it is—wild grass, leaves, twigs an' such. I'll have to use it when we run out of good hay fodder."

"I don' think Tessie'll like it much."

"That's right, Janie. It's no good, no good a-tall."

"Did ye see any Injuns on yer trip?"

"Nay, this time of year they're prob'ly camped way out in Ohio country—up near the English Lakes, mebbe. We won't see Injuns 'round here—not till this snow breaks."

He threw back his head and took a long swigger of cider. It grew real quiet-like in the barn. Felt so good to carry on growed-up talk, I thought.

"Who's Tom the Tinker?" I asked.

Cider sputtered out from the corners of Father's mouth. He turned to look at me in disbelief.

"Where'd ye hear talk like that?"

"Grandma," I replied honestly.

"I should've knowed," he said with a wry smile. "That's a made-up name, Janie. It's more like Tom and the tinkers. Ye see, those men're downright mad about the new tax laws on whiskey makin'. Do ye know what a tax is, girl?"

I thought a bit. "It's the money we give to our country— like the offering we give at church."

"No, not quite, girlie! It's one thing to be offerin' up a copper to praise the Lord an' a whole other business to have the greedy Federalists snatchin' at me meager coffers! The tax is unfair to us farmers in the West. Now, I despise the whiskey laws as much as the next man—that's the honest truth, but Tinkerin' Tom an' 'is gang—out shootin', burnin', an' scarin' God-fearin' people to death—that's a whole different matter. It's hard enough knowin' what to do without his turnin' neighbor against neighbor."

He didn't seem to be talking with me any longer.

"But Father, ye always said it was important to obey the law." I tried to understand him.

"That's right, Janie. That's right."

His eyes seemed wild and far off. I didn't mean to upset his happy mood. Quietly, I slipped the cloth wrapper inside my apron, picked up the shoulder-yoke, and left him to his work and worries.

III

THE VISITOR

Equal taxation and no excise
No asylum for traitors and cowards

—Inscription on a Liberty Pole, 1794

A freckled face shined back at me. Oh, it wavered a bit with the cut of the window pane. I supposed it had to be my own. The mouth pursed, then smiled, trying to seem more comely. With serious blue eyes and red-brown hair pulled straight back into braids, I doubted I had a chance to appear comely. Mother said there were more "important matters" to worry about and she wouldn't allow a looking glass in the house. I guess the "important matters" were working and praying. . . . Grandma said I had a good singing voice, though. I checked the window as if it could tell.

The grey clouds in the afternoon sky caused Mother to light the window taper early. Our window pane was the only place I ever caught sight of myself—except down by the run in the summertime. Absently, my eyes focused on the path outside. What a strange sight!

"Mother!"

"Come away from the window, Jane. I need your two hands here."

"But Mother, someone's out there. I'll go see."

"Just a crow-shootin' minute, young lady," said Grandma, already opening the door and scooting me out of the way.

"Hallo? Hallo?"

No answer. From the window I could see an old horse with the rider slumped over in the saddle.

"Why, it looks like Zachariah, the pastor's horse," Grandma reported.

The glistening animal came to a halt right by our hitching post. The old man was all dressed in black. His head bobbed on his chest—he was sound asleep!

Father'd run up from the sheep pens by this time. "Reverend Clark! Reverend Clark?"

He stirred somewhat. Tired eyes blinked open slowly, then he wheezed and gasped for air. The Reverend's horse was well-known throughout the area. And what a sly one! Zachariah'd made the rounds of the pastorate so often that the turns and stop-overs were second nature to him—with or without his master's rein!

"James? James Miller?" His eyelids fluttered as he straightened in the saddle. He was more alert now. "Zachariah," he announced, patting the horse's mane, "we have arrived. Praise the Lord!"

"Mary's put your name on the pot, sir. We'd thank ye to bless our prayers," Father offered.

He reached up, easing the weary pastor off his horse. His long, spindly legs were so stiff that they kept the shape of the saddle. For a while he stayed bent at the knees, just like Baby John!

Once inside, Grandma pulled her sacred rocker up to the fire and seated the Reverend. The whiskey jug was fetched from the corner cupboard, served with water, and passed between the two men. Their conversation escaped me. Not wanting to be seen, I planned to hold off on any Bible reciting as long as possible, so I stayed out of the way helping Grandma prepare supper. All the same, it was hard to keep my eyes off that snow white wig tied back with a black ribbon. Flashes of metal sparkled out in the firelight. Silver buckles! Below his solemn black suit, silver buckles hooked his breeches at the knee. Such dignified finery was a rare sight to behold!

"Our Lord is with me this day," Grandma whispered. "I shore is grateful we saved that last pumpkin an' have fresh meat in the house." Brushing a few loose strands beneath her house cap, she donned a fresh apron and bid everyone for grace.

Two new tapers, saved for company, brightened up the supper table. Reverend Clark closed his eyes and reached out his long skinny arms, "Save us, O Lord, in this land of Bethel which Thou hast blessed with the light of pure religion. Neither he that planteth, nor he that watereth is anything. But God maketh the seed to grow."

There were those *-eths* again! He paused. Sarie and I peered up through clasped hands, awaiting the amen.

"Lord bless this nation," he continued, "that religion and virtue may season all sorts of men, that there may be peace within all our borders . . . ."

Sarie reached for her trencher, but I yanked her pigtail till she resumed a prayerful pose.

The pastor's voice strengthened, "Maintain our president that he and all who are set over us may maintain Thy laws. In time of war, defend us; and in peace, preserve us from corruption. We beseech Thee to spread abroad the spirit of justice and amity, that there may be an end to boastful rivalries, jealous fears, and cruel threatenings, that all nations may have peace and security, through Jesus Christ our Lord. Amen."

"Amen," added Mother.

We scrambled into our seats at the small table, glad to be eating at last.

"We're pleased to have ye with us, Reverend," said Father. "Been a long time since we've seen much of anyone—much less our preacher!"

Reverend Clark nodded agreement and picked up a pewter knife as the roast turkey was passed about. Mother's pewter was only brought out for important company.

"Ye know," said Father, thoughtfully, "Mother always tells us how folks used to come from miles around just to catch sight of this log house when it was first raised."

Grandma'd served the adults and was busy dishing up johnnycakes for us. Father's words sparked her interest though, so she handed the serving duties over to me.

"I dare say she's speakin' truth," Reverend Clark admitted. "It's still a pleasure to behold a well-built log house with a split shingle roof!"

Father didn't want the Reverend to think him a braggart, so he made his point. "I think she's even prouder that one of the first ministers this side of the Alleghenies saw fit to preach right in this room."

Grandma beamed. Her eyebrows jumped so—it was plain that she was itching to join in the conversation. "That's not the all of it, Jamie. It was November of Seventy-six, it was—the same year we 'scaped the Injuns by runnin' to the Monongahela forts. Such a young lad ye were then, but your father an' I were burstin' with pride to be gatherin' our friends an' neighbors here. Reverend McMillan stood right where I'm a-standin' now, tall as Goliath he was—with a voice even Old Lady McKee could hear—preachin' the gospel accordin' to Leviticus: You shall keep my Sabbath an' rev-er-ence me sanctuary. I am the Lord!"

Grandma's eyes were bright with the memory of it. She sat down to her meal for the first time. "I'm so glad your father lived to see that first meetin' grow into a real church, son."

She heaped another portion of pumpkin stew on his plate. Father held our grandma in high regard. Oh, she was a feisty little lady, apt to get carried away with her long-winded tales—and she did trial Mother with her ideas on handling the chores, but she was the backbone of this family—in matters both spiritual and ordinary. And our father didn't begrudge her the position one bit.

"How is your health, Reverend Clark," my mother inquired.

"I can't complain, madam," he replied, not wanting to bring up rheumatism, ague, gout, and a host of other ailments he never could shake.

"How is Margaret an' that fine son of yours?"

"They're fine, just fine, thanks. Willie's been a real blessing for us both. Ye wouldn't believe how that young man can play the violin. He's learned so much about music."

Gradually, Mother inched the conversation around to her liking. "Any news from Cross Creek?"

"Not a word, Mary. I haven't talked to Thomas Marquis, the new pastor out there—not for months. I wouldn't be fretting over your kinfolk, though. This time of year, I'm sure the Indians are camped way off in Ohio Territory."

"That's what I've been tryin' to tell her," said Father, passing the whiskey jug. "What brings ye out here anyway, sir? This isn't yer normal time fer makin' the rounds of the pastorate."

"That's true, James, but lately I've been anxious to get around to all of my congregation—even through this snow."

He lowered his voice, glancing over at our small table. "I've been worried ever since I heard rumors in Pittsburgh about some tar an' feathering! It seems a federal inspector rode out last week to one of the farmers who'd paid the excise tax on whiskey making. . . . Before he could reach Cochran's place, a band of men showed up on horseback. Well, ye'll not believe it, but they passed up the inspector and by the time he'd arrived, they'd already fired Cochran's still house!"

He thumped his fist on the table just like he did at church meetings. "Then, as if that weren't enough, they rode over to your neighbors here—the Kiddoos—and shot up their still! Left a crude calling card: Tom the Tinker—come to mend your still. But, forgive me," he pushed back his chair, "I'm sure ye've heard most of this by now."

Father heaved a sigh, "Yes sir, I'm afraid we have. We're related to Elder Kiddoo by marriage."

"That's the Tidball side of the family," explained Grandma. "His wife's my niece. They're 'xpectin' a young-un, too, come spring."

All eyes turned to Mother, making her feel uneasy.

"All the more reason for me to get over there," said Reverend Clark. "By the way, who's handling your whiskey making these days?"

"My father willed the still to my brother, Oliver," answered Father.

"He's been laid to rest some years now," mused the Reverend.

"Aye, it's my older brother, William, who operates the still."

"William," pondered the preacher, "he belongs to the Mingo Militia, doesn't he?"

"An' a good one he is, too," Grandma assured him. "All my boys are God-fearin' men."

"I don' doubt that, Mrs. Miller, but there's talk that this Tom the Tinker group has its roots in that Mingo Militia. And ye must admit, ma'am, it's outright wicked to be scaring hard-working farmers when they're just trying to comply with the law."

"Some say that law's unfair," Father suggested.

"Well, ye've got representatives in the Congress. Work together to change the law or repeal it legally. Until that time, we must learn to accept it," counseled the pastor. He eyed the adults carefully and went on, with conviction: "The ministers of this presbytery—including Reverend McMillan and me—feel the tax laws on distilling spirits should be obeyed. Folks should feel free to register their stills without fear of terrorizing bandits. Why, they're probably the same scalawags who've been interfering with the revenuers. President Washington, himself, warned against tampering with federal tax inspectors over a year ago!"

"*President* Washington, pooh," snapped Grandma, "he's still the same *General* Washington fined for swearin' over in Washington County, not ten years back!" She still smarted over the conduct of Washington when he'd come by to inspect some of his holdings. He'd found some farmers on the property and when they couldn't meet his terms, he forced them off.

The Reverend faced Grandma calmly. "He's also the same *General* Washington who led your oldest boys, John and William, in the fight to birth this nation.[2] Don't be forgetting that!"

Grandma's mouth quivered as fast as her eyebrows, but she held her tongue.

"Look, friends," he said in a compromising tone, "I know whiskey is the main source of what little cash we see around here. And I understand that taking it across the mountains is the only way to make a profit, but it saddens me to see suspicion and fear creeping into my flock." He shook his head in dismay. "We've got to abide peaceably and obey the law."

---

[2]   According to researchers Ann and Bill Barton, William and John Miller served in the Pennsylvania Militia in 1774 against the Indians. William was seventeen years old and became a sharpshooter with a rifle at the time.

By August 1776, William, John, and neighbor Guion McKee enlisted as privates in Capt. James Montgomery's Company in the 8th Pennsylvania Regiment. The stated purpose of the regiment was the defense of the western frontier. During the Winter of 1776, they were ordered to leave their garrison in Kittaning (Pa., 38 miles northeast of Pittsburgh) to join Gen. George Washington in New Jersey. William, John, and McKee all marched east with the regiment. Due to winter conditions and lack of shelter, there were numerous deaths.

The Spring of 1777 found William (now 20) as a member of Col. Daniel Morgan's Rangers in Morristown, New Jersey. Because many of "Morgan's Rangers" were expert marksmen from years of fighting Indians, they were given a prominent role at Saratoga.

Colonel Morgan was instructed to "begin the game" at the Battle of Bemis Heights on October 7, 1777. The Rangers mortally wounded British General Fraser, which took the heart out of the British fighting. The Americans stormed British lines, moving General Burgoyne into a general retreat. Soon, Burgoyne's army was surrounded at Saratoga Heights, whereupon he surrendered, on October 17.

Saratoga, of course, is known as the turning point of the Revolution. It also had the effect of bringing France to side with the Americans.

After Saratoga, William and John Miller returned to the 8th Pennsylvania Regiment. Morgan's Rangers were disbanded in late 1778.

Mother and Father stared hard at each other, holding back their unspoken doubts.

It was meant to happen. It was going to happen. They were no longer absorbed in their politicking confab and the shadows could hide me no more. Reverend Clark pulled me out of the corner and seated me on the high stool. Reaching into his saddle bag, he brought out a Bible and a small leather-bound book, *The Shorter Catechism.*

He thumbed through it to the well-worn page, cleared his throat, and began. . . . "Jane Miller, ye've grown a lot, I see. How's your Bible study, lass?" I braced myself taut as the pastor leaned closer. "What is God?"

"God is a spirit, infinite, eternal." I finished the rest soberly.

"That's right," he commented, obviously pleased. "Now tell me, 'What satisfaction hath the soul in the enjoyment of God?' "

"Unspeakably more gladness than when corn, wine, and all the earthly comforts do most abound," I answered, looking to Grandma for reassurance. I tried to keep my mind on reciting, but couldn't help admiring the way he rolled the *R*'s in his Scottish brogue.

"Now, Mistress Miller, what about the psalms? Have ye committed any to memory yet?"

"Yes sir, I know Psalm 100, and the Twenty-third. . . ." If only he'd pick one of these. I knew them so well! I waited hopefully, but the Reverend raised his eyebrows prompting me to continue. "An' I started to learn another one, too: One Hundred and Forty. . . ."

"Aye! One Hundred Forty—now there's a psalm to ponder. Let's hear it, lass." He settled back in his chair, crossed his arms, and shut his eyes in anticipation.

Slowly, I began, "Deliver me, O Lord, from evil men. Preserveth me from violent men who plan evil things in their heart an' stir up wars c-con-tinually."

I hardly recognized my own voice saying the part about the sharp-tongued serpents and the poison-lipped vipers. It was difficult to keep my eyes off the oversized wig that framed the pastor's face. Cousin Oliver had heard, back East, that French King Louie and Queen Marie somethin'-or-other wore bigger, curlier wigs just like it—but they got axed! I broke out in goose bumples just thinking of it.

"I say to the Lord: 'Thou art my God.' " The Reverend seemed to be repeating the words.

"Thou art my God," I said, trying to pull my thoughts together. "Grant not, O Lord, the desires of the wicked. . . . Let the mischief of their lips ov-ov-over . . ."

"Overwhelm them," roared the pastor. His impact startled the rest of the words right out of me.

"Let burning coals fall upon them," he continued, "let them be cast into pits, no more to rise. Let not the slanderer be established in the land."

I wrung my hands in fear and wonder, but he'd taken over the reciting himself and his attention was centered on the grown-ups now, as if the message was meant for them.

"Let evil hunt down the violent men speedily. . . ." The Reverend paused solemnly, then rose to his full height. "The Lord maintaineth the cause of the afflicted and executeth justice for the needy."

The fire crackled in the silence. Everyone was lost in thought. "Mama, I tired," broke in Sarie, at last.

"I've tarried long enough, friends. I'd like to call on the Kiddoos down the lane yet this evening." The preacher donned his cloak and hat, heading for the door. Our family gathered around to see him off.

"Thank ye, ladies, for the hearty repast." He kneeled and took my hand, "Jane Miller, ye've got a pure heart and a beautiful spirit—well-molded in the way of the Lord."

Now what did that mean? It sounded kindly enough.

Once Father hoisted him atop Zachariah, Reverend Clark raised his arm again for a final prayer. "Almighty God, who knowest our presumptuous thoughts and perverse rebellings, who seest also sins that we commit in secret—as though we could hide anything from Thee—Hear our humble confession and pardon all that we have said or thought or done amiss. Let it not ripen to its bitter harvest, but let Thy mercy interpose, and do away as the night our transgressions and scatter our sins as the morning cloud."

Sleep was beyond me that night. The pastor'd left hours ago, but the voices below droned on and on. Straining to hear, I crept to the top of the foot ladder without rousing Sarie or Ollie.

"He didn't mean that William's involved in the Tinker's group, Ma." It was Father talking. I glided down the ladder to catch the rest. "The Reverend knows there're plenty o' good men—like Parkinson and Phillips—in the militia."

"That's fer darn sure," Grandma agreed. "And where was the gover'ment when my boys were off fightin' that war of independence? They sure weren't out here protectin' us from savages! Fend fer ourselves, we did. Why, if it weren't fer the local units, like Capt. Billy Fife's militia an' the Mingo group, we'd prob'ly all be buried at Bethel Cemetery."

Grandma's words squeaked when she was angry. Crouching on the top stair by Grandma's bed, I pulled my bed gown under stockinged toes and wrapped my arms about my knees for warmth. I wasn't missing a word now.

"Mother, ye know I'm not like Eastern folk—beholden to Washington an' that money-schemer, Hamilton, but . . ."

"Fruit flies! If yer father, Oliver, were alive, he'd be spittin' mad to see us plagued with excise. It was Britain's taxin' that drove him out of County Antrim, Ireland, in the first place. One of the main reasons we trooped out to this backwoods was to be rid of the money mongers an' their stranglin' tariffs."

"But we've got to obey the law, like Reverend Clark said."
My mother's voice trembled, quiet and strange.

"Would ye be bringin' Tinkerin' Tom to our very door,
woman?"

I climbed onto Grandma's bed and pulled her quilt around
me. The sampler about the "dreadful book" stared down at
me through the gloom.

Father sounded confused: ". . . I'm torn. Seems like
there's no way out. How can we refuse to pay the tax when
our own pa was one of the first justices in the area?[3] Why,
this family's always stood for law an' order, but this
excise—it's unfair!" His voice grew louder. "Come June,
Will's goin' ta have to pay a tax just to register our still."

"We'll be payin' at least four cents on every gallon after
that," Grandma figured.

"What's so dog-gone dander-raisin' is the injustice of it all.
The law's unfair because it's unequal. It'll hurt every
farmer this side o' the Alleghenies much more than the big
whiskey distillers in the East."

"Payin' the tax, obeyin' the law looks like a sure step
toward reprisals," said Grandma.

"The Lord won't let that happen," vowed Mother.

"It's a real possibility, Mary. Open yer eyes!"

Father never shouted so at Mother. My insides pinched
and tugged. A dull pain squeezed my brow. I gulped back a
sob as the squabble downstairs grew louder.

"But the law'll catch up with us, if we don't pay," cried
Mother.

"Hen's teeth! Next thing ye know, they'll be taxin' the air
we breathe!"

---

[3] The Miller property was once part of Yohogania County, Virginia. In 1776,
Grandma's husband, Oliver Miller, was among those appointed Justice of the
Peace. On August 26, 1777, the Court met at he house of Andrew Heath (near
Elizabeth, Pa.) and ordered several members to tour their districts and "tender
Oath of Allegiance and Fidelity to this (Virginia) Commonwealth to all free
male inhabitants above a certain age." Oliver Miller was to start from the
"mouth of Peters Creek thence . . . up the Ohio and Monongahela to the
beginning."

Talk below ceased. My ears took no note of it. I could no longer choke back the cries that sprang from deep inside. My bleary eyes opened to find Mother and Father close-by. Their presence was both fearful and comforting to me and I cried all the harder.

"Janie-babe, what's the matter?"

Father got no answer and looked to Mother for assistance.

"Don't cry, Jane. You're my big girl now. We were both mighty proud of the way ye handled yerself with Reverend Clark this evenin'."

"Yer mother speaks truth, lass. Ye've got a keen memory—like yer Grandma."

My mind flashed with thoughts of the pastor. His long, grim face had nodded slowly as he spoke the lines about burning coals and the desires of the wicked. I saw how tired and helpless my parents looked, but couldn't stop crying.

"My crackies, what a pair!" exclaimed Grandma, bustling into the room. Her arms encircled my shoulders and drew a noggin of catnip tea to shaking lips.

"It's plain to see all this heavy talk of violent men an' Injuns an' outlaws has scared the child to tears. Why, it's enough to make a strong-willed ol' biddy like me want to sit down an' bawl like a babe."

"I'm not scared," I thought, my breathing still jumping and hic-coughing. I just couldn't understand how I had made everyone so unhappy. Then the warm tea worked its miracle of sleep.

IV

FAMILY GATHERIN'

Remember the days of old,
Consider the years of many generations.

—Deuteronomy 32:7

The ice was melting on Catfish Run. A thin line of silver moved freely through icy banks for the first time in months. I tested the water. Brrr! It was colder than Sarie's feet last night. The March air gusted, but the sun felt pleasant on my skin. Dropping my bonnet back on my shoulders, I tilted my head to inspect the sky. The sun beamed down warmly through a grey cloud or two—strange how it had snowed last night. The thawing ground was a slush of icy puddles. I picked up my basket and zigzagged a dry path to the barn. Chickens clucked contentedly from their straw beds. The warm breezes had perked them up, so there'd be plenty of fresh eggs for baking.

Father ambled up the hill with a fleece under his arm. But the shearing was weeks off! Fleece this morning could only mean dead sheep. I was scairt to hear the truth.

"Don't go down there, Jane," Father stopped me. "Wolves got into the sheep pen last night. Killt a lamb an' one ewe."

"Not the newborn?" I'd visited the new lamb every day since its birth last week.

"Aye, 'fraid so. We're lucky it wasn't worse. Sheep're such timid critters. Just stand around—even when a bloodthirsty wolf comes a-callin'. Guess I'd better keep a closer watch."

I hung my head to hide the tears. The lambs and other small animals around the farm were the playmates I didn't have. As often as we'd lose some of them, I couldn't get used to it.

"Look," said Father, catching my expression. He held out the fleece for me to stroke. "Mebbe there's enough fer a new meetin' dress, huh girl?"

The wool was soft and oily to the touch, but even the prospect of a much-needed meeting dress couldn't wipe away the empty feeling at the pit of my stomach.

"Mama wants ya," Sarie waddled up to tell me. I dried my eyes and turned toward the cabin.

"Here, take this," Father handed me the fleece, "and cheer up—this is a sugar snow, girlies!"

The melting mess looked anything but sweet to me. My sister tasted a few flakes to be sure.

"Not the snow," laughed Father, "the sap in the trees!"

"What's sap, Fawder?" She was obviously disappointed at not being able to lick up all the snow, like candy.

"Sap is the juice an' life-blood of a tree, Sarie. If we catch some before the leaves bud out, we'll have maple syrup an' sugar."

She had visions of doctoring that hot gummy porridge served up every morning. And now, Grandma could sweeten a cake for Sarie's birthday, a few days off.

"Wouldn't surprise me a-tall to see Uncle William drop by fer a sugarin'-off party," said Father.

"And Cousin Lizzie?" I asked.

"The whole family, I 'xpect." Father was already moving off to the barn.

"Sugar snow, sugar snow!" squealed Sarie with delight, and hopping all the way up to the cabin door. I hugged the sheepskin and followed her, hoping there'd be no more bundles like this till the shearing come May.

As predicted, the sound of bells jingled around the backside of the cabin before I could even start my fetching chores in the root cellar. The horsepath from *Milville* . . . As I rounded the corner, I set eyes on more people than I'd seen since Thanksgiving last. The whole family gathered out front. Uncle William helped Aunt Rachel off her mare. Cousin Lizzie was pulling little Tommy from the farm sled. My oldest cousin, Alex, managed the ox team.

I braced myself for the display of hugging and kissing that Grandma and Aunt Rachel'd started up. They were the only two enjoying it at all. I didn't mind Grandma, but Aunt Rachel pooched up her two lips and smacked a wet one right on me.

"Janie Miller!"

She tickled my sides. I wiped it away with my sleeve, thinking I'd like my plump, freckled aunt much better without her sloppy kisses.

Father and Uncle William slapped each other on the back a few times, looking restless. "I 'xpect a Miller knows a sugar snow when he sees one," grinned Uncle. He was a strapping big man with Grandma's grey eyes almost buried behind grizzled brows and chin whiskers.

Grandma wanted to feed everyone, but the men were eager to be off.

"There's no stoppin' 'em now, Mother Miller," Aunt Rachel assured her. "Will's been whittlin' sugar spouts an' hollowin' out syrup troughs fer months on end!"

"Come along, Jane," Father called.

I was proud to be included with my older cousins. Maybe it'd be a good day after all. "Who'd have guessed ye'd get sugar out of trees?" I wondered, trudging up Orchard Hill behind the farm sled.

"My pa says the Injuns were tappin' trees long afore any white folk set foot in this new world."

I looked up to my Cousin Lizzie. Only three years older than me, she knew as much about these backwoods as a grown boy. She was brave and not afraid to find her own adventures. Under that mob cap flowed a loose mass of red curls. These I admired even more than her carefree temperament or secret dancing ambitions. Why, if I had hair like that, Mother'd braid it back quick as a whip-stitch!

"Yessirree," agreed Uncle William, "the savages knew what to do after a sugar snow."

"Why's it called a sugar snow, sir?" I asked.

"Cause we'll be makin' candy an' sugar an' . . ." Lizzie got carried away with sweet thoughts.

"No, girl," corrected her pa, "the first sap to flow is the syrup makin' sap. It runs afore the sap the tree feeds on. The best time to catch the sugarin' sap is after a cold night—with some snow, mebbe."

"A sugar snow," concluded Lizzie.

"It's only a sugar snow if it warms up come daylight. When ye get a day like today, the juice races up these trees!" Uncle William threw back his head and whooped out his eagerness.

Just past the apple orchard, the hill was thick with sugar maples. Grandma called them sugar bushes. Cousin Alex halted the oxen and the men began unloading the sled.

"Jane, help your cousin hang these buckets," Father instructed. While Lizzie and I set about our task, he used an auger to bore a hole into the nearest tree. The wooden buckets were easy to place, but it took both men to lift the log troughs.

"Look," pointed Lizzie. "Here's a healed-over mark from last year's tappin'." We found other spots that looked even older. When the last bucket was in place, we ran back to watch the grown-ups. Father cut holes and Uncle William hammered in wooden spouts. Sometimes, he stopped and whittled down the ends to fit the hole better.

"I helped Pa cut those spouts out o' elderberry bushes," said Lizzie.

"You mean Aunt Rachel 'lows ye to carve an' whittle?" I asked, wide-eyed. My mother felt that was boy's doings.

"I can do most anything Alex does!" Lizzie announced with pride.

"Look, girls," nudged Uncle William, "It's running already. A day like this, James—'twouldn't surprise me a-tall to get near five gallon a tree."

"I'm hopin' for a good year. We sure could use the extra syrup an' sugar for barter." They agreed. "You girls stay within earshot—'twon't be long 'fore ye'll be needed to run the sap buckets down to the boilin' fire near the orchard." Cousin Alex was already loading his sled with freshly chopped wood for the bonfire.

"Janie, I've got a secret," announced Lizzie, ready to bolt.

"Wait," I called. "I'll take you to my secret hidy-place!"

I turned sharply to make sure we weren't overheard. Arm in arm, we hiked the rest of Orchard Hill. The slippery leaves and sloshy ice drifts hampered the steep climb, but we were too full of giggling and grinning over the prospect of a secret confab to care. Lizzie leaned back against a chestnut tree at the summit, catching her breath.

"Where's this secret spot?" she demanded.

I laughed and started up the tree. "Yore restin' on it!" I called down.

Lizzie darted after me, spry as a polecat. Together, we roosted high up, where the branches thinned out enough to let the wind rock us gently.

"Shucks, what's so secret 'bout this?" asked Lizzie.

"We're the only ones who know about it," I answered, desperately struggling to think up a more impressive reason. "An' it's the only spot I know where ye can see both our houses."

Sure enough, across a sea of grey branches, the roof and chimney of *Milville* stood out—and far below, smoke poofed up above the orchard at *Mansfield.* Lizzie smiled her approval.

"Now, what's the secret?" I couldn't wait any longer.

"We're movin' to Kentucky!"

I was stunned at this strange prospect and didn't know what to say. "Where's that?" I asked at last.

"Well, Pa says we'll take a flatboat down the Ohio River, then head south into Kentuck. Says there's plenty o' good, cheap land an' more huntin' . . ."

"An' more Injuns!" I added. The tears started to well up at the idea of her going.

"Injuns! By jiminy, my Pa knows how to whup Injuns good! I'm not a-scared neither! Don' cry, Janie. We'll all be fine—'sides, we're not leavin' fer a long while yet—not till next fall, after our new babe's born."

Another new baby—that was news to me. I wiped my eyes. Fall did seem a good ways off.

"C'mon," shouted Lizzie, "that's Alex whistlin'—I'll race you back to the sugar camp. Last one back's a pokey numbskull!"

We reached the maple grove, just as Alex disappeared down the trace with the farm sled piled high with chopped wood. Father and Uncle William were deep in the midst of grown-up talk.

"But why so far, Will?" Father asked. "I mean Cross Creek is one thing, but Kentuck—that'll split this family apart."

"I told ye, Jamie, there're miles of unclaimed land out there. Just like this land when our pa first ventured this way . . . an' ye know I'm nearly as foot-loose as that horse-packin' cousin of ours." He cracked a convincing smile, then said seriously, "Ye've got the main plantation, Jamie, and the bulk of the property, to boot. Me, I jus' want to get out."

"Yer sure it's not yer Mingo friends who've got ye thinkin' 'bout leavin'?" Father demanded.

"What're ye sayin', Brother?"

"I want to know yer stand, Will." Father's words echoed down the hill. There was an uncomfortable pause in their converse.

"All right, so the Mingo boys are more outspoken than most outfits. An' David Bradford, that loud-mouthed lawyer, is tetched in the head with ideas of breakin' off from the Feds an' startin' a 'Western Empire' . . . an' Holcroft . . . that man's up to his eyewinkers in tinkerin' . . ."

There was that word again: tinkerin'—Tom the Tinker. Was he really this man called Holcroft? I tried to ask Lizzie, but she was intent on listening to her pa.

"An' yerself, Will, what about you?" Father wanted to know.

"Mebbe some folks need scarin', James," his brother answered. "After all, why should I be taxed for drinkin' my grain when I can feed that same grain to my horses or serve it up at my table fer free?"

Uncle William wouldn't give in.

"What if we rode over to Bower Hill together an' talked with Neville?" Father suggested. "He's chief tax inspector now. Mebbe he'd listen. I hear he voted against the excise in the legislature, an' Ma says we've got some kind of marriage ties with his family."

"Save yer breath to cool yer hotch-potch, Brother. It's clear ye've stayed too close to the cook-fire these past months. General Neville's set up a tax office in his very house, an' others acrosst several counties. He oversees the swine they send to these parts an' call tax collectors. I heerd he no longer has any *regard* for the goodwill of his neighbors. Do ya think he'll be supportin' our contempt o' the excise now, man? Ye've got to be clean daft!"

There was an undercurrent of feeling between them as each turned back to his work. Every swing of the axe cracked louder. Lizzie and I backed away.

"Ow-ow-wow-ooie!"

Shrieking Injuns! I dropped behind the closest stump.

"Get up, Jane," said Lizzie, unruffled. "It's just Alex doin' his savage singin'. Pretty good, ain't he? There's scarcely a bird on a branch or a critter in a hole that he can't coax out in the open. You should hear his wild turkey call."

"Stop yer chitterin', Lizzie," Alex ordered, poking his nose from one bucket to the next. "Come see this sap a-racin'."

We drew closer for a look-see.

"Doesn't taste sweet," I noted, licking my fingers.

"Cow cookies! Ye've got to boil it first, Cousin," he reproached.

"Get the shoulder yokes from the sled," Father directed. "Looks like it's time to run the first batch down to the cook fire." He and Uncle William kept a close watch on all the containers now. "No sense in allowing an overflow!"

"It may not be sweet yet, Janie," said Uncle William, tying a scrap of cloth over the top of the buckets, "but there's a passel o' pesky bugs just clamorin' to get into the stuff! Hurry back!"

We headed for the boiling kettles, trying not to slosh away a drop. It wasn't easy to keep up with my older cousins. "Wait for me," I called. "How much runnin' will we have ta do?"

"There's 'bout five gallon here," Alex guessed, not slowing down one step. "Takes forty gallon to make one gallon of syrup."

It sounded like a heap of running to me. We wore a path to the orchard that day. It was hours before Aunt Rachel noticed me straggling half a trip behind the others and asked me to help at the bonfire. It was a kindness, I discovered, for all I could really do was keep out of the way.

A sturdy cross-timber was braced between two trees. From the beam hung a huge iron kettle. The air was choked with heavy black smoke that spewed up from a roaring fire. Aunt Rachel picked up a metal plate punched through with holes. The plate was attached to a long wooden handle that she pulled through the sap.

"What's that?" I asked, pointing at the greenish-white foam that bubbled to the top.

"Just dirt an' such that has to be scraped away from the good part. Here, try it." She handed me the skimmer. I stirred the sap slowly, enjoying the tingle of hot steam on my face.

"Couldn't we make the syrup inside?"

"Nay, chit! It'd steam away the roof if we didn't smoke it off first! 'Sides—it takes hours to boil sap down to the syrup stage, an' hours more 'fore it hardens."

"Jane!"

My mother let out an ear-splitting scream. She dropped the dinner basket she'd been toting.

"Get away from that fire!"

Her arms swung across her eyes and she tore down the trace back to the log house. Her scream scared the devil out of me and I dropped the skimmer in the fire.

"Here, child," said Grandma. She retrieved the skimmer and seated me a safe distance away. After dipping into the brew for a long while, she'd ladle the sap into the air to keep it from boiling too fast. Droplets streamed down her red, weathered face from the constant smoke and steam. Finally, she handed the skimmer to Aunt Rachel and sat down beside me. I was confused and shaken.

"Yer mother's a good woman, Janie," Grandma began slowly. "She's had a hard time of it, though—saw her own sister burnt to death, at just such a boiling down. The hem of the poor girl's apron caught a spark an' she was a ball o' fire. That's why Mary cried out to catch ye near the flames. Mebbe that's why she's let me do the cookin' chores fer so long. An untended coal—even a stray spark is a dangerous thing—it can bring down a whole house 'fore anyone wakes up to know better. Yer ma called out in fear, girl, but she didn't mean to scare you. She loves you so much, Janie. Why not go to her now?"

The door to the cabin was wide open. Mother sat spinning by the window. Her foot clicked the wheel in motion as her practiced fingers eased the wool onto the spindle. It was the fleece I'd brought in this morning. She looked up, her eyes a-glisten. I never knew she lost her sister. She'd never said a word about it.

"You an' Sara'll be needin' a new meetin' dress," she said softly. "Ye won't be spoilin' the surprise, will ye Jane?"

"No, ma'am."

Grandma was right. I had much to learn from my mother and now I held her in a fresh, new light.

It was a late supper that night. The men stayed out in the sugar camp till long after dark. They finally returned with the farm sled loaded down with sap.

Squirrel stew and rye bread with butter rumbled through my stomach. I'd gotten so used to lard drippings, I'd almost forgotten the taste of real butter—the smooth sweetness of it—melting over my tongue. It was a treat from Aunt Rachel. I stored a big wedge of it myself down in the springhouse.

Grandma and Mother were whispering over the dish pan. I pressed closer to hear.

"How 'bout a farewell quilt with a signature design?" Grandma was asking. "We'll work up a bee come first church meetin' next month."

"Rachel will be right pleased," Mother replied.

Cousin Alex was arm wrassling his father at the puncheon table. My twelve-year old cousin was rough and tumble, but his arm soon gave way and Father was drawn into the contest. Their cavorting came to a halt at the sight of Grandma dripping hot maple syrup over a trencher of snow. She let it cool, then pulled it up like taffy and dropped it into Sarie's mouth. Soon everyone was out dishing up clean heaps of snow.

"There's nothin' like sugar-jack!" grinned Father, licking the gooey candy from his beard.

Now I wished I hadn't eaten so much butter bread at supper. Who could believe it?—maple candy and a whole houseful of visitors—all in one day! And Mother didn't even send me off to bed with Sarie and the babies.

Grandma sat down and opened the family Bible. My name was writ in there somewhere—my name and all my kin from way back. I'd seen it once.

"Then the Lord said to Moses, 'Go in to the Pharoah, and say to him: Let my people go, that they may serve me!' " Grandma's voice rang with conviction and she looked fondly at Uncle William and Aunt Rachel. She spoke of the Israelites' bondage in a place called Egypt and how the Lord sent a plague of frogs and boils and locusts to torment the Egyptians.

"Bet he even sent Tom the Tinker," whispered Lizzie.

My eyes popped wide at the thought of it, but Grandma raised her voice to squelch out any further interrupting.

"All their oldest children died, but the Lord spared the Hebrews, an' even parted the great water to pull them out of slavery. It reminds me of my grandfather an' his family," she reflected.

Father and Mother shared a "heaven help us" look as Grandma's face shined with a light of deep recall.

"Grandfather 'scaped consider-able torment himself." She defended her digression to my elders. "Did I ever tell you children about the hanging of my grandfather?"

Our mouths dropped wide open and we scrunched closer to her rocker by the fire. Grandma ignored the skeptical sighs of Mother and leaned back in her chair as if to conjure up just the right words. Her gentle rocking was hypnotic. I locked eyes with hers.

"My grandfather—now that would be your great-great grandfather—was hung. He was a doctor. My crackies! We never see a doctor in this untamed part of Pennsylvenny, but Grandfather was surgeon to none other than the king of England an' the story of his life is a true-un."

I never doubted that the stories told to me by my grandmother were true. There was something about the firelight that let her look inside herself and bring out all those things she'd learned as a girl. All those kinfolk, long dead, were well-known to me through her lips. She had a talent for maneuvering her wrinkled face into the character of her subjects. Her thin arms flailed with the action and her voice—it crooned and teased, it ranted and hooshed. It lifted me out of my chink-logged house in the Pennsylvania backwoods and made me part of the adventure.

Grandma's eyes didn't see me now. Her spirit was beyond us, and I settled in for the telling:

Back when William an' Mary were king an' queen of England—about a hundred years ago— Doctor William Brownhill (that's my grandfather) set off on a sailin' expedition. He was ship's surgeon. What a fine man! Out at sea, a frightful bout of sickness spread amongst the crew. 'Fore long, there was nary an officer left to command. The dwindlin' crew picked Doctor Brownhill as the best person to take charge.

Long about this time, another bugaboo hit the unlucky seamen. Out of nowhere, a fleet of hostile Portuguese appeared—an ornery an' shiftless lot they were—ready to do battle. They stripped the English ship of its valuables an' captured my grandfather an' his crew. The varmints weren't satisfied with the plunder they'd already pilfered, so they threatened the skipper, "Show us more!"

"Ye have the lot of it," Grandfather told them honestly.

These Portuguese weren't ready to believe it. They had grand visions of a tremendous treasure hoard of rubies and diamonds and gold. "Show us your treasure or we'll show ye yer death," they vowed.

The brave doctor stuck by his word and was unfortunately hung. He dangled from the hangman's noose like a sausage out in our smokehouse, but soon the menacing pirates cut him down hoping he would talk. They combed the vessel from stem to stern looking for a boodle of gold. Try as they might, they learned nothing from Grandfather and he was strung up again. His life-spark was a-flickering when they cut the good doctor down again and partially revived him.

"Where's the loot?" they demanded.

Desperately, Grandfather choked out the same reply.

"Fer the last time, Brownhill, where's the gold?"

Their ungodly sneers and murderous greed was met with silence. Hoppin' mad, they carried out their threats and Grandfather was hung for a third time. It would've been the end, if his own men hadn't finally managed to convince the pirates of the truth. The good Lord intervened that day and my poor grandfather was saved. It was a miracle.

Grandma Miller heaved a sigh of relief and patted her Bible. "Ah," she remembered, "but that wasn't the end of it:

It wasn't enough that the Portuguese tried to hang Grandfather . . . the connivin' ferinners decided to carry him back to Portugal an' lock him in prison for seven long years. Doctor Brownhill endured his share of torment before he was eventually freed. At last he could return to London-town where he hoped to find the wife an' child he'd left behind so many years ago. He was excited as a pup!

Once in London, he made a beeline to his house and rapped on the door. A little girl bid him inside. She was none other than his own little young-un, Lizzie! She'd grown so much since he'd seen her last that he decided not to let on whom he was at first—just asked if Mrs. Brownhill was at home.

"My mother shan't return until nightfall, sir," she replied.

"And where is your father, miss?" He wondered what she must think of him after all these years.

"My father left home years ago an' died at sea."

"Ah, yes," said her visitor, "I remember now. He was hanged, I believe."

"My father was an honorable man, sir! He never died a coward's death," the lass insisted.

"I tell ye, Sis, your father was strung up by the neck like a common sheep thief!"

This was too much for her little heart and she scorned the persnickety scamp, as she thought him to be. How dare he speak so falsely of her dear papa, whom she'd always loved and honored?

He left the house to seek her mother, leaving Lizzie alone till evening. The very thought of her mysterious visitor left her smarting. She seethed over his insults.

Imagine her confusion at seeing this same stranger returning down the street. Why was her mother holding his arm and even resting her head on his shoulder? The sight was too awful and she burst into tears.

At long last, the secret was revealed and Lizzie hugged her dear papa whom she'd long given up for dead.

The wind wooshed down the chimney and through the cracks in the chinking. I hated to break the spell cast by Grandma's hanging tale. Maybe she'd go on.

"What happened to Lizzie after that?" I coaxed.

"Why, she grew up, of course, but mercy child! That's a whole other story and a romantic one at that." Grandma had that knowing smile that made us clamor for more.

"Romance, yech!" scoffed Cousin Alex. He clenched his throat and poked out his pimply blue tongue, pretending to be hung. He held his gruesome pose till he'd scairt us up the stairs.

That night in the attic as my mind wandered through the whole tale, I was grateful for the company of my older cousin, Lizzie.

V

ATTIC PREACHIN'

*Steal not this book
The owner says —
Lest the rope
Might end thy days.*

—Inscription in James Miller's Bible

Saturdays were awful. There was no getting around it. They were just out and out awful. It was always the same. Every last lick of Sunday's work got moved up a day, making Saturday the workingest day of the week. Oh, I was used to it. My double chores made the day go quickly. Then Sunday rolled around, slowing things down to a dead halt. Meals were warmed over, conversation hooshed to a whisper, and things got dull, dull, dull. In the morning we'd take turns reading from the Good Book and later, I'd practice reciting, or pray by myself. Sometimes, it got so still I'd hear my own heart beating and wonder if the day would ever end.

This particular Saturday was even more awful than usual. Tomorrow was the first spring meeting at Bethel Church and everything had to be perfect. Mother said so. Sometimes, she reminded me of that Bible story about Mary and Martha. Jesus visited them once and Martha flew around the house fixing meals and redding up. When she called for her sister to help out, Christ rebuked her while praising Mary for sitting at his side a-listening to his words.

Yes sir, my mother was just like Martha. This morning she got me up an hour early to wash clothes, buff shoes, and mend the holes in my old meeting skirt. She added a new pocket and said that would have to do. There'd only been enough wool to cut a skirt for Sarie, so I'd just have to wait, Sarie having the birthday and all. It wasn't easy. Every time I saw my faded, patched skirt hanging next to Sarie's new indigo blue, I felt sick with envy.

Father'd shooed me out of the barn after my egg gathering chores. He was busy giving Old Dan and Dolly an extra going over for tomorrow's ride. Even Grandma was bossy. She had me toting water to fill up the wash tub. That was another awful thing. Tonight everyone had to take a bath! I thought my arms would stretch down to my ankles with all the hauling. Then I was sent to the loft to fetch down at least a week's worth of potatoes, turnips, beans, and other vittles. Every other trip, Sarie'd tag along, getting in the way or wanting to stop and play dolls in the attic.

"That's fer babies," I informed her.

My feelings weren't at all friendly toward Sarie this day. I was tired of babies. At least on Sunday, I'd see Lizzie and plenty of other grown-up girls. I tromped down the stairs, leaving her to pout. By about the tenth trip, I was ready to play. We sat down among the pumpkins and squash and dressed some sorry-looking corn cobs in skirts of husk.

"Now, I'll be the mother an' you ken be the lil' girl," I told her. "My crackies!" I cried, assuming a strict tone of voice. "If ye don't stop that cryin' I'll give ye somethin' to cry fer."

I got carried away pretending till Sarie grew tired of her role. "Yore too bossy. I quit!"

"That's all right by me 'cause I got a better game." That sparked Sarie's interest. I seated her on a pumpkin with her cob dolls and pulled up a big barrel. I took an empty linen sack from a corner, stuffed my braids inside, and wore it on my head. Then, I tied the end of my sack-wig at the back of my neck. Now I was ready.

"This is called 'church,' " I announced, folding my hands piously. "I'll be old John Clark an' you can be the congregation . . . ." Sarie clasped her chubby fists together, going along with the game.

"And now, me children of Bethel," I mimicked the slow wavering voice as best I could. "What sins have ye committed since our meetin' last fall?" I craned my neck over the barrel and slowly scanned my pumpkin flock. "How many've broke the peace of this Sabbath Day by cookin' or quiltin' . . . or cursin'? Was it you, Sara Miller?" I shook a pointed finger under her nose. "How many've broke the peace of this settlement with gossip an' backbiting? Was it you, James Miller?" I looked off accusingly at the imaginary sinner. "And how many of ye fergot to seek the Lord's word from the holy book each day? Was it you, Grandma Miller?"

With each question I thumped my fist on the makeshift pulpit then turned to pace up and down. "Oh, children of Bethel," I said, thrusting out my arms with exaggerated fervor, "get down on your knees, lift your eyes to the heavens, an' pray for forgiveness . . . for the plain truth is we're all weak, wretched sinners in need of the Lord's help. The plain truth is . . . that . . . uh . . ."

By this time I was running short on sermonizing words, but with Sarie's laughing encouragement, I went on aping the jerky movements of the aged pastor and repeating his favorite phrase.

"Yes, me children, the plain truth is we're all sinners. The plain truth is . . ."

"Jane! Jane Miller! What is the meanin' o' this?" Grandma poked her head up into the loft and saw in a glance the cause of the merriment. All my antics and pacing harangue'd dropped the wig down over my face, and Sarie was rolling around the floor giggling.

"Come downstairs here, where I ken speak with ye proper."

I pulled off the wig and we hung our heads in guilt. Obediently, we descended the ladder to the second floor.

Grandma brought out the family Bible from the stand beside her great off-the-floor bed. Carefully, she unlocked the metal clasp and leafed through the thin pages to the middle.

"Here," she said sternly, "I want ye both to see this." She ran a finger down through all the family records—births, deaths, marriages, long lists of children and grandchildren. It was all neatly recorded for posterity.

"Here's yer grandpa, Oliver Miller," she read, "died March 18, 1782. Reverend Clark was there to lay him down to everlastin' rest. And, here's me eldest—yer Aunt Sara, born June 17, 1745 . . . almost fifty years ago. She made me a great grandmomma last year. The Reverend did her baptizin' back at that other Bethel Church in Chester County an' he did the new babe's, too. Fact is, he's served all ten o' me children as well as their young-uns—right down to weddin' me youngest. That'd be the year afore he baptized you, Janie."

Sure enough, there at the bottom of a long list was my own name. It was clearly entered in Father's firm script. Grandma saw the wonder on my face.

"Who knows, Janie, mebbe one day ye'll have yer own gal an' her name'll be right in here with the rest." Her voice grew strict again. "Now, aren't you ashamed? If ye only knew all the trouble the Reverend's seen me through—ye'd be givin' thanks 'stead o' pokin' fun. Lord knows, I never cease to marvel how all that service comes out of such a sickly body. Pastorin' ain't ever been easy—not then—an' it shore ain't gettin' any easier now . . . ."

Her voice trailed off and her mind seemed to wander. She laid the Bible on her bed and continued, "So, tomorrow when yer sittin' at meetin', I want ye to remember all the good things Reverend Clark's done an' give him yer prayers, not yer funnin'."

She started down the stairs, then paused to add, "Ye know, Janie, I think the Reverend would've liked the part about needin' the Lord's help an' 'the plain truth.' 'Twouldn't surprise me a-tall to hear it come up in his sermon tomorrow."

She gave me her kindly, knowing look. "Now, redd up you two, an' come down to help me shell corn. Bring that wig poke, too. Ye ken fill it up with seed corn to take to Dido fer spring plantin'."

After Sarie and Grandma left, I went over to look at the brown, leather Bible. I felt the fine tooled grain and gently opened the cover to the first page. There in beautiful script was written:

Steal not this book
The owner says —
Lest the rope
Might end thy days.

My eyes bulged at the words and my hands sprang to my throat. "Lest the rope might end my days," I repeated. "Just like the hangin' of my great-great-grandfather . . . ."

An involuntary gulp escaped my lips as the severity of the warning sank in. I closed the book quickly, wondering whether Grandma would mention my church prank to anyone. Making fun of the pastor was a sin, and I was beginning to realize that church-going was serious business in this family—real serious business.

VI

THE ANNIVERSARY

Remember the Sabbath day,
to keep it holy.
Six days shalt thou labor
and do all thy work:
But the seventh day
is the Sabbath
of the Lord thy God.

—Exodus 20:8-10

Something was wrong. This just didn't feel right. I pushed myself up off the bed ticking to figure it out—too much light in the room for things to be so still. The whole family was usually up and fed by now. My eyes followed an amber line that splotched the floor up to the parchment tacked onto the window.

There stood Grandma in a glow of morning light, running her crooked fingers gently along the oiled paper. "Oliver Miller wed Mary Tidball on April ninth, in the year of our Lord, Seventeen Hundred and Forty-four," she read.

I stepped toward the light and peered at the badly faded script.

"Fifty years," Grandma muttered. "We were married fifty years ago this month."

"Yer weddin' parchment was tacked up at yer first cabin, too, wasn't it Grandma?"

"That's right, girlie. It's seen years of window service . . . peculiar how the years soften the lookin' back. Almost makes a body long for the lean livin' back in Friend's Cove, near Bedford. Yer Grandpa Oliver ran the trading post there an' I was workin' at his side—keepin' the ledger, countin' up figures, easin' his dealin's with the widows an' other pore folk—always addin' a tad extra to the order fer the young-uns. Oliver never did approve of that!"

"An' here at *Mansfield,* Grandpa was justice of the peace," I added, proud to take part in the family narrative.

"Aye, the stubborn old coot," she recalled fondly, "I s'pose it was his high ideals an' honorable repute—along with his writin' skills that made him a justice . . . well, he never could've handled all his legal duties an' still run this plantation without me—me an' my boys."

Grandma pulled her old house-skirt over her head. "Ten children an' fifty years later . . . funny how I've quit hankerin' after that Brownhill frippery."

"You mean yer mama's riches?" I asked, pulling on my apron. "I've dreamed of runnin' me hand over her fine furniture or wearin' her bonnet laced with silk ribbons, or havin' her petticoats trimmed with fancy ruffles . . ."

"Whoa, Janie," Grandma put a sympathetic halt to my ramblings. "I used to dream 'bout wearin' all that finery, too. Even liked to imagine meself walkin' through a real town like Phil'delphy—used to be all a body could think of . . . .Now, it's the family. The family's what's important."

I followed Grandma downstairs and through the latch door. Morning color still streaked the bottom of the sky. Grey-pink beasties and purple hued banshees . . . the shapes and tints were never alike from one morning to the next. It gave a body hope to know that something was fresh and changeable. It was a favorite time—a cool, private time before the struggle began. And privacy was a rarity amid the tall butts of the backwoods and the endless daily chores. The wilderness air was clean and the sun was so fresh it cast a yellow glow across the barnyard.

"Ideas snap up at me in the morning," Grandma was saying. "Problems straighten themselves in my mind. Things make sense, Janie. Even Will's goin' . . . he's got his father's bullish sense o' justice—makes it impossible for him

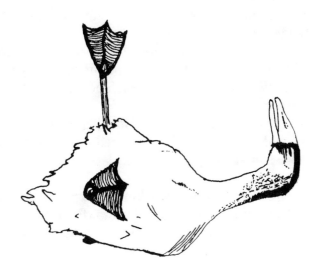

to reconcile with the local politickin'. Too bad he's got the wanderlust as well. He'll be a-leavin' . . ."

"But Father won't go. He'll keep us here at *Mansfield*, won't he?"

"Not to worry, lass. Yore daddy'll stay on the land. He's a solid one—always ready to tackle a tough job—ever since he broke in those oxen at such an early age. He. . ."

Grandma's converse broke off suddenly and I noticed a far-off look in her eyes. "What's the matter, Grandma?"

"Oh, Will's goin' an' I have this strong yearnin' to see my youngest gal over in Cross Creek. This family's breakin' apart—by distance an' by principle—with this excise turmoil. There's got to be a way to keep us together."

The old woman shook her head and grabbed a sack of corn grit from the henhouse. It was warm enough for the chickens and geese to run loose now. She hummed and clucked along with them, scattering feed along the path. Sarie showed up just as we spotted the gaggle of geese down by the run.

"Lady Tidball," hooted Grandma. "Lady Tidball!"

"Lady Tidball," Sarie joined in the call.

"She's a mean one," I observed, "look how she hisses an' snaps an' edges out the little-uns for seeds!"

"Why, there's nothin' mean about her," grumped Grandma, always oblivious to the temperament of her prize pet and I knew she wasn't always fond of us children barging into her morning solitude.

Sarie bent down to stroke Lady Tidball's long neck, but before she could touch it, the bird plopped down on its back and stuck two feet straight up in the air!

"What a silly goose," she giggled.

"She's ready for a good pluckin', I 'xpect," grinned Grandma, starting a song: "Go tell Aunt Rhody. Go tell Aunt Rhody."

We joined in, "Go tell Aunt Rhody the old grey goose is dead. The one she's been savin' . . . to make a feather bed . . . ."

"Mother Miller!"

Mother had arrived sight unseen. The stern expression on her face told me that we were all in trouble.

"How could ye?" She was asking, " . . . singin' worldly songs an' makin' light mockery on the Sabbath—it's a sin! And you, too, Jane Miller. I'm ashamed of ye. Now, inside girls. Run!" She pressed her Bible to the bosom of her grey meeting dress and swooshed back to the house.

"I must be gettin' on," Grandma sighed, following Mother into the house. "Forgettin' the Sabbath!"

I felt guilty. I'd forgotten, too. No wonder. There'd been no one astir. All the cooking and wood chopping—everything was prepared. A smoked ham was brought in from the smokehouse to be sliced down for a cold supper. Only the basic tasks like feeding the stock and milking the cows were permitted, out of necessity. Even a bathing down'd been indulged in by all. The last Saturday bath'd been before the husking bee last fall because of Mother's fear that washing was unhealthy. Too bad—Grandma said the hot water had a soothing effect on her old bones.

Back inside, Grandma picked up her fig jar from the corner cupboard by the hearth. It was brought all the way from Ireland—a gift for her wedding day, fifty years past.

"Yes, this is a day to be set apart for prayin' an' hymn singin' an' Bible discourse." Grandma sounded as if she were reminding herself, as well as the rest of us.

"Father Miller, what are ye thinkin' of me this day?" she mused. "Forgettin' the Sabbath, an' this the first meetin' of the season at Bethel Church. At least I didn't forget our anniversary."

"No, I'd never forget that," she repeated softly. She replaced the fig jar tenderly in its spot of honor beside the whiskey jug.

"Strange how things make sense in the morning." She twisted her wedding band with rough, gnarled fingers and headed upstairs in search of her old meeting dress.

VII

SABBATH MEETIN'

O God of Bethel, by whose hand
Thy people still are fed;
Who through this weary pilgrimage
Hast all our fathers led.

—Scottish Psalter, 1615

"Janieeee! Wait fer me!" Lizzie raced to catch up to us on the trace along the high side of Catfish Run. Her meeting shoes were strung across her shoulders and red hair was flying as she bobbed up the path.

"My folks are comin'—'bout half a mile back," she reported. After all that running Lizzie wasn't tuckered in the least. I quickened my pace to keep up with her.

"Good morning, Elizabeth." Mother smiled approvingly at the loosely braided tresses. I don't think she noticed my cousin's bare feet or mud-spattered hem. Mother made Sarie and I wear moccasins. We toted the shoes Father'd repaired during the winter. As we continued along the narrow, puddly trace, I was grateful for his leather skill.

Father headed our caravan with Ollie atop Ol' Daniel. He led us southwest toward Bethel Road. Just ahead, the oak-slat creel squeaked with each step of Grandma's little brown mare, Dolly. The basket contained vittles for between the services. Grandma sat arrow-straight in the saddle and Mother walked, carrying Baby John and leading Sarie between the puddles.

At the crossing, the new neighbors appeared.

"It's the Crocos, whispered Lizzie. We stared awe-struck at the husky man who barely spoke a word of English. "I heerd he's from Poland."

" 'S that near Ireland?"

"Don' know."

" 'S that near King Louie an' Queen Marie somethin'-or-other?" I remembered my Cousin Oliver's axe tale.

"Don' know. Further, mebbe. Pa says Peter Croco grew up in Germany an' come to America with some 'Hesshun' soldiers, then deserted and packed west—like us."[4]

Mother joined Mrs. Croco, who also clutched an infant. Mr. Croco greeted Father and soon they fell into a silent march leaving the Croco boys—Henry, Peter, an' John—to gaze at us, tongue-tied.

"Wee beastie brains—the lot of 'em!" Lizzie poked her elbow into my side.

"Bet they're just shy," I said, "prob'ly never saw hair your color afore."

That did it. Lizzie twisted up her nose at them and crossed her eyes. They quit their staring and moved off fast, keeping well ahead of us.

Sarie had stopped in her tracks and reached up to Lizzie, imploringly. Not missing a step, my cousin swung her around pig-back and tromped up the never-ending hill.

"Would ye be needin' a boost, too, Cousin?" She heard me huffing and puffing along behind.

"It takes over an hour walkin' to church, Lizzie. That's a good hike."

"Pfff, 'tis barely a jaunt in the cornpatch, Jane. Come along with ya."

Sun glittered through naked trees. I looked for patterns in the branches, trying not to think of my sore feet, but it

---

4 Peter Croco's father, Andrew Krackau (Croco), was born in Kracow, the ancient capital of Poland. He emigrated to Germany, where Peter was born. Peter served as a grenadier in the German army and came to America in a regiment of Hessians. He was severely wounded in the Battle of Brandywine. After recovering, he was assigned picket duty where on the first night, he deserted to the American side. He married an American girl, Catherine Uldrich, and came West in 1792. He purchased a tract of land at the headwaters of Lick Run. One of the first log schools was built on a section of the Croco Farm.

made me dizzy. Cold swirling air brought out the goose bumples. I felt hot and cold all at once. At last, we reached the crossroads at the crest and turned down toward the meetinghouse.

"James! Hallo, hallo man!" Neighbors approached from the other side. Father slowed Ol' Daniel to a halt and waited for Robert Smith and his family.

"Mother Miller—and Mary," Jean Smith squeezed their hands like the long lost friend she was. "Ye've fared well, I see." The long months of isolation set their eyes a-sparkle with a keen eagerness. Mrs. Smith's bartering talent was well-known throughout the backwoods. Her business knack had eked out many a bargain for her family and others, too.

"I'll bet ye've cooked up some good ones, Jeannie!" Grandma was always ready for swapping ideas, but they set a perfect Sunday example—no worldly talk on the Sabbath. Business would have to wait for another day and now it was enough just to be among friends.

When the church came into view, we sat down to tie on our Sunday go-to-meeting shoes. Sarie whined about her blisters, but no one paid her any heed because now the road was buzzing with "hallos."

"Hush Sarie, I don' fancy wearin' shoes either," I tried to console her.

"But my toes pinch." She took my hand and walked along gingerly. Father tethered Ol' Daniel and Dolly with the other horses at the side of the meetinghouse. They whinnied and sniggered as if they enjoyed each other's company as much as the folk in the churchyard.

Grandma pulled her footwarmer and coal tin out of the creel, then we entered the log church together. It was filled to overflowing. Mrs. Croco slid over to make room for us on a long split-log bench. Father joined the men and boys who lined the walls at the side and rear. Some wore overcoats like my pa, but others draped heavy wool blankets over their shoulders. They shifted to strike a comfortable pose and propped their guns against the wall.

Reverend Clark's shaky voice rang out, "Let us worship God!" All squirming stopped for the pulpit was high enough that all could see and be seen by the minister. His tall frame looked stooped beneath the weight of his black wool coat. The great white wig on his bald pate was tied neatly back with a swatch of black ribbon.

"His crowning glory," I murmered.

He lifted up his arms, bidding us rise. Below him stood the Precentor—Elder Kiddoo. It was his solemn duty to lead the singing, line by line. He started "Old One-Hundred" in a low, monotonous rumble, then slid up to a high note—our starting pitch. Voices resounded through the church—firm and austere. This was my favorite part of worship. I loved the singing, though sometimes it wasn't easy.

"Sing to the Lord with cheerful vo—ice," Precentor Kiddoo hit the lead-in pitch with authority, but Lizzie never quite found it. As much as I enjoyed sitting next to her, her singing had a sour ring.

I cupped a hand over one ear to better concentrate on the tune. Then, a voice began warbling behind me. I recognized the shrill, tremulous tones of Old Lady McKee. Several beats behind the congregation, she was singing with great gusto at an ear-shattering volume. Mrs. McKee's work in the Lady's Aid Society was widely admired, but her singing was endured by all. Most folk tactfully chose not to sit directly in front of her at services, for as the momentum grew, her high, off-key chirp was impossible to ignore.

Unable to hear my own voice, I stood on tiptoe and looked around. My ears found her first. The purest, clearest sound came from the far corner. It stilled the strange noises around me and carried sweetly and effortlessly throughout the room. Dido! I was agog! Reverend Clark's servant lady had such a beautiful voice and the kindest face—creamy brown in color, like milk and chickory brew. I liked her Maryland stories, too, but most of all I loved to hear her sing. I wished I could sing just like her.

Mother's scolding look pulled me back to the end of the hymn. "His truth shall from age to age endure . . ." I joined in with great zeal and drew out the 'amen' with a little trill, just like Dido. Pleased with myself, I plumped down beside Grandma, ready for the long morning sermon.

I well remember that April Sunday—crunched between Lizzie and my grandma, praying for my soul, and observing the ancient ritual. The serious nature of my Scotch-Irish kin is clear to me, now. Looking back, I see faces stamped with the bleakness of the Highlands and the spirit of grey-green moors. They were proud, honest faces, intolerant of government restraint and easily enraged over injustice. They were invincible faces, revering Calvin and Knox, battling Indians, banding together—a fearless lot, well-suited to wilderness struggle. Life was a serious matter. Their intense hunger for religious soul-searching made each part of the service food for thought.

My grandmother was a perfect example. One bony hand clasped the thorn brooch at her throat, while the other followed Psalm 107 in her Bible. She knew the passage by heart, but this would be the sermon text and she chose to ponder each word. "Oh give thanks unto the Lord, for He is good . . . the redeemed are gathered out of the lands, from the east, from the west . . . They wandered in the wilderness in a solitary way." Her expressive eyebrows punctuated the text and she nodded in agreement with its content. Skillfully, the minister wove the verses into a sermon of hope and redemption for all the sinful mortals of Bethel—who wandered in the wilderness, where there was no way!

"Have you kept the Ten Commandments," asked Reverend Clark soberly? The service had run a long while now and I fidgeted uneasily. I was sure the pastor pointed directly at me. Maybe he'd found out somehow 'bout me preachin' in the attic.

"Are you still wandering in the wilderness of lying, gambling, promiscuous dancing, or backbiting? Have you broken the sanctity of the Sabbath with frivolity and work?"

 Grandma looked at me and shrugged her shoulders in guilt. Surely, the Lord would forgive a forgetful mind. She untied a thimbleful of coriander seeds from a kerchief, popped several in her mouth, then dribbled the rest into my ready palm. A row ahead, Mrs. Smith was passing out ginger balls to keep her children quiet and alert.

No one dared to sleep through this part of the sermon, but farmers were active sorts, not accustomed to sitting. Sometimes a lid or two would fold, making it perfectly acceptable to stand for a spell. Capt. Billy Fife was first to blink back the drowsiness and stand, then James Dinsmore. Reverend Clark wisely quickened his pace and waxed louder in his speech. He proceeded to the climax—the sovereignty of God's grace and the need for repentance and a change of heart. There was a holy calm as he outstretched his hands and made one last earnest appeal to his 'children of Bethel.' The familiar words told me the end was near. Letting out a great sigh, I looked forward to racing Lizzie down to the spring.

We filed out into the churchyard after the final prayer. I followed my mother into a group of women who scurried about, setting out pot pies and breads, comparing recipes and catching up on all the winter's news. Many remarked on how I'd grown, some asked about my stitchery skill, but most commented on the passel of babes to be born.

"There's Mary an' Rachel Miller," they counted. "An' you, too, Jean Smith! I heerd Mary Kiddoo's feelin' so poorly she had to stay abed . . . an' this our first chance to visit in so long . . . ."

Mother handed me a bucket and I tore down the hill, glad to be rid of their well-intended questions and considerable cooing.

"Lizzie! You can't play in that spring water—not today!"

"Who's playin'! By jiminy, Janie, I was pooshed—an' when I get a-hold o' that bullyraggin' brother o' mine, I'll . . ."

"You'll what, Miss Sassbox?" Alex was snickering along with the Croco boys nearby, but he didn't stay to hear the rest of Lizzie's threat.

"I'm sorry, Lizzie, are ye all right?" I helped her out of the icy pool.

"No great shucks," she replied, clenching her teeth to keep them from chattering. "Those blunderin' cads can't make me cry. 'Sides, Ma says if ye fight a skunk, ye get a bad smell." She untied her shoes and pulled off the soggy wool socks. "Sometimes I wish we could leave Alex here an' move off to Kentuck without 'im!"

"What's this about movin' to Kentuck?" asked Hannah Dinsmore. She and her sister Sarah were fetching water, too. Lizzie was delighted to tell them the news of her leaving.

"Wish we could ride down the Ohio on a flatboat!" The older girls were enthralled, but I felt left out. My cousin was my closest friend and I just couldn't share her excitement over a trip that would take her away from me forever.

"My grandma's planning a signature quilt for Aunt Rachel," I explained, trying to worm my way into their conversation. "It's for the farewell."

"Sounds like fun, but it'll take a lot of stitchin'," said Sarah.

"We'll all help," Hannah decided, turning away from me. "Come on, Lizzie, looks like you could use some dry moccasins!" They laughed their way up the hill, leaving me alone. I was feeling very sorry for myself when I heard Mother holler. I picked up the old wooden bucket.

"What kept you, chit?" she asked. "Can't you see yer grandmother's ready to do the biddin' over this meal?" Inside and out, the church was dotted with families preparing for their noontime feasts.

"Find your sister, Jane," she added, "an' be quick about it."

"Take care not to disturb James Dinsmore up on the bury-hill," Grandma warned. "He's keepin' vigil over Rebecca's grave." She empathized with the man who'd been my Grandpa Miller's friend in the early days of organizing the church. A few years back, his wife had died and he was still fretting. We could see him now, standing tall and portly beneath a giant oak tree. His oldest girls—triplet daughters—were all talking at once and redding leaves from the simple marker.

"I'll bet Rebecca herself had trouble sortin' out that trio," remarked Grandma.

I knew exactly where to find Sarie: behind the church with the Gilfillan tots. What I didn't expect, though, was to find her barefoot and sitting in a pile of hay meant for the horses.

"Look at your new dress," I admonished. "An' where's yer shoes an' stockings? You're lucky Mother didn't catch you like this."

"Don't tell." The tears started to roll. She wiped her face and retrieved the footwear.

"I'll be keepin' yer secret," I laced the dreaded shoes back on her feet and brushed off her new wool skirt, "but . . ." I just wish she were older, I thought, and more like Lizzie.

After the noon meal, I wandered around the feed trough as the horses munched contentedly. Each was so different. Grandma's Dolly was small and gentle while Ol' Dan'l was a big, solid chestnut—better suited to working than to toting people around. Down on the end was the Reverend's Zachariah. Always first to arrive, he was as black as coal and very sure-footed. The senior member of the lineup was Elder Kiddoo's MacTavish. The poor beast was so old his back'd sunk into the shape of his horseshoes. I chawed a piece of oat straw, considering the scene before me. The boys were in one group while Lizzie and the Dinsmore girls were in another. Ollie an' Sarie joined the little-uns, who clung around their mothers' skirts. Not wanting to get my cheeks pinched again by the church ladies, I sneaked around the other side of the meetinghouse to where the men were talking.

"Seems like they've come up with this whiskey tax just to punish us pore western folk."

"And who else would the president be taxin'?" It was Mr. Smith talking. "Not those mollycoddled rich-uns back in Phil'delphy. Oh no, not with all their money an' influence!"

"There's where the shoe pinches," James Dinsmore concurred. "With all those Easterners sittin' in Congress, they'll never gather the revenue equally by passin' a land tax."

"Aye, James," said another, "this snarl over the whiskey tax is gettin' worse. Now, it's our own John Neville who's crammin' the law down our throats!"

"Those Feds must be payin' him a pretty penny to be tax collector. 'Tworn't so long ago that he voted our way, against the excise, in the state legislature."

Craning my head around the corner, I saw my father bickering along with the rest. His fists were clenched tightly behind his back.

"That turncoat! When I think of all the times he came around *Mansfield,* askin' me to vote him in here an' vote him in there."

"Well, I've seen the swine he calls tax collectors," broke in John Connor. "Nary a one of 'em could fill our shoes an' do a decent day's work."

"Shiftless bums an' ferinners, they are!"

"Aye, they're a corrupt lot," Robert Smith admitted, "but who's worse—the tax collectors . . . or the hot-heads out tar an' featherin' 'em?"

There was a rumble of muttered debate.

"Ye may not think it so bad when they've taken on the tax men," he went on, scanning the group fiercely, "but now they're takin' reprisals on men like yerself—who've decided to comply with the law. "

"I heerd Richmonds an' Strawhan had their barns burnt," said a deep voice I couldn't see.

"Met Will Cochran over at Croco's tannery last week—he told me they threatened to tar an' feather 'im when he registered his still."

"I'm afraid it's closer to home than that, friends," said Father. He looked at his neighbor, James Kiddoo. The debate grew still as they hunched in closer to hear the latest.

"Aye, Miller," said the elder, coolly, "ye may not know," he looked at the rest, "but Cochran's mill was destroyed." There was a buzz of talk. "General Neville came out to discuss the violence with me, my mill bein' close an' all. That same night, a mob broke into my stillhouse, shot the still full of holes, then set the place afire." He paused at the memory of it. "I still haven't recovered from the damage."

The elder received an outpour of indignant dismay.

"That's ugly news, neighbor," said Thomas Tidball, offering his help. "Have ye any idee who these men were?"

"It was dark, Tidball," said the disgruntled churchman, "but they tacked up a note signed 'Tom the Tinker.' "

The name brought a tumult of converse and suspicious looks. Most stared at Father and Uncle Will who stood toward the rear with Peter Croco.

Capt. Billy Fife found his tongue first. "Some say those men are from the hills of Mingo and Peters Creek; that John Holcroft, a Mingo militiaman, is their leader."

All eyes were on Uncle Will.

"You're in that group, Miller," continued the captain. "What say ye—is Holcroft the Tinker?"

Everyone knew Billy Fife was on the side of law and order. His militia ran whiskey east to supply the federal troops. I couldn't believe it! How could our own neighbors be so mistrusting when Uncle Will'd worked alongside them in the fields and at their cabin raisings? How could they think my uncle would take up with a hoard of bandits? It was a tense moment as everyone awaited a reply.

"Come now, gentlemen," interjected James Dinsmore, "this is no way to talk on the Sabbath."

" 'Tis all right, brother," said Uncle stepping forward. "I'll speak me mind on the issue. I've wrassled it aroun' in me own head long enough." He shifted uneasily at being put on the spot. "Shore, I've been with the Mingo outfit, started out as a bunch of boys drillin' in a field with cornstalk poles, but we're a right crack militia now—done pretty well on our Injun campaigns, if ye recall. I don' know any more than the rest of ye concarnin' the private goin's-on of the membership. I just follow orders. You can be understandin' that Cap'n Billy?"

The group looked doubtful.

"Aye, Miller," allowed the captain, "but how will ye stand, come June, when the law requires you to register your still in the office of John Neville?"

Again, the crowd was intent on my uncle, as if each man was trying to make up his own mind.

"It's a sore question, Billy," he replied, red with anger and struggling to keep his temper. "Like straddlin' a fence an' not wantin' to land on either side, so I reckon."

 The sound of a handbell interrupted the fiery discourse. Elder Vance was calling people back for the afternoon sermon, leaving the men in a dither of an upset.

VIII

OLD JOHN CLARK'S FAREWELL

In yonder church I spent my breath
And now lie slumbering here in death
These lips shall rise and then declare
Amen to truths they published there.

—Reverend John Clark's Epitaph in Bethel Cemetery

Mary Miller was piqued. She was uncomfortable in the small of her back with the unborn babe, but that wasn't the real problem. With all her years of church going, she could sit through most anything. It was her mood that vexed her.

"It's been a while," she thought, "a good while I've been here in this church." She felt a twinge of pain, but kept it well hid behind her stoic, at-meeting face.

"Still cain't decide whether I'm at home here," her Cross Creek family figured clearly in her mind's eye. " 'Course I never was much on decision makin' . . . prob'ly wouldn't be here a-tall if my father and Mother Miller hadn't stirred up the weddin' proceedin's after those revivals. James is a good man, of that much I'm sure." She looked for her husband, but couldn't find him in the crowd of somber faces. "Always carin' an' providin' for our young-uns like they's royal pups. If he just weren't under his mother's thumb so much . . ."

She glimpsed the Miller matriarch now, clutching her hymnal, singing "O God of Bethel." Mary's role in the house of her mother-in-law was a private struggle faced a hundred times a day. Openly respectful and fond of the lady as she was, she just couldn't shake the notion that, for all her babes and years of household duties, Mother Miller treated her as a child.

"She's the one who rules the house." Mary couldn't stop her jealous thoughts. "She's the one James turns to in times of crisis. She's the one with the ready answer. Even the children rally 'round *Grandma* most of the time."

"This won't do," she felt sinful at heart. "It's me that's the trouble—if only I weren't so timid 'bout settlin' things," she stormed at herself, "if only I didn't get so befuddled every time someone asks my opinion . . . if it were just in my nature to be more strong-willed, like Jeannie Smith."

Mary admired the take-charge character of her neighbor and closest friend outside of Cross Creek. Why, Jeannie could run her own household, cater to the young-uns, trek down to Coal Hill Market, and still have time to meet all the folks who sought her out for bartering advice. She had real business know-how—"spunk," Grandma called it.

"Heavens," thought Mary, startled at her change of outlook. "A few years back, I wouldn't've seen the good in a woman like Jeannie . . . I'd be thinkin' like my kin folk back in Cross Creek—that she was too outspoken, pushy, an' should keep her mind on more spiritual matters." Mary had a secret longing for the stricter mores of her youth.

Shutting her eyes, she tried not to think how Rachel let her children romp around, scot-free . . . or how awful she felt this morning when Martha Gilfillan asked after James' nephew, Oliver.

"That'll be the livin' end when he gets back," she fumed. "That coarse-mouthed drifter'll spoil my children an' have James off to some ungodly shootin' match, all in the same afternoon." She resolved to speak to her husband on the subject.

The shrill kee-yoo of a distant hawk tore at her irreconciled conscious. Mary shrugged off the foreboding noise outdoors and tried to regain her peace of mind. But there had been a change in the mood of the congregation. Everyone sensed it. The warm fellowship of the morning service had dispersed, leaving a cloud of doubt. The

Precentor lined out the opening hymn as usual, but the vim of the singers was lacking. Harsh stares were traded among the men, especially toward James and William.

"Oh no," thought Mary, "how could they get so worked up over politics on the Sabbath?" There was no question in her mind that they should obey the law and follow Reverend Clark's advice. She felt sorry for the poor minister. He's so feeble now and after all his years of spreading the gospel through this backwoods, he has to make his farewell address to this gloomy throng. It wasn't fair.

He read, from Matthew, the parable of the sower and the seed:

> The kingdom of heaven is likened unto a man who sowed good seed in his field. But while men slept, his enemy came and sowed tares among the wheat and went his way.
>
> But when the blade sprang up and brought forth fruit—appeared the tare also.
>
> So the servants . . . came and said unto him, "Sir, did thou not sow good seed in the field? Whence hath it tares?"
>
> He said unto them, "An enemy hath done this."
>
> The servants said, "Wilt thou then that we go and gather them up?"
>
> And he said, "Nay . . . let both grow together until the harvest: then I will say to the reapers, 'Gather ye together first the tares and bind them in bundles to burn them, but gather the wheat into my barn.' "

"Friends, it is my duty to say farewell." The Scottish minister's brogue and correct speech were soothing to Mary's ear.

"What a blessing it is to have a man of learning in our midst," she thought, remembering his Princeton training.

She hoped all her young-uns'd learn to read and write. Of course, the most important thing was that they grow big enough to help out with the heavy work at home. "My oldest is a-tryin'," she had to admit, "but it'll be a long while 'fore lil' Ollie is ready to work a-side his pa." She looked at her son, his feet dangling from the pew. He was waving slyly at Rachel's youngest, Tommy. Just then, Grandma turned him around—letting him nibble a costmary leaf that she kept in her Bible as a marker. Mary abhorred this kind of child-pampering that went on at services.

"Sakes alive," she vowed, "I'll be powerful glad when they're older."

"Although I will continue to live among you as a neighbor," the Reverend was saying, " 'Tis Reverend Joseph Patterson who'll be your spiritual advisor until a permanent replacement is found. I am sorely pressed to find myself giving a final address in this company. The plain truth is—I'm sad. Sad to call an end to my years of service to the Lord—and deep-down sad to leave my far-flung flock during these trying times . . ."

"I've given farewell sermons before. In the past they were just a means of leaving one calling to take on the burdens of another. This farewell will be the last." His crooked fingers trembled and whitened as he straightened his sermon notes and gripped his Psalter tightly. "The Clark family will be ever grateful to all of you."

Mary eyed Margaret Clark, sitting neat and prim in a black taffeta dress in the front row. Some said she was a mite uppity, but they seemed to forget how she'd taken in that young-un whose father died and how she was always organizing to make clothing for the young men studying for the ministry. And, who amongst us wants a house full of complaining elders and traveling ministers who stay forever and eat you out of house and home? Yes, Margaret was a fine, charitable woman.

Margaret had confided to Mary at noontime that she'd never seen her husband lose so much sleep over preparing a sermon. He'd gone through all his material from Mount Bethel, back in eastern Pennsylvania, and Bethel Church, down in Baltimore County, just to find the right text.

"He's determined to reason with the congregation about the taxation problem," she'd explained. "Nevermind his rheumatism, chills, an' shakes—he was ready to take that grueling trip back East to plead the farmers' cause with the federal authorities. Why, it took every ounce of persuasion I had to convince him that he was too weak and the only strength he had to offer was his strength of conviction—his faith in the Lord."

Mary agreed with Margaret and tried to give her comfort. "In my lifetime, I have served many Bethels," continued the pastor. "I've performed the Lord's work through all kinds of suffering and privation. I've seen Indian massacres and famine. I've buried those who died of loneliness in this solitary wilderness and I've buried those who fell in the war against the tyranny of England. During times of tragedy, I've tried to instill faith—into a woman widowed by the kick of a horse, and a father made childless by the bite of a mad dog."

"This rough land." Mary thought of her own dead sister, burnt in an instant. "It has no reverence for life." Tears welled up in her eyes as she realized she'd just been wishing time away.

"During times of joy, I've joined you in wedlock and baptized your bairns—most recently the young lass returned to us from Indian kidnap." Everyone knew he was speaking of the Fife family. Capt. Billy Fife found the poor child wandering in the wild during one of the Injun campaigns last fall. The Fifes had accepted her as their own daughter and given her a Christian home.

"Through it all, we've been a tight-knit congregation—working together and prospering our plantations to grow with each succeeding generation.   We've shared great renewals of faith during our revivals and have worked to provide education for those who will carry the message of the gospel across this great land." He looked proudly at his son, William, who planned to enter the ministry at Jefferson College.

There was a long silence from the pulpit, Mary noted, as if the Reverend was trying to get up the courage to say the next part:

"Now, we must remain a tight-knit family; we must support our president. Every man here who fought in the Revolutionary War struggled for a system of representative government where all disputes are settled by amicable means. Now, an enemy has stolen among us and sowed bad seed. One of our number, who felt it his moral duty to pay the federal tax, was visited in the night—his still shot full of holes and his family terrified . . . I sense in my flock a growing discontent—a hardness of heart against each other . . . . There are tares amongst the wheat!"

Mary sensed the uneasiness around her.   She was engulfed in it. The pastor's words had struck a sore spot in many who felt the excise on whiskey was unjust and the system of changing the law too slow and unyielding.

"Let those who plan to defy the law repent, for as the parable says: In time of harvest, the tares will be gathered up and burned, while the wheat . . ."

But before the final words of the message were uttered, Mary's attention was drawn to the side of the church where the Miller brothers stood. William grabbed his gun from the wall, pushed his way through the crowded meetinghouse, and banged the door behind him.

IX

THE NAMESAKE

The ship is sailing down the bay,
Goodbye my lover, goodbye.
We may not meet for many a day,
Goodbye my lover, goodbye.

—Sea Chantey

This beat all. Sunday evenings were usually dull, but tonight, everyone was on edge. Sarie, Tommy, Lizzie, and I banded around a taper, reciting our psalms and trying to stay out of the way. Poor Ollie got snapped at and went off to bed without being told. Mother had retired, though from all the pacing going on overhead, it didn't sound as if she had her mind set on sleep.

The church meeting was responsible. We all knew that. Uncle Will storming out at mid-service—it shook-up everyone. Somehow, Reverend Clark had managed to finish his farewell without further protest, but he was plainly worn out when he shook my hand after church.

There'd been times before when someone'd disagreed with a sermon and walked out, but none so shocking. People were aghast and full of sidelong glances for the whole Miller clan. They took Uncle's hasty exodus as cause for further mistrust. They didn't understand. I wanted to defend my uncle to anyone who'd listen, but no one was talking.

Aunt Rachel left Lizzie and Tommy here at *Mansfield* and went home alone to await her husband's return.

"She'd never do that 'less they have some serious talkin' to do," figured Lizzie.

Now, Grandma was dragging out the evening vespers as if she was doing a month's penance. She rocked at a furious pace, rattling off one psalm after another.

"Hear my voice, O God, in my complaint," her eyes left the page as she recited, "Hide me from the scheming of evil doers, who whet their tongues like swords, who aim bitter words like arrows, shooting from ambush at the blameless, shooting . . . suddenly and . . ."

"Grandma, could we have a story, now?" asked Sarie.

The old lady took in the moping faces aroud her and closed the heavy family Bible. "Reckon we've done our share of soul-searchin' this Sabbath," she decided.

"How about the rest of that story about your grandfather?" I suggested.

"Oh please, Grandma," begged Lizzie. "You promised to tell us the romantic part."

"Never would've guessed you were so keen on romance, gal," teased Grandma, "not the way you was ignorin' those Croco boys this mornin'!"

Lizzie blushed as red as her hair.

"Well, let me see . . ."

It was good to see Grandma put aside her personal fretting and act more herself again.

" 'Tworn't long after my grandfather returned to London-town . . ."

"After he escaped the hangin' noose?"

"An' left the Portuguese prison?"

"Aye, girls. Now, would you be hearin' me story, or not?" She tried to look cross, but her wavering eyebrows told us she was pleased we'd remembered the tale. Sarie climbed into Grandma's lap and they commenced a-rocking. Again, the creak of the chair and the snapple of the fire set a spell over the telling:

> Grandfather returned to London an' built what you might call an "honorable repute." He was the king's surgeon—the most skilled doctor in all London-town! One day, the king heard that my grandfather took a nasty spill—broke his thigh-

bone clean through. Why, quicker'n you can say "Jack Ketch," the king fetched in a troop of doctors to take a look-see, but it was all in vain. The good doctor died of his fall—a man held in high regard with many to weep over his bury-hole. On his deathbed, Dr. Brownhill . . .

"That's our great-great-grandfather," I informed Tommy.

. . . advised his wife to take Lizzie an' their younger gal to America.[5] So, they gathered up their belongings an' set sail, in 1714. By this time, Lizzie'd become a young woman. Under her silk bonnet were a pair of sweet blue eyes an' hair the color of Nebbychadnezzar's fiery furnace. What a handsome lass!

During the voyage, Lizzie set eyes on a young sailor named Thomas Tidball. She fell for him right off. They said nary a word, for it wasn't proper for them to converse. She was a wealthy English lady and he—only a common sailor. Still, he thought of her day and night—through his dreams an' at his work.

Once in a while, he'd see her promenadin' on deck with her mother. He sometimes thought she glanced at him. This set his heart a-burstin' with emotion, for all the fires of first love raged inside him. He pained in silence throughout the long voyage.

Months passed an' Miss Brownhill was also feelin' peculiar. She thought her sailor to be better than the rest. He had a noble, manly face,

---

5 Dr. Brownhill served King William from 1699-1702. When Queen Anne ascended the throne in 1702, changes in English religious, political, and economic life were so great that the doctor advised his family to emigrate to America. His acquisition of land in Jamaica may have also been a factor.

a politeness of manner, an' somethin' in every word an' action told her he was no ordinary man. Her feelin's ran strong an' she resolved to strike up a converse. Twice, she pretended to be ill so that she could walk the deck to get fresh air, but her hopes of a secret meetin' were thwarted. Her mother never left her side! Poor Lizzie! She knew she could never politely speak to the sailor an' her pretended illness became real.   She was heartbroken.

Thus, the voyage ended.   Their differences of rank kept them apart.   On the eleventh day of August, 1714, they landed in Philadel'phy.   Here, the lovers were doomed to part, though nothing had passed between them.   Lizzie settled in Chester County with her mother, while her beau returned to sea.

Now, Dr. Brownhill's wealth was built up through his holdin's on the island of Jamaica. His widow'd barely set up housekeepin' here in America before this scoundrel of a nobleman showed up. He'd followed her over from England an' wormed his way into her affections. Soon after he wedded Elizabeth's mother, he left to tend the property in Jamaica. That rascal was never heard from again! Folks politely figured him for lost—murdered mebbe. The truth was— he nabbed the Brownhill fortune and absconded!

But, gettin' back to Thomas—the sailor boy we left aboard ship—the return to England made him restless. Once the ship weighed anchor, his hopes sank down deep. Wakin' or sleepin', Lizzie was always on his mind. He was desperate.

The storyteller paused, as if the hopelessness of the situation was too much to bear, then picked up on the telling:

So it was, for our young hero. Full o' spunk an' ambition, he was, but sore-troubled to see the miles growin' 'tween him an' his Lizzie.

As if that weren't enough, the poor seaman faced other heartaches: His father died in London-town an' his sister-in-law, a sly, uppity woman, stole his inheritance.

Still smitten with Lizzie, the penniless lad turned back to his life at sea. He shipped off to America an' began a diligent search. Finding Miss Brownhill was no easy task. He didn't know where to turn, or who to ask, but he kept on a-tryin'. Finally, his persistence paid off. The lovers were reunited an' agreed to an engagement.

On a glorious day, the sixth of July, 1715, Thomas Tidball wed his Elizabeth.

"Elizabeth," repeated my cousin breathlessly, "just like me..."

"That's right, Lizzie," affirmed Grandma. "Elizabeth Brownhill Tidball was your great-grandmother an' your namesake. A grand lady she was, too, with elegant clothes, fine china, an' furniture from France."

"What happened to her?" Lizzie asked.

"She was a brave one," Grandma's eyebrows arched up proudly, "left all those worldly comforts an' trekked out into the frontier."

"Must've been hard on her," I said.

"Aye, Janie," Grandma patted my hand, "but Elizabeth had great faith an' she knew her problems would work themselves out for the best. She didn't complain an' she learned, as I have, to find joy in the little things in life."

"Like havin' a secret hidey-place?"

"Like havin' a passel of healthy grandchildren at her knee," Grandma smiled down at Sarie, asleep in her arms. She'd dozed off back at the part about the king's doctors.

Lizzie gazed far beyond the hearth flames. The coals cast a fiery glint around her "Nebbychadnezzar" hair, making her look like a queen.

X

APRIL GREENS

The big butts stood around,
more lordly and toplofty than ever,
shouldering one another,
crowding out the sky,
keeping the humans down under their thumb.

—*The Awakening Land,*
Conrad Richter

"Ah," gasped Grandma. Her sharp eyes had a way of spotting the things I overlooked. She brushed back the dead leaves to find a whole mat of watercress standing no higher than her thumbnail in the black, moist soil. The tender stems and shiny leaves sparkled in the sunlight as she plucked and folded them carefully into her apron.

"Bit early for watercress, Janie. The mild weather must've helped 'em along." She tasted the tangy plant. "Snappy as ever ..."

A stiff April wind whipped my skirt about my legs as we hugged our gatherings tight and meandered down the run. Spying a cluster of curly dock, Grandma fell to picking the crinkly edged leaves.

"What a tasty mess this'll make," she told Sarie. I shared her preference for the young sprouts of early spring.

Our search took us through the woods and up into the old pasture. Last year's poke stalks were shriveled up along the edge. In a month's time, we'd be back to pick the new growth that was sure to spring' up around the old. I stuffed my apron full of dandelion greens and Grandma's favorite: wild mustard.

"It's a joy to have things growin' here, where once was naught but trees. A miracle really. When I think of all the grubbin' out we did here," Grandma recalled, ". . . plowin' through roots an' around stumps, always fightin' off coons, crows, pigeons, an' every other hungry critter. Lost a good horse to snakebite—not to mention pounds of human sweat. I can see your Grandpa Oliver now . . ."

I glanced around the pasture. Seeing no one, I thought Grandma was acting mighty peculiar. Maybe the early morning light was playing tricks on her senses.

"Yes, girls, an' he's as young an' strong as the day he marked off *Mansfield*. What a glib tongue he had in his head that mornin'! Why, one look at this virgin woodland risin' up aroun' Catfish Run an' he tramped off a claim, blazed the sides of that boundary oak, a-talkin' all the while."

"Just look at these butts, woman," he'd say, " 'Tis a sign of land worth havin'." His mind was stubborn set. "Soil's rich here—well drained." He'd sift the dirt into my fingers. " 'Twill clear into good farmland." Dreamily, she stared up into a leafy bower. Sarie and I traded stares, not sure whether Grandma was speaking to us or not.

"Well, he was right," she went on. "My old legs met this forest almost half a century ago. They're well acquainted. The boundary oak, that old white oak," she repeated.

"Where is the boundary oak?" I asked, trying to pull her back to reality.

"It's been years since I've seen the marks on that tree, but it must be nearby." Determined to find it, she led us up the ridge, then cut through the new clearing.

A woodpecker was rapping away. "Pop-op-op! Creak!" The sharp noise sent Sarie and me scampering. Thinking better of my flight, I turned to see Grandma frozen like a scairt deer. "Crash!" A dead gum tree gave way in the wind, pinning her down in a tangle of branches.

"Oh, no!" I cried, gathering a screaming Sarie tight.

"Merciful heavens," groaned Grandma. She tried to raise up, bumped her head, and collapsed to the ground.

"Hold still, Grandma," I directed, snapping some of the thinner dead branches away. Sarie helped me clear the rubble.

"The Lord spared me by a few inches," she said, rubbing a sore spot and looking glad to be alive. Her old bones were locked into a crouch—her feet snagged in the folds of her skirt. I rolled Grandma onto one side and she was able to twist free of the debris.

"Hadn't we better turn back now?" I feared she was hurt worse than she knew.

"Aye, Jane, but let's salvage our pickin's first." Back on her feet, she began to regather the greens dumped in our panic. Her chest heaved and she swiped at a trickle of blood on her cheek.

"Forgot how treach'rous these new clearin's can be. Guess I'm not the hale woman I used to be."

Father girdled these trees two years back. Now they were lifeless hulks ready to be niggered off. He'd be ready to plant around the trunks by the end of May. As the wind picked up, another limb fell nearby. Grandma took Sarie and I by the hand and hurried us into the safety of the green wood.

"Bad cess to ye!" she yelled back, riled at the skeletons that loomed over the clearing. "I've done battle with these trees right from the start," she explained. "That first spring, yer Grandpa an' I bivouaced on a forest floor smooth an' unspoilt by undergrowth. The lean-to served well enough; it was livin' in the half light that bothered me. The foliage was so thick I had to light a taper in the middle of the day. What was it Oliver used to say? 'Tree cover was so tight . . . a squirrel could start out in the Poconos, live off acorns, an' never touch ground till he's clear past Ohio Territory.' Finally he hacked out a clearin' big enough for the log house."

"An' that was the beginning of *Mansfield*," I added.

"That's right, Janie . . . such a blessin' to see that first splotch of sunlight in the clearin'. A holy marvel, it was, for with the sunlight came the grass an' with the grass the cow could feed proper—the livestock grew, an' the plantin' began. It's an eerie feelin' livin' under the constant gloom of this big woods. Makes ye sick in the head. Menfolk don't mind much. They're out there huntin' an' such, but woman's work keeps her on the improvement. Plenty of women go clean daft in the darkness."

I remembered her story about Minnie Coots, back at Friend's Cove. That woman got so depressed, she couldn't remember her own name. "That's why I'd rather work aside Father out in the fields . . ."

"Nay, chit, the trees are hard on the body, too. I've helped pull out enough stumps to see the big butts sap the life right out of a man. And let up for just one season an' they start a-creepin' closer. Why, dead or alive, the trees can get you—body an' soul. Ye'd best stick with your Grandma an' the near-house chores, Janie." She shivered at the thought of this loathsome struggle. She shivered with cold, too, for her skirt was drenched and stained, her moccasins squishing wet with slick dew.

"Guess trees are like that stubborn ol' barn cat of Jamie's," decided Grandma. "You fight with 'em so long an' go through so much that you end up gettin half fond of 'em."

It was beyond me how anyone could hate something so much that she started to like it. But I didn't question my Grandma. In fact, I gained a fearsome respect for the trees that'd almost taken her from me this day.

Grandma was jittery from her fall. Anxious to get her home and into dry clothes, I didn't notice Sarie darting into the near woods on some secret mission of her own. She reappeared soon enough with a sly smile on her face and her chubby fists stuck behind her back.

"Close yer eyes an' hold out yer hands," she demanded.

I obeyed, then peered down at handfuls of tiny blue violets. "The first flowers of spring," I admired softly. "Do ye think there's enough sugar to make candied violets?"

"Hoity-toity, Jane," Grandma had changed her skirt and appeared more like herself now. "Ye know we're low on sugar till yer Cousin Oliver gets back. 'Sides, those flowers can go right into the mess with the other greens."

"But they'll get all brown." Sarie and I dipped a mug in the water bucket and filled it with fresh violets to brighten up the dim room. Grandma didn't mind. She spread out her whole collection for us to see. I recognized the mustard leaf—rounded and deep green—but the others looked alike.

"Looky here," pointed Grandma. "This-un with the rough toothed edges—it's chickory. Yer dandelion leaf is just plain-toothed an' pointy. Heap 'em together, boil 'em down twice, an' ye got yerself some fine eatin' . . . . Almost forget," she dug into her apron pocket, "chickory roots boil down to a hearty brew."

"I know these!" Sarie picked up her favorites. "Dandy roses!"

"Now, how'd that get in there," laughed Grandma, removing Sarie's treasure. "The leaves of an old plant like this are too bitter," she explained. "They'll sour my mess even if it is cooked twice."

It was a treat to find fresh things to liven our usual diet of corn mush and rye loaf. Grandma sure knew her wild plants. Maybe one day I'd know them, too.

"You'll catch on," she said, reading my thoughts. "Just need to know what yer doin'. Take poke—saw some this mornin'. Poke sprouts make fine eatin' 'fore the plant stands hand high, but after that the greens sour an' the roots'll kill ye. Ye might see birds gobblin' down those purply pokeberries, but don't try it—to young gals like you—they're poison!"

"Poison berries!" Sarie considered it seriously, skewing her face into a sour pucker.

"When will Mother an' Father get home from the log rollin'?" I asked, changing the subject.

"They'll be along with yer brothers sometime this evenin'. Now, let me work on me greens, girls. Ye've got hens to set afore noon."

It was cool and pleasant outside. The leaves were still tiny, letting the sun beam through. I was glad to be about the outdoor chores again. Oh, there was always plenty to do inside the cabin, but finding greens and running after chickens—that hardly seemed like work a-tall.

Checking the barn, we found only one of the older hens nested. The rest were scratching up corn grit and running around loose. "Cluck, cluck, clu . . ." I grabbed a fat one and set her over the eggs nestled in the straw.

"There," I said, clapping a basket over her head, "now just you stay put."

"Why'd ye do that?" Sarie wanted to know. She was afraid of chickens and looked around suspiciously for Ol' Red, the rooster who liked to sneak up and peck her backside.

"We've got to keep 'em settin' on the eggs to warm em up, so the lil' chicks'll hatch." Sarie thought eggs were just for cracking up and beating into bread puddings.

"Ockeroo-eeoo. Eeoo!" The pesky rooster found his target. Sarie wailed and held her backside while the hens scattered to the far corners of the barn.

"Quick, Sarie, catch 'em," I ordered. But she'd had it with

fowl and sat down on a bale of hay and played at blowing
hen feathers into the air! Meanwhile, I raced around the
barn, gathering the nervous hens and trying to coax them
atop their eggs.

"Janie!" Sarie was hollering again. It must be Ol' Red. I
followed her voice and found her kneeling in the cow stall.
She was calmly stroking a hen who'd nested in one corner.

"See, Janie, I didn't even need a basket," she smiled
proudly, as if to make sure I knew she wasn't always a
scairt rabbit.

"Well, I just hope Tessie doesn't up an' tromp on her!"

After a dinner of bread and fresh milk, Grandma started
churning outside the front door. She hummed and got

going at a lively clip, then must've decided that there were
too many idle hands.

"Bring that straight-backed chair out here, Jane. Looks
like Lady Tidball needs a good pluckin'."

I toted out the chair and hung her feather sack up over
the back. "Well, what're ye standin' aroun' fer? Catch those
geese!" We didn't budge. Sarie'd had her fill of birds this
day an' I knew their nasty natures.

Grandma threw up her hands in dismay, set me to
churning, and approached the gaggle herself down by the
run. Sure enough, as we watched, she reached out for
Tidball and plop, the old bird fell over with her feet in the
air. Grandma pulled out a strip of cloth, tied the webbed
feet together, and carried her pet up the hill.

"There's a good grey goose," she soothed. Holding Tidball
by the feet, she tucked its head behind her arm and plucked
the down and small feathers from the soft white under-
belly.

"Does it hurt?" asked Sarie.

"Nay, these feathers'd fall off anyway," answered
Grandma. "This way she keeps cool an' new feathers have
room to grow in."

Sarie tried to pat Tidball, but the bird responded with a
hiss.

"See, Grandma, she is mean!" I agreed with my sister's
assessment, but Grandma was too busy plucking to hear
any complaints. She finished the downy stomach, then
turned her over and pulled back a few long feathers to get
to the smaller ones around the wings and neck. Sarie
played with the big feathers, for their stiff quills would
make an uncomfortable spot in the bedding. After a spell,
she set Tidball free. The old bird waddled off awkwardly,
honking a protest of her recent indignity.

"Now, it's your turn," said Grandma, getting back to her
butter churn. We romped around the slope, finally cor-
nering a goose. She seemed friendlier than Lady Tidball, so

while Sarie held her down, I tied up her feet. At first, we were afraid to tug at the feathers, but Grandma nodded approvingly and we got used to it. Several handfuls of down got carried off by the breeze, but we managed to bolster the supply.

"Maybe this'll be enough to stuff Cousin Oliver's pillow," I said, hopefully.

"Could be, Janie. Careful! Don't pull out the green feathers. Those are the new-uns. Got too much moisture in 'em so they'll take too long to dry."

We captured a few more geese. The more we tried, the easier it got. Little by little, the sack filled up. At last Grandma fluffed up the feathers and hung up the sack in the air to dry.

Supper was delicious that night!

"Being outside all day has a way of heppin' up an appetite," Grandma claimed.

One taste of that mess of greens and I had to agree. She'd fixed it with a dab of lard and sliced bacon—the first fresh food of the season. Sniffing at our bouquet of spring violets, I decided that with the feathers ready, I'd better keep pace with my pillow stitching. I brought the cows home and rushed through the rest of my evening chores so I'd have enough time to add a whole new letter to my sampler.

Long after dark, Mother and Father still weren't home. They weren't back next morning either and I wanted to know why. "Do ye think the horse went lame, Grandma? Do ye think someone got hurt? Mebbe they met up with John Holcroft—that Tom the Tinker fellow . . . ."

Grandma hooshed me with a look and tried to keep me busy, but I could see she was worrying, too. It was late afternoon before we heard familiar voices and saw Ol' Dan'l clip-clopping up the trace. I dropped my water bucket and ran to greet them. Grandma flew out of the house where she'd been preparing supper.

"Not a mort too soon," she cried, then we all took in the glum expressions on my parents' faces.

"Thought you two'd have a good time at the log rollin'," said Grandma, puzzled. "What's the matter with ye, Jamie? Not enough pot-pie an' whiskey to go 'round?"

"The rolling off was fine, Mother." He was not amused. "We were just finishin' up in the afternoon when Will rode over to give us all the news. Benjamin Sweet was killt yesterday mornin'. He was out grubbin' in a clearin' when a tree fell on 'im."

"The dear old man!" exclaimed Grandma. "Edna never could get him to slow down."

"Most of the folks rode over for the wake." He put his arm around Mother and Baby John. " 'Course, we went along, too. Been up all night."

"I should've been there. I should've been there." Grandma wrung her hands, then took charge. She took the baby from Mother and shooed us all inside. Steaming noggins of hot chickory brew were cut with whiskey and served to my parents. I laid out supper, glad at least, that they hadn't run into the Tinker's men. It was a quiet meal.

"Lord have mercy!" Grandma repeated over and over as she rocked the baby by the fire. "It could've been me 'stead o' that pore man. She explained the source of her scratches and her near miss in our clearing the day before. "To think, I was pinned under that limb about the same time he was killt. The Lord works in mysterious ways."

"Almost like an evil spirit was turned loose acrosst these woods," whispered Mother. She looked haggard from the long couple of days and sleepless night.

"Nay, Mary," disagreed Father. "Life has enough real evils for us to contend with, without conjerrin' up imaginary ones."

Somewhere off in the night, a mourning dove cooed.

XI

THE BLACK SHEEP

As I went down to Derby,
all on a summer's day.
'Twas there I saw the biggest ram
'twas ever fed on hay.
The wool on that ram's belly,
it dragged down to the ground
They sold it there in Derby
for forty thousand pounds.

—Favorite English song of
George Washington

The threat of frost was gone now and the ground was warmed by the May sun. For days, I'd helped Mother till the truck patch by the side of our log house. All the stones, twigs, and deepest dandelion roots had to be dug up and the clods raked smoothly. When every inch of soil was loose and feathery—to Mother's satisfaction—we set in planting. Potatoes, turnips, cabbages, and onions—all were neatly covered underground.

Mother'd made a trade for some sunflower and dipper gourd seeds at the log rolling. I was helping her start a patch in the back where they'd have plenty of room to grow.

Father called me out to the barn. "Look at this, Jane!" he said, angrily. I climbed up the stall gate to see. Alexandra lay in the straw with two newborn lambs huddled at her side.

I was delighted. "What's wrong, Pa?" I asked, not understanding his mood. He'd been so pleased with the lambing this spring. Maybe he didn't like Alexandra birthing so late.

"For one thing, those're males an' I'll have to trade 'em off." Father only kept a few rams. Sam-the-Ram was enough! It was the females that he prized, for their wool and for their ability to increase the flock.

"For another thing, . . ." he nodded straight below. There was a tiny black lamb all by itself. I swung over the gate and knelt beside the wee beast. I'd never seen a black sheep before. It was barely breathing and trembled with cold. Gently, I picked it up and carried it over to nurse with the others.

"Baah. Baah." Alexandra's low bleat was unfriendly. She stood up and nudged the black lamb away.

"How can she do that when the poor thing can't even stand?"

"She's shunned it, Jane. Best let nature run its course."

I thought about the lamb killt by wolves and my feelings ran strong. "We can't let it die, Father. We just can't! Is it a ram? Is that why ye won't save it?"

"Nay," he replied, surprised at my outburst. "The black-un is the only she-lamb in the litter, but show some sense, girl. Can't think of anyone 'round here who's got time to play nursemaid to that young-un. 'Sides, I'm countin' on your two hands at the shearin' tomorrow."

I pleaded with him to save the black lamb, but before I could convince him, he set off to work and would hear no more. Wrapping the newborn in an old seed bag, I carried her into the house.

"What have we here?" asked Grandma, looking up from her work. Sarie and Ollie were down with colds and the itch, so she'd spent the whole morning dumping out old stuffing from the bed ticks. Now she was hackeling dried cornhusk for fresh mattresses.

"Well, I'll be!" she exclaimed. "Wait till yer mother sees this!"

"Sees what?" asked Mother, coming in from the truck patch.

My father'd been skeptical and Grandma was amazed, but Mother was superstitious.

"That one's bad cess," she stated. "It has the mark of the devil! Why, it could change yer brother's cold into croup or somethin' worse. Now get it out of here!"

"Why, Mary," soothed Grandma, "don't ye remember what Jamie said the other day 'bout there bein' enough real evils without us makin' up more? 'Twon't hurt to let Janie help this lamb along." She dipped the end of a cloth in some milk and tried to get the lamb to suckle.

"You try, Janie," she said after several unsuccessful attempts.

My mother'd seen enough. "I've gone along with most of yer ways concernin' the chores an' the raisin' of me children, Mother Miller," her voice sounded strained, "but I'll not be weavin' black wool an' I'll not tolerate that evil critter around our house."

I agreed to take Olivia—for that is what I named her— back to the barn. It seemed right to name the lamb after Cousin Oliver; my mother had no great liking for him, either.

"You couldn't be bad cess to anyone," I told my pet. It was hard to tell whether any of the milk had dribbled down her throat. I stroked the dark wool and contemplated my new black oddity. "Feels like any other lambskin," I decided. "I wouldn't mind havin' a pair of black mittens a-tall." My mother was as heartless as Alexandra to shun this weak, suffering animal. When I left to start my supper chores, Olivia showed no sign of improvement.

Inside, Grandma was softening bits of brown soap in water. It would be used to wash the sheep down in the run tomorrow. Mother was covering the red sores of Sarie's itchy flesh with a black, greasy mixture. How strange she looked!

"What's that?" I asked.

"Hog's lard an' brimstone," answered Mother. "Quit yer scratchin', Sara Miller, an' be still. Fetch me some tea," she directed.

I filled a noggin and whiffed the vile odor of Mother's cure-all: boneset tea. She brewed the stuff in large quantities whenever anyone had a cold. Personally, I felt it'd be better to die than drink it, but Sarie'd have to learn that for herself.

"Here," winked Grandma, dropping in a lump of maple sugar.

I stirred it up and watched Mother coax my sister into taking a sip. It was hard to tell who looked worse—Sarie, her face streaked with black, contorting with every taste of tea—or Ollie, who lay whimpering on his corner pallet— covered head to toe with Mother's gooey ointment. Even his scalp'd been rubbed down, so that his yellow moppet was a dark, oily mess.

"He looks like a black sheep himself," I said without thinking. One look at Mother and I knew I'd better not mention the subject of black sheep again.

"Aye," concurred Mother. She leaned over Ollie with her hot tea remedy. "He's scratchin' himself raw, but I 'xpect he's cryin' over that bear rug more than anything else."

"Had to take his bear-skin blanket away," Grandma confided. "Found it crawlin' with lice an' bed ticks, so I took it out back an' set it afire."

That was disastrous news for my brother. His bear-skin was his prize possession. He couldn't sleep without it. It hadn't been an easy day for anyone.

When the chance arose, I sneaked back to the barn, where Olivia was still looking poorly. I wrapped her in my arms and tried some boneset tea. She took a little from the end of the cloth and my hopes started to grow.

"I see ye've got yer mother's patience fer doctorin'." Father looked down at us in the hay. He was right, I realized, half regretting the harsh things I'd been thinking about Mother this day. She was particular about things, but she knew her herb remedies as well as Grandma knew her greens.

"Gettin' late, Janie," said Father. "Time for bed."

I agreed, reluctantly, but as it grew dark I found it difficult to leave. Olivia was swallowing now. Intent on my task, I was unafraid of the deepening shadows, and the noises of the barn animals seemed protective company.

The next morning, I awakened to find Olivia tottering before my eyes. She stood! I flipped back a blanket that someone'd spread over me and ran out of the barn to share the news.

My feet were barely touching ground as I stopped short at the latch door and confronted an empty room. Grandma was off somewhere. The creak in the floorboards overhead told me Mother was upstairs tending Sarie and Ollie. She'd be in no mood to share my discovery anyway. There was a faint sound behind me and I turned to find Olivia standing at my heels. She'd followed me all the way from the barn!

"Ye found yer walkin' legs," I patted the tiny black head. She bleated to me softly, as if in reply. Sounded just like those two white lambs calling to Alexandra. As I poured some milk, Olivia teetered along at my side. Dipping the end of my apron into the liquid, I fed my young charge. She was more eager this morning, licking my fingers and slurping in each new offering. I helped myself to the porridge pot and rushed through my meal before Mother could get down to scold.

Our whereabouts were not to go undetected, however, for just as we stepped outside, Father hollered. He, Uncle Will, and Cousin Alex were building a dam across Catfish Run near the sheep pens. Leaving his work, Father waded out— his mouth set in one grim line.

"Ye know your mother's feelin's 'bout havin' that critter in the house."

"Her name's Olivia, sir, after Cousin Oliver." I was surprised at my own boldness.

"That's a good one, Janie!" Uncle Will slapped his knee and doubled up in laughter. "Looks like yer missus ain't the only one this side of the Tuscaroras that thinks of Oliver as a black beastie!" He elbowed Father in the side, unable to control his mirth.

"Jane Miller, take that animal out to the barn an' get back here to lend a hand. Be quick about it, lest ye get your first laced jacket."

I moved quickly, for my father was a man of his word. He'd never whupped me before, but I didn't plan on there being a first time. Couldn't figure what Uncle found so all-fired humerous. I'd given it considerable thought, and Olivia was the most honorable name I could imagine.

Back near the run, the sheep were huddled at the far end of the pen, as if they sensed what was about to happen. I wished Lizzie were around to help as I approached them, uncertainly. Before long, I was well behind in the chase.

"Who's herdin' who?" Grandma queried, pokin' a fat stick through the fence corner to clear the flock out into the open. This allowed me to circle around the closest two, clap my hands, and drive them down to the water's edge. They bleated and whined all the way. The one Uncle took hold of let out a terrified, "Baah!" Using softened globs of Grandma's brown soap, Uncle lathered up the struggling animal. That ewe-sheep was stubborn strong and terrified, but Uncle jostled his footing and kept his balance.

After he soaped up the first sheep, he dragged her into the waist-deep water where Alex was waiting for the scrub-down. They splashed about like babes in a tub, but Alex did a thorough job and shoved the sheep toward the holding pen. The suds rinsed away in the current as the ewe swam through the cold spring. Father met her at the bank and standing in water up to his knees, hoisted her into a clean pen.

"Keep 'em comin', Janie," Uncle shouted impatiently.

They were hardly cooperative, but I ran rings around those sheep and worked hard to keep pace. By noontime we were almost done, and I was as wet as the men in the run. "Storm's brewin'," cried Father, checking the grey clouds on the horizon. "Get a move on, girl."

I understood Father's worry. A storm would slow down tomorrow's shearing. Sheep had to be perfectly dry or their shorn fleece would mold.

Suddenly, I was airborn. I felt an unexpected sensation of upheaval. It was Sam-the-Ram! The ornery critter'd been holding out on me all morning—hiding in corners or scampering away. He'd seen his chance and butted my backside halfway into the run. The rough landing knocked the wind clear out of me, not to mention my pride.

Father offered me a hand up and bit his lip to check a smile. I didn't know whether to laugh or cry as I watched him join the chase. It took all three men to corner Sam and drag him into the water. The stubborn old ram baahed worse than any of the others and I felt a twinge of satisfaction to see him get his come-uppance just like the rest. He hopped up the bank, cocky as could be, and joined the chorus of bleating protesters.

Sam-the-Ram and Alexandra were the only named sheep in the flock besides my Olivia. Father gave names to horses and cows—animals that'd be around while, but he said it wasn't worthwhile to name the smaller livestock. They were often traded off or met the chopping block.

Alexandra was worth a name. She came from a Merino strain with very fine wool and was a gift from the prize flock of my Uncle Alexander's. But, Sam was nothing special—I never thought he deserved a name of his own. It came from a soft-hearted field-hand, who once said he stood out like a tall hog at the trough. So, the dubbing was based on Sam's antics and cantankerous disposition.

Early next morning, the sheep were let out. Their hour of reckoning had come on a clear and glorious day. Being outside through the brunt of the winter, their coats had protected them well and now hung heavily.

Alex drove the flock into the sheepfold. His father took a firm hold of one, lifting her up on a platform. She put up a squealing good fight till Father turned her over, at which point she lay there agape, docile as could be.

"She just gave up," I muttered. Out came the old shears. "Uh-oh!"

"Not to worry, girlie," Uncle Will reassured me. "These sheep'd thank us later, if they could. They'll be glad to be rid of this growth, an' yer father's hand is steady as a wart on a toad." Father snipped away, rolling the fleece back with one hand and shearing with the other. There was a steady click of the shears as he cut the fleece up to the back bone, trimmed off all the leg wool, and molded the coat into one shorn piece. Alex caught the fleece as it fell and the bare-naked ewe leaped down among the rest. At the sight of her pinkish-blue skin, the whole flock started bawling and bellering.

Next, Uncle crabbed Sam, but the belligerent ram slipped through his grasp, yanking him sideways.

"Not so fast, Sammy," hooted Uncle, with grit. "Ye'd best get it over with, boy-o!" Sam-the-Ram was pounced upon. It took considerable grunting and muscle for the men to heft him in place and flip him belly-side up.

"Ye plan on lollygagglin' all mornin'?" asked Alex in his jeering voice. He indicated that the shorn fleece was ready for bundling. I watched as he spread the wool outside up, then lapped the leg and haunches from each side. Rolling from tail to neck, Alex gave a neat twist to the neck wool and used it as a binding.

"There," he said with a final flourish, "you try it." I caught on, but he made me re-roll several fleeces tighter and I couldn't get the hang of the binding.

"Here," he said, finishing one for me. "Now, tote these out to the barn loft—quick!"

"Just a dad-gum minute," interrupted Grandma, arriving on the scene. Her eyes poured over the fluffy white bundle. "Ye've left the cut side out—that's good," she praised meagerly. "A woman has to be able to see what she's workin' with!" She pinched her boney fingers through each plump, oily fleece and set the best aside. The others, I hauled to the barn. On every trip, Olivia bleated out to me, but after yesterday, I planned on staying in my father's good graces. There was no time to dally.

Back at the sheep shed, Grandma was all a-dither. "This won't do, Sonny," she scolded. "Some of the wool is still damp in places an' moldy wool ain't worth a hill of beans. Now, spread this out on the hay rick an' see it dries proper."

It was fun to see Alex get bossed for a change. He leered at me on his way out, so I kept my smile to myself, but couldn't wait to tell Lizzie.

XII

THE RED EAR

Now as for those sheep:
they're delightful to see.
They're a blessing to man on his farm.
For their meat it is good;
it's the best of all food.
And the wool it will clothe us up warm.
And the wool it will clothe us up warm.

—"The Sheepshearing,"
English Folk Song

My talk with Lizzie was a long way off, for most likely, she was being kept as busy as me. Mother wanted to get the bulk of the spinning done before hot weather set in.

"It'll take a heap of wool to stuff Rachel's farewell quilt," said Grandma, sorting through the strong prime staple cut from the sheep's back. She picked up a hank and whisked it across the metal teeth of her carders. Outright fussy, Grandma marked her carders "left-hand" or "right-hand," and never let me use them. Plenty of eggs, seeds, and maple sugar had been swapped before she'd been able to afford those fine-tooth combs.

My carders were a couple of spikety teasel from the back pasture. I combed through the fluff, picking out bits of burrs and twigs. Careful as I was, I just didn't have Grandma's touch. Whisk! Her carders flew one way untangling the snarls. Whisk! She brushed back the other way. With a catchy motion, she peeled off the springy mat and patted it on the smooth wooden side of her carders, making a rollog.

Mother stretched out the first bit of combed spinstuff and sat down at her spinning wheel. She eased the rollog onto the spindle, which twisted the wool into yarn. The whir of the wheel and the "pat, pat, pat" of her foot on the treadle began a working rhythm for us all. "Spinning in the grease," she called it, preferring to spin the wool raw, then wash and dye it later.

In a few day's time, my fingers were pricked red by my teasel ˈcombs. Finally, Grandma took pity and instructed me on her coveted carders.

"Now, don't grate the teeth together," she admonished after my first try. "Just fly over the top like a whisper." She watched over my shoulder for quite a while before approving my strokes.

Day after day, I sat there carding away till my joints stiffened up, but Grandma was insistent. She was pushing for her quilt stuffing, and Mother wanted the finest shoulder wool combed out to spin baby shifts and blankets. Baby blankets! I figured we needed a bevy of them. Whisking and picking, brushing and rolling—it never seemed to end.

Such a mortal shame it was to be penned inside on such a beautiful day. My only break came each noon when I toted out the dinner pail to Father in the far clearing. He was working the soil with the big ox team, trying to get ready for corn planting. My outdoor escape didn't last long. Ever since our neighbor got killt and Grandma had her mishap, Father was quick to shoo me out of the treacherous clearing.

"And don't bother yer cousin while he's training those bull calves," he added. Uncle Will'd loaned out Alex a few mornings a week so he could work the young oxen.

"Back off, Janie," ordered Alex, when I met him on the path.

"Alex-the-Boss," I thought, resenting his stint here with the calves. I'd sure rather curry Buck and Bill than comb out sheep's wool. If Father'd just give me a chance, I could get their coats gleaming and teach them to mind, too.

I carried my fretting inside, but couldn't suppress it. "Why can't I work in the fields with Father or train the oxen like Alex?" I asked them. "I could learn just as good as any boy."

The spinning wheel kept whirring and Mother had no reply.

"Your work here is just as important, Janie. An' don't let anyone tell ye diff'rent." Grandma bent over to thread her drop spindle.

"But, you worked in the fields with Grandfather . . ."

"Only 'fore Alexander an' Thomas were old enough to help. Neighbors were scarce back then, too. Let yer father do that gruelin' work, Jane. Ye'd best help out in other ways."

Longingly, I peered out the doorway watching Alex put the calves through their turns again.

"This is a right nice day. Why don't we work outside?" suggested Mother. Grandma carried the spinning wheel and Mother started working the drop spindle so she could walk around minding the children. Hauling out the fleece basket and my block chair, I sat basking in the sun. The warmth in the blustery air was refreshing, but if I had my druthers, I'd be out training that ox team.

The next day it rained, keeping everyone inside. Father repaired tools in the barn. As for me, it was more of the same. When I wasn't carding, I wrapped the spun yarn into skeins on the niddy-noddy. Grandma kept the spinning wheel whirling while Mother washed and dyed the hanks. If I didn't comb the wool just right and get out every last nit-picking fleck, Grandma handed it back saying, "We ain't makin' horse blankets," or, "Comb it again—soft as Tidball's down."

It rained all that day and the following two. The longer it rained, the shorter the tempers got inside. Sarie and Ollie were up and about now, their red sores still doused with sooty ointment. Our work didn't interest them much and they started to whine. Mother diverted Ollie for a while with a gourd rattle. She slipped a few corn kernals inside and let him play.

"What 'bout me?" sulked my sister, wanting a toy of her own. Grandma had the answer: she opened up a corner of their new bed ticking and pulled out some cornhusk to fashion a crude doll. Taking a strip of husk, she tied a goose feather behind the head, creating an Indian maid. Sarie was enthralled, but Ollie was more difficult to amuse. Too fidgety for Grandma's stories or even the ever-faithful coriander seed treats, his face twisted up in a terrible pout.

"Ye'd better not cry," warned Grandma, getting crotchety. "Else I'll give ye somethin' to cry fer." She didn't like being house-bound any more than the rest of us. Ollie turned purple as pokeberries, then just like someone'd popped the stopper off the whiskey jug, he bust out wailing. Baby John woke up and joined him. That made Mother cross and she chided me to keep working. Soon, Sarie was snivveling, too, and I thought my head would split with all the jabboring clack. I just had to get out of the house, but the rain continued, turning the barnyard into a marsh and washing rivulets down the slope to Catfish Run.

That night, I still felt vexed—cooped up. I pushed a pile of stewed pumpkin around on my plate. I'd had so much pumpkin and mush that the stuff clogged in my throat refusing to go down. Father was too busy to hunt fresh meat, so it was back to the old stand-by: jerked beef. Grandma couldn't get away from her spinning long enough to gather fresh greens and the truck patch was nowhere near ready. Keeping my mind on the blackberries I'd be picking in a few months made the bland food a little easier to swallow.

"Eat yer mush," I snapped at Sarie, feeling I had as much right to be cross as anyone else.

"Howwww!" It was an astonishing yell. My eyes bugged out of my head and Sarie jumped about that far off her chair and started shreiking.

"Now, stop that screaming," ordered Mother. "Jane, don't stand there with yer mouth open! Ye both know Indian Peter as well as ye know yer own father. Now, stop that screamin', Sarie, stop it!"

But, it didn't make any difference. Ollie and John were crying too, but Indian Peter paid us no mind. His business was with Father.

"How does he do it?" I wondered, unable to take my eyes off his dark, sullen face. None of us heard that Indian come in. Why, when any of us opened or closed the latch door, it's creak could be heard a quarter of a mile, but when Indian Peter came—he opened that door, stepped inside, closed it, and there wasn't a sound. He'd sure put some excitement into a dull day!

Mother served him some supper, averting her glance from his fierce, swarthy eyes. His weather-beaten face was a coppery color—his cheeks hung in loose folds around a great hooked nose. There were folds around his mouth, too,

putting his face into a permanent frown. The chin was firm and square-set and his lower lip protruded giving him a look of proud strength.

Other than his curt greeting, Indian Peter had little to say. He offered to help Father with the corn planting, accepted the meal Mother handed him, and left for the barn. There was a mad dash to the window so we could watch his every step. I worried about Olivia being out there with him, but Mother turned a deaf ear.

"Strange how that savage has a habit of showing up around mealtime," she noted.

"Don't be fergitten' he's the *savage* that warned us 'bout the Injun up-risin's. Oliver an' I gathered up all our young-uns, 'cludin' lil' Jamie here, an' hightailed it acrosst the Monongahela to safety. An' just in the nick of time, too!"

"That's right," Father recalled. " 'Sides, he'll sure take some of the plantin' load off my back."

"That's all well an' good," Mother conceded, "but I never can tell whether he plans to stay a day, two weeks, or two months, even."

"Not to worry," Father tried to ease her mind. "I'll only need him for a spell, an' he'll stay in the barn."

"Why's he named 'Indian Peter?' " I asked, recovering from the shock. "Peter's a white man's name, ain't it?"

"Isn't it?" corrected Mother.

"Isn't it?" I repeated, eager to hear the story.

"Don' know if I can answer that or not, Janie," Grandma thought for a while. "Long as I can remember, Indian Peter's been helpin' the settlers in this backwoods. Spends a great deal of time fishin' along the creeks. Come spring, he'll work aside the white folk plantin' crops an' he'll turn up somewhere else to harvest in the fall."

"But how come he doesn't live with his own kind?" I wanted to know. "That's a good question," replied Grandma. "All I know is what I heerd when I first got here—that Indian Peter's the son of William Peter, who's the only Indian who was ever sold a tract of land by the Commonwealth of Pennsylvenny. William Peter an' his wife owned a whole hillside acrosst the Monongahela River."

"Their oldest boy was also called William Peter, but the settlers called him 'Indian' Peter. When the white men came into the area, the Indians resented them for taking their land an' moved west across the Ohio River. They'd sneak back on the warpath burnin' cabins an' takin' prisoners, but Indian Peter had no part of it. He stayed with the settlers, an' they liked him. 'Indian' Peter they called him, which wasn't his Indian name a-tall."

"I heard his ma was a half-breed," said Mother, suspiciously. "Maybe that's how he got so friendly with the whites."

"Stop talkin' down a rain barrel, woman. That's just hearsay," Father stated. "Plenty of folks livin' in the wilderness were captured an' lived with the Injuns 'fore the treaty was signed—some captives didn't want to return to their families an' some that did were shunned."

"That's right," Grandma agreed. "Mebbe some things are better left unsaid."

Mother was tongue-tied. Father seldom spoke against her in front of us all. Guess his nerves were on edge, too.

"Well, I'll not have me children thinkin' all Injuns're friendly," She spoke up at last. "Remember the massacrees an' that young-un Captain Fife found—uprooted from her blood kin by cantank'rous savages."

"Aye, Mary, aye," murmured Grandma in agreement.

I wondered what it'd be like to get kidnapped by Indians, live among them, then escape. I'd be heartbroken if I got home to find out that my own folks would have nothing to do with me. Now I knew how Olivia felt being shunned by her mother. At least she had me.

My mother needn't worry. I had no plans to take up with wild Indians. Still, deep down, I couldn't help thinking that there was something grand, even noble about Indian Peter.

"Hope Olivia fares all right out there in the barn with him." It was my last thought before drifting off to sleep.

Strange how one day I couldn't wait to take the vittles out to the clearing, and the next day, I held back, hiding in the thicket, half scairt to take the last few steps.

"Janie!" Father spied me and whoa'd up the big ox team. Feeling rather foolish, I stepped into the open, handed Father the dinner pail, and turned around, ready to beat a hasty retreat.

"Not so fast, girlie! Indian Peter has somethin' fer ye."

Apprehensively, I looked out across the fine-tilled earth. Father'd plowed the clearing crisscross so the kernals could be planted in each juncture. At a distance, I saw Indian

Peter working with a long stick. He pulled the seeds out of a pouch that swung from his neck and with a few deft motions, bedded the corn underground.

"Why's he usin' a stick?" I asked.

"That's the Indian way," answered Father. "It's called a diggin' stick." He gave a hoot, beckoning his new field hand over for the noon meal.

Indian Peter uprighted himself and approached. His upper half was naked—the coppery flesh a-gleam with sweat. Although he wore breeches like a white man, his hair was greasy-looking and hung loose below his shoulders. It was long enough to braid, like my own! I took refuge behind Father as he got closer.

"How!" he yelled.

My knees were shaking like the ague.

"*Ho! Kpet'ching-we-Xi!*" He dug deep into his seed pouch and held something out for me.

"Go ahead, Janie. Take it." Father prompted.

Feeling squeamish, I gathered my wits about me and accepted the present. It was a tiny ear of Indian corn. I opened the creamy husk and saw that each neat row was perfectly aligned with shiny, red kernels. Indian Peter's eyes flashed on mine, but I saw no other hint of kindness on his time-lined face.

"Thank ye," I mumbled, not sure he'd understand.

"*Kitchi*," he grunted. "Red ear—bring good luck!"

I rarely got presents, especially from Indians! By now, my curiousity was awakened, so I ventured some questions.

"Is that yore good luck piece?" I pointed to a round, grey stone that hung from a leather strap around his neck. It had a hole ground out through the middle and a strange design.

"Eh-eh," he replied, holding the pendant in his great rough hand. He crouched down for me to see better. "Bring me good luck—like your *Xus'kwim*. He pointed to my red ear. "Many winters ago, my father's father found stone on shore of Great Water. Made by his father, eh? Now, I keep *man-it'to*," he said, clutching the ornament, "to honor my people and remember those who've gone before."

"What's yore real name, Indian Peter?" I was eager to hear more. "*Leni Wis-a'mek,*" he said. "Mean 'Catfish Man,' but that long ago, before my people left their land."

"*Leni Wis-a'mek,*" I recited. Who'd ever guess he had the same name as our run?

"Eh-eh," said the red man. "Now, I take white man's name—Peter. Preacher say Bible Peter good fisherman—like me!"

"Of course," I thought, remembering the story of the Apostle Peter in the New Testament. "What would 'Jane' be, in Indian talk, I mean?"

"Jay-hayne, Jay-hayne," he said. "No such name. I call you *Shi'ki-ni'tis'xkwe.*"

"Shee-kee. . ." I just couldn't get my tongue around it.

"*Shi'ki,*" he repeated, "mean 'fine.' *Ni'tis* mean 'friend.' *Shi'ki-ni'tis'xkwe!*"

"*Shi'ki-ni'tis'xkwe.*" It had a pretty sound, rolling off his lips.

"Shee-kee-nee-tees-hkway," I said. "Fine friend . . ." Well, if that didn't beat all, I told myself! I'd been right all along. There was something grand about Indian Peter and I knew I'd never have to hide from him again.

That night, I hung up my red ear of corn on the wall— right next to Mother's sampler about the 'dreadful book.' I figured my good luck piece'd help even-out any of the bad things that might be writ about me in there.

Looking out the window, I saw a wagon coming. Uncle Will and Alex sat in front, lurching this way and that with every rock on the path. They'd taken the last of our rye and oats over to Kiddoo's mill for grinding. The wheels rattled over the puncheon logs thrown acrosst Catfish Run as they pulled up out front. The family gathered around, but Uncle William was gravely silent.

"Hallo, Brother," called Father. He began unloading grain bags from the back of the wagon.

"Ye needn't bother, Uncle James," said Alex. He and Uncle didn't budge from their seats. "It's still raw grain. There'll be no flour ground this day."

"What's wrong, Will?" Father demanded. There'd never been a hitch in their arrangement of trading turns riding the grain to mill.

"John Neville, that's what's wrong!" exclaimed Uncle. "An' that cursed excise, that's wrong, too!"

"Calm down, brother," Father tried to understand. "Now, tell me what happened."

Uncle Will was seething with anger. "They're still takin' reprisals on pore Kiddoo, that's what! Parts of his grist mill were carried off last night. Looks like Tom the Tinker struck him twice!"

"Galumphin' lunkheads!" cried Grandma.

"Listen James," roared Uncle, "what happened today—it's made up me mind. I'll not be registerin' the still next month—not a-tall!" He slapped the reins on the back of his horse team and clattered off. "No matter what!" The last words were flung into a cloud of dust as he disappeared up the path.

Father was speechless, the strain on his face was plain to see. Grandma looked browbeaten and Mother looked worse. We stood on the path, just as they'd left us. The baby squalled, breaking the tense silence. It was then I realized that Indian Peter, *Leni Wis-a'mek*, had been watching us.

"*A-ki!*" he yelled, drawing closer. "If you are care-worn, go up on the mount and let the north wind blow your worries away." He raised his great arm, as if to lift a prayer. "Or let the south wind talk to you and give you peace."

With that, the Indian left and though I didn't know it then, we were never to see him again.[6] I thought I'd never heard anything sound so holy.

"If it were only that simple," Father wished aloud.

---

[6] Janie later learned that Indian Peter died shortly after that, probably of a heart attack. He was found on a path heading toward the river, perhaps en route to do some fishing. He lived in a log cabin along a stream in Finleyville. There are many stories of his kindness passed down through the generations.

XIII

PAYIN' CALL

*This is therefore no country from whence to raise a revenue.
It is (yet at best) but a nursery, and from whence you are not
to expect fruit. Take your apples from your orchards, and let
these young trees grow; they will bear fruit in due time.*

—*Incidents of the Insurrection,*
Hugh Henry Brackenridge

About a week later, I stood waiting on the trace behind our old log house. A whippoorwill was crying out its name, and a pair of hermit thrushes fluttered for insects atop the swollen waters of Mansfield Run. The forest had that lush, yellow-green color of new spring.

The clatter of a rickety wagon broke into my morning reverie, as Uncle Will's powerful ox team appeared round the bend and eased to a halt nearby. I piled Father's tools and Grandma's old dye pot in the back of the wagon, greeted my aunt and uncle, and climbed aboard.

"Ye'll be slowin' me down at the smithy's, Jane," grumbled Uncle.

"Hokey-pokey," declared Aunt Rachel. "One old pot to mend won't make that much difference, William. Ye'd be a lot easier to live with sometimes if ye had an even tem'perment—more like yer ox team here."

"If me tem'perment were more like the oxen," he told her with a wink, "ye'd never hae married me! Come along, Buck. Gid up, Bright!"

The animals' massive necks leaned into the yoke, sharing the weight equally and easing the cart into motion.

"Could I run an errand over at the Reverend's?" I asked secretively, still chewing on my corn pone breakfast.

"Mebbe on the way back," offered Uncle.

"I'd say ye had a bit o' unfinished business to settle with the pastor yerself, William," Aunt Rachel urged.

I remembered the day he walked out of church during the farewell address.

"Aye," he admitted, his face turning grim. "Things are closin' in on me, Rachel, but just as soon as ye have that young-un an' I get me last rye crop in an' Oliver gets back to help me make one more batch of Monongahela Rye . . . We've got to be movin' on."

"What're ye cheepin' fer?" demanded my aunt. "We'll be ready. Ye've already sold half the property[7] an' we're gettin' the team shod today."

"Keepin' Buck an' Bright was a good idee," he said with certainty. "With their feet protected, they'll be ready to take that rough trek inland once we get to Kentuck. Why, the two of them together eat 'bout as much as one horse."

"Things are shapin' up," decided Aunt Rachel, cheerily.

We were silent the rest of the way, and I returned to thinking of Lizzie and her family leaving. I tried to keep my mind on Olivia and Cousin Oliver, but I kept coming back to the realization that I would soon lose my best friend.

"Hope we reach Tidball's early," said Uncle, " 'fore a crowd sets in. I'd just as soon avoid any talk 'bout the latest tinkerin' over at Lynn's in Canonsburg."

"It don't take more than a handful o' men these days to turn a pleasant gatherin' into a finger-pointin' harangue," added my aunt.

When we pulled up in front of the blacksmith shed of our cousin, Thomas Tidball, I knew there'd be no getting around rhetoric this day. Outside was Capt. Billy Fife, comfortably sitting on a log amid an odd assortment of wagon wheels.

---

[7] On June 9, 1794, William and Rachel Miller sold 150 acres of *Milville* to Conrad Sailor.

The captain's horse was tethered beside a black steed that looked strangely familiar.

"Looks like Zachariah," I noted, " 'xcept fer that white diamond on his brow."

"Bet that horse's seen a lot of miles," said Captain Billy, between puffs on his long clay pipestem.

He nodded toward the smithy's shop where our cousin was working on someone's mouth with a pair of horse pincers. "Now, ain't that a pretty picture?" he asked, sarcastically. "Thomas Tidball—doctorin' the teeth of the very man who ruined his own brother-in-law's mill. Pore Kiddoo," moaned Captain Billy, "he'd prob'ly thank me to smash Holcroft to smithereens! I oughta knock the hindsights off . . ."

"Holcroft!" I gasped, darting behind Aunt Rachel. "He's the Tinker, ain't he?"

"Hoosh, chit," commanded Uncle.

Holcroft swore a terrible oath as the smithy yanked a back molar from his jaw. The bloody tooth fell to the dirt floor. Cousin Thomas picked it up by the roots with the same pincers he'd used for the operation and dropped it into a leather pouch. The contents clicked ominously as he slung it into a corner.

"Another token fer me bag o' pain," he noted, unsmiling. "I reckon there's more misery laid to rest in that bag, than in all o' Bethel Cemetery, over yonder."

Aunt Rachel put her arm around me as if to ease the shock. She had no stomach for such things, and even Uncle seemed queasy at the ugly sight.

John Holcroft clapped a hand over his mouth and exited swiftly. "Hallo, Miller," he mumbled through his pain, seeing his fellow militiaman for the first time. "Don' be fergittin' the muster down in Mingo the second Wednesday o' next month. We've got important business to meet the new troop quotas required by Congress." Blood was seeping through his fingers as he swung onto his mount and galloped off.

Apparently, Holcroft's brief statement had whetted the captain's interest. "Well, well, well, Miller," he brayed, "Now, what do ye think'd bring that man out here?"

"Mebbe the Mingo smithy, John Wall, cain't handle dental work."

"Mebbe," said the captain, mocking'ly, "or mebbe the Tinker's makin' the rounds—lookin' fer his next victims—those good, law-abidin' men who registered their stills this month afore the deadline!"

"I'm pleased to pass the time o' day with ye, Captain, but I think we could find safer lines of converse."

"The devil take ye, Miller! Don' be puttin' on airs with me. Ye know that office General Neville rented from John Lynn in Canonsburg—where the stills are to be entered?" He didn't wait for an answer. "Well, last week a bunch of ruffians broke in—painted black, they were. Tricked Lynn into comin' downstairs, then whoosked him off ta the woods, lopped off 'is hair, an' tar an' feathered him. Threatened to hang 'im if he ever 'lowed his house to be used as a tax office again, then tied him stark naked to a tree an' vamoosed."

"Why are ye tellin' me this, Billy? I heerd it all afore—includin' the latest visit, when they pulled down half o' Lynn's house, obligin' him to vacate."

"A-ho!" chortled the captain, "So ye know, do ye? How'd ye find out, Willy? Mebbe yer friend Holcroft tol' ye, or mebbe ye were there yerself!"

It was happening again—just like the scene in the churchyard. Why did Captain Fife think Uncle Will was a member of the tinker's group? My enraged uncle tore after his accuser, eager to get his hands on him, but it was too late. The captain dug his heels into his horse's flanks and rode away. Seething with anger, Uncle unhitched the oxen. He mustered the quiet deliberation needed for any task involving the handy beasts. Delivering Buck into the hands of the smithy, it was plain to see my uncle's thoughts were burning hot as the red coals inside the forge.

"So, it's come down to this," he told his wife. "Defendin' me good name among me own neighbors . . . Just as soon as ye've had that young-un, I plan on vacatin' meself." He repeated it over and over.

Meanwhile, the smithy was rigging up Buck. Oxen had no skill at balancing their great bulk on three feet, so a windlass was used to lift the ox's feet slightly off the floor. The windlass was a wooden frame gadget with long canvas slings that strapped under the animal's belly.

Thomas Tidball worked steadily, for it was a lengthy task to put eight shoes on the cloven feet of each ox. Clad in a black muleskin apron, he was a burly man who didn't mince words—a habit that was easy to understand amid the endless racket of his workroom. Uncle was in no chatting mood anyway and the tapping of the smithy's hammer was talk enough for both men. The smithy's son worked as a striker—pumping the bellows, laying out tools, and working in tandem opposite his father at the anvil.

They fired the iron, watching it sputter and take heat from the blazing charcoal. At first, the iron was a dull color; then it began glowing a cherry red. Magically, to my eyes, it began turning yellow. Just as it reached a bright yellow, the iron was removed from the hearth.

"Rap, tap, rap," rang the smithy's hammer. "Clang," pounded the sledge. They created a syncopated rhythm that rumbled through the ground beneath the anvil and could be heard clear up to Bethel Meetinghouse. "Szz-szz-szz-sizzle," the tempo changed as hot iron was plunged into a tub of water. Soon, the irregular music heightened as a new set of tools was put in motion: "ringing, ringing, ringing."

I thought my head would burst, but admired my cousins' tolerance for the trade. The pounding finally let up and the shoe was fired again. The smithy pulled out the molten shoe and seared it onto Buck's hoof. A sickening burning odor filled the room.

"Don't hurt him! I cried, watching closely as he dunked the fitted shoe under water, then mounted it back on Buck's hoof with a row of small nails. I was curious about the bellow pump and the huge post that anchored the anvil in place. "What's that funny-shaped tool fer? What does it do?" The smithy and striker ignored my questions and Uncle had no patience for explaining—not today. When the last nail was hammmered into Buck's foot, Uncle Will gave our cousin twenty-eight pounds of mutton and a cord-and-a-half of wood.

With the yoke in place, we traveled uphill toward the Reverend's place, *Plain Truth*. The cart was empty now and the only sound to be heard was a hollow click of metal on the stony path.

"I shore is glad you dropped by, chile," said Dido. Her sleeves were pushed up above her plump, dimpled elbows and her strong brown fingers were buried deep in a bowl of bread dough. I was pleased to find her home alone—the Reverend being out and Mrs. Clark off nursing a sick neighbor.

"Tell me now, what's on yore mind?" she asked, setting the mixture aside to rise. Her dark brow was dusted with flour as she looked square at me, offering her full attention.

"Do ye think y-y-ye could teach me to sing?" I stammered.
"Mercy, chile!" she exclaimed, "you come all the way over
here to ask me that?"

"Oh, no ma'am," I replied, remembering the real reason.
Out came several loops of bright-colored enbroidery floss
from my pocket. "These are fer you. Grandma says Aunt
Rachel's quilt should be finished at the bee, come July."

"Ooo!" she said, admiring the yellow and blue floss.
"Missus Reverend an' me have a dee-sign all figgered out.
Yore mama must a knowed there's nothin' but black thread
in this house—what with the Reverend's duds an' the
missus preferrin' black taffety."

She caught me casting sheep eyes from her to the floor
and back again, and got back to my first question.

"Hmmm," she puzzled, "singin'. . ." Dido dragged her Dutch oven out of the embers and peeked under the coal-covered lid. "Never did think about it much—jus' took a big breath an' out it comed!" She scooped out a helping of cobbler for me and sat down at her butter churn, pondering the matter.

After the long morning at the smithy's, I was grateful to taste her baking. There was just a hint of salt in the crust, and a touch of cinnamon sweetened the apple filling.

"Singin' is how ye feel," she said at last. "It's a way of searchin' deep through yerself an' bringin' out all those worries that pop up at ye late at night. It's a lettin' loose of the hope ye feel at the light of day." The dasher in the churn slowed down as she continued. "Guess, singin' is like the gospel net, takin' in the good fish with the bad-uns. Down in Maryland, I did more wailin' than singin'—the way things were. Now, we're with the Clark's, an' they treat me an' Dave good. So, when I think back on all that ugly ol' misery, I sing fer joy. Yer joy, Janie! Course, I'll be singin' me heart out when I's free at last."

"When'll that be?" I asked. Freedom sure must be important to her, the way her smile was quivering and the tears welled up.

"When I meet my maker, chile. Heaven help me, that'll be the day."

"Well, I hope yer free afore that," I said sincerely, not wanting to think of death at all, especially Dido's.

"Thank-you, chile. . . livin' an' dyin'—that's what sweetens yore singin'. Good an' bad may happen to ya, Jane, as ya live an' breath, but no matter what kind of instrument God gave ya, the best tunes come with the livin'—from inside. An' when ya sing from yore heart, it feels as right as rain."

Her churning stopped altogether an' she seemed to be lookin' back on troubled times. A stray tear rolled down her cheek. She caught it with her apron hem and managed a smile. "Let's try somethin' together—somethin' lively that'll make this churnin' go faster."

"How 'bout 'The Devil's Questions?' " I suggested.

"That's a good-un—the Reverend's favorite. I'll start an' you sing the answers."

Intro: If you can an-swer my quest-ions nine, Sing nine-ty nine and
Devil: Oh, what is high - er than the tree? Sing nine-ty nine and

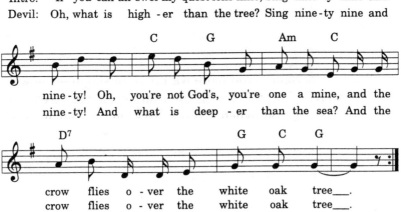

nine - ty! Oh, you're not God's, you're one a mine, and the
nine - ty! And what is deep - er than the sea? And the

crow flies o - ver the white oak tree___.
crow flies o - ver the white oak tree___.

The clarity of the Negress's voice gave me chills. Yes, there was plenty of living ringing out in that voice. While she might not get her freedom in this life, I couldn't help but think that God had truly blessed her. The dasher of her churn tapped out the beat and I chimed in with all the feeling my tender years would allow:

Child:

> Oh, heaven is higher than the tree,
> Sing ninety-nine 'n ninety!
> And love is deeper than the sea
> And the crow flies over the white oak tree.

Devil:

> Oh, what is whiter than the milk?
> Sing ninety-nine 'n ninety!
> And what is softer than the silk?
> And the crow flies over the white oak tree.

Child:

> Oh, snow is whiter than the milk,
> Sing ninety-nine 'n ninety!
> And down is softer than the silk
> And the crow flies over the white oak tree.

Devil:

> Oh, what is louder than the horn?
> Sing ninety-nine 'n ninety!
> And what is sharper than the thorn?
> And the crow flies over the white oak tree.

Child:

> Thunder's louder than the horn,
> Sing ninety-nine 'n ninety!
> And hunger's sharper than the thorn
> And the crow flies over the white oak tree.

Devil:

> Oh, what is heavier than the lead?
> Sing ninety-nine 'n ninety!
> And what is better than the bread,
> And the crow flies over the white oak tree.

Child:

> Oh, grief is heavier than the lead,
> Sing ninety-nine 'n ninety!
> God's blessing better than the bread,
> And the crow flies over the white oak tree.

Devil:

> Now you have answered my questions nine,
> Sing ninety-nine 'n ninety!
> Oh, you are God's, you're none of mine,
> And the crow flies over the white oak tree.

With the last note, she clasped my hand in hers crying, "Janie! Yore voice is lovely, chile, jus' lovely!"

I beamed at the compliment.

"Sakes alive, if ya aren't as clever an' talented as my own namesake."

"Who's that?" I wanted to know.

"Oooh, Lordie, she crooned, digging out chunks of butter that lodged in the bottom of her churn. 'Cordin' to the book the Reverend let me read, the first Dido was a fiery lady—queen of Carthage, she was." She poured the buttermilk out of her churn and offered me some.

I couldn't believe it—Queen Dido! I was all ears.

"Where's Carthage?"

"Dunno 'xactly. Prob'ly somewhar deep in Aff-ree-ka."

"Aff-ree-ka." Just the way she said the name painted an exciting picture in my imagination.

"When Dido first got to Aff-ree-ka, she was nobody—all alone without a fip in her pocket. The ruler back then made her an offer. She could have as much land as she could gather up in one bull hide."

"But that's hardly 'nough to turn 'round in," I said.

"That's jus' what the ruler was thinkin', but like I tol' ya, Dido was a resourceful woman—like yerself. She cut that hide into weeny bitty strips, pieced 'em together, an' roped off a whole city! Folks called it Carthage."

"An' they crowned Dido queen," I concluded, highly impressed.

"That they did, Janie. Now, I think I hear yore aunt a-callin'."

I was reluctant to leave her, but she promised to come to the next bee, and handed me a wedge of fresh butter to take home. As I bid her goodbye, I felt different somehow—like one of those "refined" young ladies from Grandma's stories—just out for an afternoon call and a cup-o-tea.

"Will ye help find me husband, Janie?" queried Aunt Rachel. She paced restlessly by the oxen and rubbed the small of her back. "Me unborn babe don' like waitin' anymore than I do," she said, patting her bulging stomach.

"He wanted to set things right with the pastor after his hasty departure from meetin' last month."

"You stay here, Auntie. I know just where to look." Following a hunch, I scouted the orchard behind the parsonage. It was a fine orchard filled with many varieties of apple trees. Here was a row of Jonathans, and over there were Cortlands, Rambos, and MacIntoshes. Many of these trees must've come as payment for the pastor's services at weddings, funerals and such.

Spotting the old minister and Uncle Will on their knees, I wondered if they were praying or planting, and I hesitated to intrude. Drawing closer, I saw the Reverend had layered several lower boughs of his trees and had new shoots springing up. Working in the soil, the old man carefully severed a rooted branch from its mother and set it aside for replant.

"I owe ye an explanation," Uncle was saying, "about me conduct at yer farewell meetin'. There was talk between the services, sir . . . I found me good name questioned by neighbors I've known all me life. Seems like a man's reputation ain't worth a hoot if he happens to belong to the Mingo Militia these days."

"Just what is your association down there, son?"

"I'm not in the Tinker's group, if that's what yer askin'," vowed Uncle adamantly. "My ties are strictly military, but my membership has thrust me into a real muddle. That's why I couldn't go along with yer stand on the excise that

Sabbath. With all due respect to yerself an' yer years o' service to me kin—if I were to register me still today, John Holcroft an' his boys'd be over to tear me place apart afore the ink'd dried."

"I suspect ye would be a likely target," admitted Reverend Clark. He ceased his work and appeared sympathetic to my uncle's dilemma. I was glad to see someone trying to understand him.

" 'Sides, it's pointless fer me to pay the tax now when I'm savin' every cent an' countin' on one last cash crop to cover our move."

"When will ye leave?"

"Early fall, I reckon—soon as Rachel's well enough to travel an' I can sell off the rest of me land. Then, the whiskey woes'll fall into the hands of me brother, James, an' he can make up his own mind on the issue."

The pastor looked doubtful.

"I know ye think I'm runnin' away—me own brother thinks the same, but I'd sooner confront the perils of an untamed land than get mired down in more excise trouble— an' trouble there'll be. I can see it all comin' to an ugly head."

The Reverend nodded agreement. "Ye're wrong on one count though," he eased Uncle's defensive look with a smile. "I'll not condemn your leaving. It puts me to mind of an old Scotsman I once knew. He liked to speak of the Ulster Scots—a proud lot. Nary a man would run away from trouble—rather, they were a people who preferred to choose the kind of trouble they faced. It's clear to me son, that ye've made your choice. Your mind is made up. Ye've got the mettle to face the unknown." He set down his cutting knife and pulled Uncle Will up on his knees beside him.

"Lord, look with favor upon your servant, William Miller, and his family. Protect them on their journey and keep them ever mindful of Thy words from Proverbs . . . ."

Uncle doffed his hat and I dropped to my knees beside him, feeling an uplifting of spirit as the minister's words rang true.

"Keep thy heart with all diligence, for out of it are the issues of life. The highway of the upright is to depart from evil. He that keepeth his way preserveth his soul."

And so, the two men cleared their minds and made their peace with God and with each other. At last, Uncle helped Reverend Clark to his feet and as he was taking his leave, Dave, the Negro servant, was seen leading an old horse down the hill. I ran to greet them and patted the curved back of Elder Kiddoo's MacTavish.

"Don't tell me, Dave—ye found him in the churchyard?"

"Yes, suh, Mr. Reverend, standin' there calm an' peaceful as ken be right by his own hitchin' post. Now, how'd you know dat?"

"It happened once before," explained the pastor. "Elder Kiddoo was beside himself searching for this horse. He had the whole family out combing the winding roads, the corn cribs, the near yard and the far away fields—most everywhere he could imagine. He was almost ready to give Ol' MacTavish up for lost. After all, ye'll recall the outbreak of pilfering we had that fall."

"I remember the pattern," said William. "A horse stolen here got hitched up to a wagon stolen there, then the same night, the bandits carted off some mutton from a third place an' sold the whole shabang up in Pittsburgh."

"Aye, William," the pastor agreed, stroking the horse affectionately, "a nasty business, but MacTavish here is another story. He's one of my best churchgoers. He's been to meeting so often that good attendance has become a habit. Ye know your pew, don't ye ol' boy? Just got your days of the week mixed up!"

"Ah," he told me, "What a marvelous illustration he is of the force of a good habit. Why, if more people'd follow this horse's example, we could start up regular mid-week prayer meetings."

We had to laugh. I never would've guessed that Reverend Clark had a sense of humor.

"I'll be glad to take 'im back to Kiddoo's place for ye," chuckled Uncle Will, preparing to leave.

But the minister had other ideas. "Look here," he called, strolling down the rows of trees. He pointed out two hearty saplings. "I want ye to take these. They're Smokehouse apples—about the only part of Maryland that I didn't have to leave behind. The fruit stores well and makes fine eating—cooked or right off the tree. I want a bit o' *Plain Truth* to go along with ye on your move to Kentucky."

XIV

TROUBLE

The painter needs a ladder and brush,
The artist needs an easel.
The dancer needs a fiddler's tune,
Pop goes the weasel.

I've no time to wait or to sigh,
Or to tell the reason why.
Kiss me quick, I'm off, Goodbye,
Pop goes the weasel.

—Old English Singing Game

Tuesday was cleaning day and Mother had no intention of straying from her routine. She got down on her hands and knees, scattered some sand, and scoured the puncheon floor with soft, brown soap. It was only mid-morning this first day of July, but already the heat was oppressive. Even having the fire banked and the door wide open did little to help. Mother splashed her brow and forearms with spring water and continued her drudgery. The weight of the unborn babe was driving her kneecaps into the wood, causing her to moan in anguish.

"I can finish the scrubbing," I offered. Her time was more than a month off, but already she looked overdue. Mother thought it a good sign—another boy to help Father. Determined to finish the job, she sat down on the floor and scooted herself along like a spider.

"Shore am glad you an' Baby John're the only ones eyein' me now," she confessed, looking about as graceful as a lame ox.

A hunting horn rang out from down by the run crossing, setting us into a panic. Soon the blaring noise was right outside and Mother was struggling to get her bulky figure afoot. Awkwardly, I pulled her onto a chair and hid myself in a corner as a stranger sauntered into the house.

"Hallo, Lovie!" He was grinning like a cat eating cockleburrs and slapped her a rough one on the back. The greeting jarred Mother to her feet, but the real shock came when she realized that the man beneath the wild hair and mangy chin whiskers was none other than her own in-law, the freighter, Oliver. I froze with excitement the moment I recognized him.

"Merciful heavens! God grant me patience," Mother prayed as he crossed the room to the corner cupboard. Chunks of dried mud dropped from his buckskin leggings and moccasins, but he didn't notice. Slinging the jug over his shoulder, he took a long sligger of Monongahela rye. My eyes grew wide as the whiskey drizzled down his beard, over his greasy, bloodstained hunting shirt, and splatted in fat, brown droplets on Mother's scour-cleaned floor. He didn't notice this either, and stood there looking at her cockeyed.

"Ye've filled out consid'rable, Love. That Jamie's a quiet rascal, but he's a real family man, I see." He let out a lusty laugh.

"Keep a civil tongue in yer head, man," replied Mother. "How dare ye speak of such things!"

"Cousin Oliver, Cousin Oliver!" I couldn't hold back a second longer, grabbed him from behind, and held on for dear life. My hero was home at last and I wouldn't let him go again—at least not without me.

"Janie-babe!" He whirled me over his shoulder and shook me like a rag doll. "What a slip of a lass ye are." He continued to hold me aloft and gave me his famous grin.

"What happened up here?" I asked, patting a large bald spot.

"Mebbe I should've believed that ol' wives' tale 'bout sleepin' in moonlight," he laughed, setting me down to don his pelt cap.

"Looks like yer hair ain't had more than a lick an' a promise the whole time ye've been gone," Mother scolded.

"Yer right, Lovie," he said, agreeable as pie, "but I 'xpects even Ma's hackle'd snag up in this growth." He slapped her on the back again, enjoying his own wisecrack. "Guess there's been a peck of 'xcitement 'round here—what with the excisemen gittin' tar an' feathered an' the taxpayers gittin' Tom the Tinkered." He ignored my mother's glare of disgust. "I even heerd Davey Bradford is proclaimin' hisself the 'George Washington of the West' . . . heerd he wants to set up a Western Empire—now that must be a big windy! Willie's militia meetin's down in Mingo must be gittin' right int'restin' . . ."

"That's right," I burst into the conversation, glad at last to have someone around who'd answer my questions about the mysterious Tinker's group. "Uncle Will's been in a whole lot of trouble an' he hasn't even registered his still. . . . Ye won't let the Tinker get us if he does—will ye, Cousin Oliver?"

"Enough, Jane!" Mother plied me away from the freighter and clapped her hands over my ears. "James's managed to stay clear of that business, thank the Lord, an' I'll thank ye not to mention the subject 'round me children."

The Freighter gave me a wink. "What's the matter, Lil' Johnnie, ye got big ears?" He lifted the baby out of the cradle and flung him up in the air. Mother quickly interceded, saying, "Ye catch me meanin', Oliver? Jane is 'specially curious now, an' I want all me young-uns walkin' the righteous path. I'll stand fer no wanderin' into idle gossip or worldly song."

"Why, Lovie," he said with mock concern, "the way you's talkin' jus' now, I think I sees a wrinkle poppin' out between yer eyes. Ye better take care lest ye prove that Eastern talk right."

"What do ye mean?"

"They're sayin' all western folk're jus' natural-born grumblers.

Mother had a hard time reasoning with Oliver; I could see her wince every time he called her "Lovie."

"What kind o' homecomin' is this, anyway?" he asked. "Where's Grandma?" Not waiting for an answer, Oliver stepped outside and fired off his long rifle, scattering chicks acrosst the yard. Then he proceeded to honk away on his ram's horn until Mother looked like she'd bawl, right along with Baby John.

The family assembled on the run. Mid-day gunfire was often a sign of trouble, so there was a wary look on Grandma's face as she stepped into the clearing.

"This is trouble—big trouble," muttered Mother, "almost as bad as Injuns."

I watched my siblings and cousins drop their berry pails and charge over to pounce on our galavanting cousin. He swung Sarie around like a sack of corn meal, crowned Ollie with his coonskin cap, and tossed the ram's horn to Tommy. Lizzie was kicking up her heels in a high-stepping dance and we all pranced about, pleading for presents.

"Let me through, ye beggers," ordered Grandma, eager to embrace her grandson. "So, the wild one's returned to the nest!" There was no mistaking the tearful glimmer in her eye or the loving affection she had for her will-o'-the-wisp grandson. My mother never could understand her blind spot for his unkempt person and untidy habits, but I always sided with Grandma—and would defend Cousin Oliver to the bitter end.

"What kep' ye, Sonny? We 'xpected ye home long afore this."

"I ain't been slow-pokin', Ma . . . Been on the move. 'Course, I did drop off to see the Bedford folks. Me an' Cap'n Jack got off fer a bit o' fishin'."

"I knowed it. I jus' knowed it!" Her eyebrows were flapping with enthusiasm. "That ol' codger Jack's always had more ways o' doin' nothin' than anyone I can think of. Now, what's new with Aunt Molly an' the rest o' the Miller-Tidball clan?"

Oliver slipped a packet of letters out of his saddle bag, while we swarmed around the pack horses.

"What ye got fer me?" asked Sarie, tapping the side of a large creel.

"Don't get too close," warned Mother. Her words went unheeded as Oliver gathered the little ones around and passed out hard candy. He left me and Lizzie to fidget in anticipation.

"Don't chaw on it," he told Tommy. "Ye'll break yer choppers. Jus' let it lay back on yer tongue an' melt . . ."

"Have ye fergot, Cousin?" Lizzie hopped from one foot to the other, her blue eyes sparkling and her red curls a-bob. "Remember yer promise? Remember yer promise?"

"Ma, ye got any idee what this gal's jabborin' 'bout?" He threw his mother a wink and played the bewildered role to the hilt. Just as Lizzie was ready to give up, he drew a cut of sky blue ribbon right out of his sleeve. Lizzie gushed out her thanks, tied the ribbon into her topknot, and sashayed down the bank for a look-see in the run. I hoped he had another ribbon hid somewhere.

By this time, the men had come in from the field where they'd been reaping rye. Their hunting shirts were drenched with sweat. Father and Uncle Will had their rifles cocked.

"Hallo, Gad-about!" Uncle Will smiled up at the gruff woodsy who stood head-and-shoulders above him. "Well, y'ain't no prodigal son—look more like Sam-the-Ram that summer he got stuck out in the woods."

Father was more reserved in his greeting. Clearly, he was irked to be losing daylight hours. "Yore 'bout the only man I know who could pull this family into a social gatherin' in the heart of a work day. If it were anyone else . . ."

"Whoa, Jamie, wait till ye see what I brung." He pulled Mother aside. "Dad-gum, that boy's got a bad case o' the grumps. He's livin' proof o' that Eastern talk. Ye best sweeten him up, Lovie." With that he produced a candle mold for Mother, a cone of white sugar and a copper kettle for Grandma, and a fine squirrel shooter for Cousin Alex.

Mother stroked the candle mold and her mood seemed to soften. "Think of all those crooked tapers I've lit. Well, no more!" It wasn't easy for her to begrudge Cousin Oliver when he came bearing gifts and news from all over tarnation.

Alex fingered his first gun as if it were made of eggshells. "Cain't believe yer twelve already," said Uncle Will.

"Ye earned this," added Father. "When we struck a deal for Oliver to fetch a gun last fall, I had no way o' knowin' what a fine job ye'd do with the young oxen." Alex stood there dead serious under this rare praise. "It took time an' patience an' was a job I had no time for." He turned back to his nephew. "So, Oliver, let's see the rest."

"Yes," I thought. "There must be something here for me."

Everyone was intent on the business of unstrapping the supplies from the oak frames atop the pack horses. There was salt, powder, lead, iron for tools, a keg of molasses, and pouches of seeds from the Miller kin in Bedford. While the family "oohed" and "aahed" through the booty, Oliver was busy unpacking his lead horse, Maggie. To everyone's surprise, he reached into the depths of the creel and brought out a black and white pup that wasn't more than about six months old. Holding it by the scruff of the neck, he walked over and placed it in my arms.

"She's all yours, Janie-babe. Name's Bet. Now don't squeeze the air out of 'er."

I felt whoozy with delight. The puppy licked my chin and squirmed to be let loose. I set the pindly critter down and we tumbled around the yard chasing after her. This was too good to be true. After Lizzie'd waltzed off with her hairbob, I'd just about given up on a present of my own.

"Jumpin' Jehosaphat!" quipped Grandma. "She looks like a long-legged stink kitty!" She was right. Everthing was pup-sized on the animal except her long, spindly legs.

"Thank ye kindly, Oliver," said Mother, "mebbe now, Jane'll give up that awful black sheep that follows her around, but I can't approve of a gamblin' name."

"A gamblin' name?" The Freighter laughed himself silly. "Jamie," he snickered, "ye got yerself a real stickler here!" Oliver looked at Mary and sobered up quickly. "Look here, Lovie," he explained, "yer meanin' never crossed me mind— Bet being a family name."

"A family name?"

"Yessirree, from Elizabeth Tidball, yer gal's own great-gran'momma."

"Rest her soul!" cried Grandma.

Mother blushed a raspberry red. She'd only meant to thank him, but somehow everything she said came out sounding haughty and everything he said came out sounding humorous. Mother closed her eyes on the frolicking young-uns and gave a shrug to her big lug of an in-law. Shaking her head, she held her belly as though Baby Miller was kicking at her insides.

"There'll be no routine this day," she conceded to Grandma. "But shore as there's angels in heaven—there'll be one tomorrow."

XV

WRONG WAY DOG

*He was the only dog I ever knew could run comin' an' goin'
an' barked at both ends!*

—Oliver Miller's Tall Tale

"**C**ousin Oliver, wake up."

I remembered his last visit and didn't dare shake him.
Living out in the wild as he did, he had a habit of wrassling
down intruders first and asking questions later. He was
sprawled atop an old coat cut from a government blanket
and looked quite content in his barn-loft bed. My new pup,
Bet, was snuggled in the crook of his arm. She stood up,
stretched out her hind legs, then licked her master's face.
One eye opened, then the other, and he blinked several
times before he knew where he was.

" 'S that you, Janie?" he moaned. "Guess I missed Ol' Red
cock-a-doodlin'."

"We've been up an' about fer a while now. I'm through all
me early chores."

"What ye got there?"

I handed him a trencher of mush and milk. "Mother sent
this. She wants to speak with ye directly."

"Does she, now?"

He poured off the milk, letting Bet lap it up, and downed
his breakfast with several gulps of spirits he took from a
small flask. "Who's that down there?" he asked, changing
the subject.

Olivia stood at the foot of the ladder bleating up at us. I
introduced him to my pet and explained her fondness for

trailing me around. "An' if she cain't be with me, she runs wild with the porkers or sleeps with the cows rather than be with the rest of the flock. Ye don't go along with Mother, do ye, 'bout black sheep bein' bad luck?"

"Don' see how's I could, gal, when yore 'Livia here sounds jus' like her own gad-about namesake. Myself, I'm never happier than when I gets off the main trail into the deep wood. I pass my time alone, a-whistlin' to the horses, gittin' out me fiddle come nightfall, feelin' free as the breeze. Now, get me to workin' on a farm with my own kind or put me behind a plow an' I might jus' as well be bound an' gagged. 'Bout the only kind of bad luck that finds me is a howlin' wolf or a hootie owl. 'Course, I never will start a freightin' trip on a Friday—now that's fer darn sure."

"Where did ye go, Uncle?" I wanted to hear everything about his travels.

"This trip, I's all over," he handed me the pup and raked his fingers through his mussy hair, "out Forbes Road, through Bedford, Chambersburg, Carlisle. Had to take a few side trips to outwit those pesky highway robbers, then I cut up toward Reading an' clean out to Phil'delphy, but I'll tell ye 'bout that later, Janie. I got somethin' 'portant to show ye."

Well, I had a surprise for him, too, I remembered. Just had to find the right moment for the giving.

He swung Bet under his arm, shinnied down the rope, and dropped the pup onto the barn floor. Bet immediately confronted Olivia. Up went her forepaw, and she stared hard at the black lamb.

"See that?" asked Oliver in a tone of hooshed excitement. "She's showin' eye. What a natural!"

Before I could ask what he meant, Olivia baahed her disapproval of the newcomer, Bet gave a yelp and chased her into a cow stall. There she brushed up aside Olivia, sidling her into a corner and blocking her every move.

I raced down the ladder. "What's she doin'?"

"Herdin'," he answered. "Herdin', Uncle Abe called it when he ran Bet's mother, back in Bedford. He said Bet's what ye call 'a workin' collie.' His friends brought this type of dog over from their home on the border 'tween Scotland an' England. Now, it's a sight to see, but shore as I'm standin' here, I tell ye, I've seen these collies herd sheep— even take the cows out to pasture an' back."

Just then, Olivia made a dash for the barn door and Bet chivvied along at her heels, following her outside.

"Watch this, Janie."

Out in the barnyard, Bet made a wide half-circle around Olivia, dropped down on the ground keeping a strong eye on her, then approached the lamb straight on. Oliver stepped left and so did Olivia.

"Sh-ssh," he called, and Bet swung right. She headed off the lamb with her nose close to the ground and her body lowered in a half-crouch. As Olivia changed direction, Bet swung left so the sheep was always trapped between Oliver and the pup.

I was amazed; I'd never seen a dog so smart. The only other dog around was Elder Kiddoo's Ol' Blue, which slept in a corner of the millhouse all day. But this pup was bright-eyed and playful. I was fascinated watching her head-off Olivia, this way and that, till the poor black lamb grew weary.

"How'd Bet ever learn all that?" I asked, sitting next to Uncle on the ground.

"It's not somethin' she learned, though I reckon Abe worked her along with her mother. Herdin' is an instinct that goes back to the wild dog's instinct to hunt. It's hard to believe, lookin' at a lovable pup like Bet, but her ancestors were a whole passel of horr'ble critters—jackals, catamounts, an' such."

"Like the wolf Father killt fer pesterin' our sheep?"

"Prob'ly, Janie. Now, those wild dogs survived 'cause they's able to hunt an' catch their own food. They ran in packs, 'specially when they had a victim too large to be killt by one hound. After the pack'd run down their prey, they'd head 'em off an' that's where the herdin' instinct got started. Herdin' an' runnin's been bred into little dogs like Bet fer so many years that now these traits come as easy as kissin'—like a trout swimmin' upstream to spawn, or a babe lookin' fer its mother's voice."

Soon, Bet's attention was attracted to Lady Tidball and her gaggle. She circled around, keeping them close together. When a stubborn gander strayed too far, she nipped his webbed feet, sending him squawking back to the rest. The honking herd brought Grandma outside to the rescue. Mother and Sarie followed close behind. Armed with a broom, Grandma bustled over ready to lay into my black and white pet.

"No, Grandma! Please stop!" I shrieked, racing up to block the blows. "Bet's a good worker—the best of her litter. She's learnin' to herd sheep. She'll be a big help to me come sheep shearin'. Tell her, Cousin Oliver, tell her," I pleaded.

I caught my breath as Uncle repeated what he'd learned in Bedford about collie dogs.

"Dad-drat, I don't like the sound of all those 'wild' instincts," said Grandma skeptically. "The first hen I see that mutt sink her teeth into, she's a goner."

She shooshed me with a wave of her hand. "Don' go singing' her praises to me, Janie. I've seen these so-called 'tame' dogs afore."

"But, Mother Miller, a workin' critter could be right handy 'round here," Mother defended. "Did I hear ye say this dog can herd cows, Oliver?"

"Shore as shootin', Lovie; I seen Bet's momma at it. What's more, I got another idee for Bet while I's in Phil'delphy. There's a lady there, gots what she calls a dog mill. She puts the animal on a boxed-in tread-mill, hootched him up to her butter churn an' ding dang, if that critter didn't run all day an' earn his keep, too!"

Sarie got the giggles at the idea of a dog churning butter and I had to wonder: Maybe Bet could take over half my chores.

"I'd be glad to rig up a contraption fer ye."

"Thank ye, kindly," replied Mother, "but first ye'd better earn yore own keep. James's been out reapin' rye for hours now with some of our neighbors. I'm shore he could use some family help."

"He can do that tomorrow," corrected Grandma. "I needs him today to help me an' the young-uns pick berries."

"But ye managed just fine yesterday," retorted Mother.

"That was nearby. Ever since last May when Benjamin Sweet died, rest his soul, I've had that far hillside in mind. There was a powerful windstorm several years back—blew down the timber an' left the whole slope open for sun-lovin' plants. I'm shore the blackberries I saw last May are ripe for the pickin' 'bout now. 'Course, goin' out that far, we'll need some protection. This is just the time of year those ornery savages start sneakin' back into the area."

"Don' worry, Ma, soon as I tend the pack horses, I'll get me gun an' be right along. We wouldn't want those plump, juicy berries goin' to the crows, would we, Love?"

As he turned on his heel, I was sure he could feel Mother's icy stare piercing into his back. To her, it was a waste of time for Oliver to be traipsing off on a gathering party, filling his stomach with berries all day. To me, I couldn't wait to get started.

Lizzie and Tommy showed up, buckets in hand, to gather for Aunt Rachel. "Where's yore ribbon?" I asked, surprised to see Lizzie's curls braided tight.

"Ma got tired of seeing me primp, so she hid it away for 'safekeeping.' Says I can only wear it on 'special occasions.' "

"Like the day after tomorrow?" That'd be a real special occasion. All the nearby Miller kin'd been invited over to Uncle William's for a Fourth of July frolic. There'd be a turkey shoot, throwing contests, and singing and dancing to the tune of Oliver's fiddle. Grandma was hoping to get today's pickings into fresh blackberry pies for the doings.

"I reckon 'Lizabeth has Sunday meetin's more in mind," teased Grandma. "One look at her fine coppery hair done up with that silk doo-dad an' the Croco boys'll be dazzled, for shore."

"I 'xpects I can catch me a sweetie better than any of those wide-eyed skinny-ninnies."

"Phew!" whistled Oliver. "I like a woman with some sass." He chimed in singing 'Haste to the Wedding,' which made Lizzie mad. She grabbed a bucket and stalked off with her hands clapped over her ears. Tommy, Sarie, and Grandma joined in the song following behind her. Oliver balanced his long rifle acrosst his strong shoulders and Bet tagged along at his heels as we headed out the trace along Catfish Run.

"How long will ye stay?" I asked. We'd left the valley bottom for the thicket.

"I've got to get over to me folks. Pa has some road work lined up fer me, but I'll be around. Ain't missin' the cornhuskin' this year. Reckon when I sees that big ol' hunter's moon, I'll be off."

"Hunter's moon?" I wondered if that'd be enough time to hear about all those far off places he'd seen.

"October, Janie—best time of year. The air turns crisp, leaves crunch underfoot, an' the full moon hangs so low ye can reach out an' grab it. Corn-huskin's 'bout the only chance a man gets to kick up his heels 'round here. 'Sides, I plan to be the first one to shuck a red ear an' kiss me sweetie."

"I didn't know ye had a sweetie. 'Course maybe Aunt Mary'll bring the Wallace girls up from Cross Creek . . . ."

"Those Bible-totin' sour mouths?" He gagged and spit in the dirt. "I'd sooner spark the Dinsmore gals. Now there's a triple dose of fun!"

Oliver admired the new calves in the clearing. Their bells clanged out as they looked up wondering what I was doing back so soon. "Well, I'll be . . ." He scratched Tessie behind the ears that bore the familiar Miller mark—a small hole pierced through the left ear and two slits in the right.[8] "Jamie's got the young-uns ears bobbed, I see."

---

[8] On December 22, 1777, in the minutes of the Court of Yohogania County, the marking brand for Oliver Miller was described as a hole in the left ear and two slits in the right ear. This date marked the first recording of animal branding in the area.

"Come on, Ma, let's get a move on," called the Freighter. Grandma'd wandered off to inspect a fine stand of fall grapes growing up among some fallen trees.

"Don' rush me, Sonny. The Lord doth provide for those who take the time to help themselves." She scouted about for elderberry, gooseberry, and other late fruit-bearing bushes.

We took to the woods for a mile or so through the vines and shrubs. At last, a steep slope opened up—cleared by nature's hand. The party split up with Grandma taking the younger children along the edges where the picking was easy while Oliver, Lizzie, and I moved slowly into the middle of the field. Here, the berry bushes rose high and formidable with sharp thorns that tore at my skirt and short gown. Even with my sleeves rolled down the briars, pierced through. Oliver resorted to a stout stick to whack against the stalks. He beat a path through the patch and as the branches fell down, we sucked in our breath to see large perfect clusters of purply, sweet berries.

"Hmmm!" Lizzie dropped one in her mouth. The slightest touch knocked several ripe berries to the ground, so she held her bucket under a batch and shook them right in. We stooped down to pick off the rest. Some patches had shriveled in the sun, while others were still sour with two or three red ones to every deep shiny black berry. It was just like unearthing buried treasure. One picker'd give a shout, then another—each certain he'd found the fullest, most perfect berry bushes.

"Wait'll ye see this," announced Tommy, his high-piping voice carried easily across the sunny field.

"Lookie here, Janie," exclaimed Lizzie. "Come help me!"

Cousin Oliver waded in amongst the tallest bushes and picked as high as he could reach. Lizzie and I stuffed our mouths and buckets full of berries till our hands got so red we couldn't tell the briar scratches from the berry stains.

Oliver broke out singing:

> Oh, I'll take the high road
> 'N ye take the low road,
> 'N I'll be in Scotland afore ye!
> Where me an' me true love'll
> never meet agae
> On the bonny, bonny banks
> of Loch Lomond.

We all joined in and sure enough, the singing made the picking go faster. It took my mind off the stifling heat that seeped up out of the wild grass and helped me forget how the weeds were itching me all over.

By mid-afternoon, we'd picked as many blackberries as we could tote. The warm sun and our full stomachs made everyone drowsy, so Uncle found a beech grove. It was cool and sweet smelling in the shade as I stretched out on a bed of soft leaves.

Bet showed eye and took off after some critter in the woods below. She wasn't like a horse or cow that had to walk one leg at a time. Bet's all fours sprang straight out— all in the same instant, making her about as long as Sarie was tall. At a standstill, Grandma might poke fun of Bet's skinny legs, but set in motion, the pup was a joy to watch.

Her running was a thing of beauty. Bounding through the woods like a white-tailed deer, she'd stop short for a scent and dart off again. Tommy watched her closely, then got up and took a couple of springing leaps before tripping over his own two feet.

Oliver had to laugh at the mimicry. "Sorry Tommy, I's afraid bouncin' Bet has ye beat!" He leaned back lazily on one elbow. "Had me a lil' dog once . . ."

"Grandma 'lowed ye?" we asked in disbelief, knowing full well that Grandma never trusted anything on four legs that got near her geese. She gave Oliver a half smile before he answered, "Yeah, shore, he was a good-un. 'Bout the best coon dog ye'd ever want to see. Well, one day he was chasing a coon an' some fool left a sickle layin' in the field with the blade straight up." He paused, reading the "what happened?" look in every eye.

"My pore lil' dog ran smack dab into that blade an' he split clean open from the tip of his tail right on down to the end of his nose."

I figured he was spinning a yarn, but shuddered all the same and held Bet tightly.

"Well, I saw 'im fall apart, so I slapped him back together. I pealed off me shirt, wrapped him up right quick, an' run him up to the house."

"What'd ye do then?" asked Tommy, believing every word.

"Why, I set him in a box, poured whiskey all over that shirt an' kept him warm by the hearth. On a nice day like this I'd take him out in the sun part of the time.

"Was he livin'?"

"Oh, well, I could see him breathin', so I hoped he'd pull through an' after a spell I seed him a-wrigglin', but I kept him bandaged a couple more weeks. Then, one mornin', I heerd him bark, so I started unwrappin' an' 'fore I knowed it—out he jumps, spry as ever. But, would ye believe, in my 'xcitement, danged if I hadn't put 'im together wrong way-to—two legs up an' two legs down?"

Cousin Oliver played dumb, scratching his bald spot and making everyone laugh. "Well anyway, as it turned out, he was twice as good at coon chasin' after that. Why, he'd run on two legs till he got tuckered, then he'd flip over an' just keep a-movin' on an' on . . . He was the only dog I ever knew could run goin' and comin' and barked at both ends!"

"Dawg-gone," punned Grandma, starting an extra burst of giggles that made my sides ache.

I couldn't remember ever being so happy. The only bad thing happened on the way back. Sarie got sick and up-chucked her berries. Red blotches broke out on her face and arms and she was in tears thinking how Mother'd be covering her up with sooty ointment again.

"This is different," Grandma assured her, "just a berry rash. We'll get ye home an' settle yer tummy with a good noggin o' peppermint tea."

Sarie kept whimpering because no one'd get close enough to her red blotches to haul her pig-back. Finally, Oliver slung her over his shoulder where she fell asleep, exhausted.

XVI

JOO-LIE FROLIC

What use is in fighting, and gouging, and biting,
Far better to let it alone;
For kicking and cuffing, and boxing, and buffing
It makes the flesh ache, and the bone.
But give me the whiskey, it makes one so frisky,
But beating, and bruising makes sore;
Come shake hands, my cronies, come near, my dear honies,
And think of your grudges no more.

—'Song of Clonmel'[9] from *Modern Chivalry*, Hugh Henry
Brackenridge

July Fourth dawned grey and drizzly, putting the *Milville* festivities in question. Mother didn't seem to mind, but the rest of us were itching to be off. The rain dragged on and on till noon, when the patter on the roof finally stopped. I was mighty glad to see Father lead Dolly out front. He strapped on the creel and boosted Grandma into the saddle. Now we were ready to follow the uphill trace along Mansfield Run.

Bouncing Bet led the party, even ahead of Father. She pranced along the trail, swished her high-plumed tail, and leaped into the brush after grey squirrels. She'd tree the critters quickly and bound right back to her lead spot. It put me to mind of my sister, Sarie, who also had a habit of wanting to be first. First to see, first to eat, first to know—everything but first to bed—that was my sister.

---

9 Clonmel was a fictional ballad singer associated with Tom the Tinker's boys.

When we arrived at Uncle Will's, the place was already crawling with Millers. There was Uncle Alexander, Aunt Jane, Uncle John, Aunt Sara and a hoard of other aunts and uncles that I barely knew at all. The ruckus of romping children made me uneasy, so I stayed by Mother, helping to lay out the food amid a gathering of all the Miller women. My usual slobbery greeting by Aunt Rachel was reduced to a tweak of the nose. That was all she could manage, having rounded out so much with the unborn babe.

My hugging aunt'd gone all out for the celebration. I could tell. Tables were propped up under the trees in front of the cabin and, for a fancy touch, sheets were stripped off the beds for tablecloths. Spread on top was a savory array of vittles—five kettles full of chicken potpie and squirrel stew, steaming bowls piled high with green beans, turnips, sweet peas, and hominy. At one side there were jugs of hard cider, whiskey punch, and fresh milk from Uncle Will's cow. The biggest tempter was an assortment of breads and sweet cakes. One young snitch couldn't resist doing what everyone else was thinking. He stole into a basketful of corn dodgers and promptly got his fingers smacked. Loaves of oat-rye and corn-rye bread were sliced around a big dipping pot full of honey. That must be Uncle Thomas's contribution. I liked to see him at family get togethers because of that beehive he kept in the orchard right behind his house. It sure sweetened up the eating. My mouth was watering as I saw Grandma setting out her oat cakes and blackberry pies next to a batch of ginger balls and fruit cobbler.

"Git it while it's hot!" called Aunt Rachel, clanging the bottom of a skillet with a big wooden spoon. Needing no further encouragement, the grown-ups assembled, ready to dig in. I was forced to join the mob of cousins who shoved to secure the better spots at the end of the line. Sarie sneaked in among the older children, but was quickly elbowed to the back.

"See what comes of always wantin' to be first?" I asked. Her lower lip popped out as she considered my query and we patiently awaited our turn. Juggling my punch in one hand and a heaped high trencher in the other, I found a seat on a log beside Lizzie.

"Guess what?" she asked through a mouthful of corn didger. "I's enterin' the tommyhawk throw!" She licked the honey off her fingers, then flashed a grin so proud I thought the freckles'd pop right off her cheeks.

"The boys'll never let you."

"We'll just see 'bout that. I ken throw as good as them. 'Sides," she pulled out an old tomahawk for me to see, "Cousin Oliver says I got a good arm. He seed me throwin' an' sharpened this up for me. He's been up here all mornin' showin' Alex how to handle that new gun of his. An' he taught me a new dance for tonight—the *Irish Trot*, it's called. Goes like this . . ."

Still sitting down, Lizzie kicked through the steps. Soon she was up on her feet jigging this way and that. I was just catching on when a gun shot rang out. Uncle Will set down his rifle and held up a hand trying to get the crowd's attention.

"Hold it down, everybody. Now, ye know this wouldn't be Joo-lie Four without gettin' in a little target practice. So, gentlemen, I'm officially announcin' a turkey shoot an' drive-the-nail contest in the clearin', yonder. Prize'll be a barrel of Monongahela rye an' one day of me labor in the field of the winner." The announcement met with a burst of approval because everyone knew Uncle Will could cut more grain in less time than any other man in the valley.

"With stakes like that, what're we waitin' for?" asked Father.

As the men trooped off, Grandma had her own announcement. She'd been in her glory since arriving, moving from one group of relatives to another, catching up with all her grandchildren. Somehow, without even trying, she drew everyone's respect and became the hub of all the doings.

"Mercy!" Grandma rolled her eyes in mock dismay. "I thought those boys'd never leave." She motioned her daughters and nieces to her side and I felt a flutter of excitement, knowing what was about to happen.

"Reckon, now's the best chance we're ever goin' to git to carry out some 'portant business of our own. As ye all know, there's some amongst us we'll be losin' soon an' we just canna, we canna. . ." Her lack of words was more than made up for by the emotion on her face and the ever-jittery brows. "We canna let them go off to Kentuck without takin' somethin' along to remember us by."

As 'she spoke, Aunt Rachel was led to the front of the group while Mother and Aunt Sara unfolded the farewell quilt for everyone to see. "There's a bit of us all in the dee-sign, Rachel, includin' our neighbors. We got some more stitchin' to do, here an' there, but we'll take care of that this afternoon, won't we girls?"

Aunt Rachel was engulfed in a buzz of well-wishers. "I'd no idee ye's all bein' so sly. Ye got me feelin' like a nervous bride at her own shiveree. Jus' wait till William sees this!" Tears welled up in her eyes as she ran her fingers from one bright colored square to another, admiring the intricate stitch-work.

Soon, the ladies sat down to their bee an' Lizzie saw her chance. Grabbin' my arm, she dragged me out to the pasture where the boys were having their contest. The redhead rolled up her sleeves, took a couple practice throws, and confidently joined a rough-looking group of my older cousins. The minute she lined up, the griping began.

"No girls!"

"Go play dollies!"

"Ye ain't lettin' her get away with this, are ye Alex?"

"Quit yer bellyachin'! What's wrong Stubby? 'Fraid she'll beat ye?" Lizzie's morale was boosted considerably to hear her brother taking her part. His words had stilled the complaints to a rash of muttered grumbles.

"Ye got to let me throw. I brung the prize—a bag of marbles for the winner—fired them meself out of clay." She tossed the bag at the boy's feet and bit her lip awaiting a favorable reply. Hedging on the issue, the cousins looked reluctantly from one to another.

"All right!" She couldn't wait another minute. "I got another prize." I was astonished to see her unknot the blue silk ribbon from her hair and wave it in the breeze. She sure didn't offer it up lightly. It'd been her dream for years and she'd talked of nothing else waiting all these months for Cousin Oliver to fetch it. Guess the throwing match meant a lot to her.

"What do we want with a girlie bauble?" scoffed Abe, the oldest cousin.

"Yore too ugly to have a sweetheart who'd take it," retorted Lizzie, irked at his disregard for her treasure, "so give it to yer ma. An' here," she dropped her tomahawk into the booty pile, "I reckon this is enough to get me in the runnin'."

"Let's get on with it," urged Alex, eager to end the debate.

So it was settled. Lizzie was in. They marked off a distance of five paces—the target being the burl of an old chestnut tree and the contest began. Each boy took careful aim, whirled the tomahawk through the air, and hit the wood with a sharp "crack." Their skill was impressive. At five steps, the edge struck wood with the handle down.

Lizzie was last to compete. What a relief to see her give an overhand heave and find her mark with a solid rap. Cousin Abe ignored her exultant hoot and nonchalantly marched off the next round at seven and a half paces.

The new distance gave some of the boys trouble. A few of them missed the tree altogether while others were disappointed to find they'd hit the target, but hadn't put in enough muscle to hold the blade fast. Eventually, everyone was eliminated except Alex, Cousin Abe, Lizzie, and Stubby McKee.

The final round was exciting. I was so hopeful and nervous for Lizzie that I forgot my own shyness and moved up with the group of boys awaiting the outcome.

Abe was first. He squinted his eyes, giving the tree a long look. The crowd groaned when the wrong end of his tomahawk hit the tree and thudded to the ground. Next was Alex, who gave an accurate clean-cutting throw. At seven-and-a-half steps, his edge struck with the handle up. There was a rousing cheer. He'd be hard to beat.

But Stubby McKee aimed to try. He was an unpleasant boy—short for his age, and short on humor, as well. It was difficult to believe that sweet, soft-spoken Aunt Elizabeth could be the mother of this scrapping bully. He reminded me of a scruffy, little bantam rooster. Everyone knew Stubby was quick to brawl and brag on account of his height—or his lack of it. At last fall's cornhusking, he'd taken his lumps over some teasing that cost him a couple of teeth and a broken nose.

As he stepped up for his turn, I hoped against hope that he wouldn't win, but with a snap of his wrist, he let off a near perfect throw. There was a smug look on his face as he yanked his tomahawk out of the tree and raised his nose in the air, trying to look taller.

If he meant to rattle Lizzie, it didn't work. Wiping her hands acrosst her skirt, she found a good grip and let the handle fly. The edge lodged solidly in the wood, off-center by a few inches. I whooped for joy and leaped into her arms. She'd beat out most of the boys and was among the top three! It took me a minute to realize that she didn't share my enthusiasm. Peeling herself away from my grasp, she walked over and pulled her tomahawk out of the burl, then calmly presented it along with the marbles and hair ribbon to Stubby McKee.

The bully was taken aback by Lizzie's gesture and the silence of the other boys bespoke their respect for her skill. She cast her eyes down, clearly not wanting to break down in front of them, then ran off through the field. I tore after her, yelling all the way.

"Wait up Lizzie! Ye did good! Yore one of the best!"

When Lizzie finally slowed down, she just hung her head and twisted the red curls around her fingers. She didn't want my sympathy. "C'mon Janie," she said at last, "let's go see if the races've started—like Abe said—what do I want with a girlie bauble?"

She sounded convincing, but I didn't believe a word.

Over in a far corner of the field, the girls and younger children were in the middle of a relay race. It didn't take Lizzie long to organize her favorite event: the pig-back race. There was a mad scramble to pair off and line up. I hopped on Lizzie's back, but she let out a grunt.

"Janie! When'd ye get so big? I'll never win hauling you!"

Glad as I was to be growing up, I couldn't bear to miss the pig-back. We'd always run it as a team—came in first the year before last. Never one for giving up, Lizzie had a scheme. Capturing my brother and sister out of a game of "duck, duck, goose," she ran them over to the starting line. Sarie an' Ollie were ridin' pig-back before they knew what happened. All the cousins took off at a trot with Lizzie and Sarie in the lead. Hard as I tried, I was always a few strides behind my sister's moppet of gold curls.

"I-yi-yi-yi-yi!" screamed Sarie, her voice bumping along with every step of the race. They won handily and Sarie was radiant to be part of the feat. I dumped Ollie on the grass, gasping for air.

"I winned! I winned!" Sarie shouted.

"We won," corrected her partner. There'd be no living with Sarie now—she'd never learn her lesson about being first.

Next came the three-legged race, bringing Lizzie and me back to our usual twosome. We tied our legs together and were off at a reckless pace. Lizzie was eager to press ahead, and her strength was so overpowering, I couldn't keep up.

The grass was still slick from the morning rain, causing a spill that brought us tumbling down in a fit of laughter. We landed in a lump, laughing too hard to even try for the finish line.

The merry shrieks and hollering fun of the racers sounded small in the big sunny pasture. From acrosst the field came the twitters and gobbles of the boys who were showing off their bird calls and way off, from the far clearing, gunfire from the shooting match echoed through the hills. The strange chorus fell happily on my ears. These were the sounds of living people, not the usual moo cows or bleating sheep. Lazily, I chewed a blade of grass and remembered all the lonely times when I'd longed for a day just like this.

With a sudden burst of energy, Lizzie was on her feet. "Let's go see how Pa's farin'."

A raucous cheer went up from the men as we approached. They'd been shooting nails at fifty paces from a wood slab target. Uncle Alexander had just driven one home and they huddled around him—slapping his back, admiring his accuracy.

"Do it again an' I'll throw in a day's labor meself," challenged Oliver, stepping into the middle of the group.

The oldest Miller rubbed his chin whiskers in disbelief. "Am I dreamin', or did I hear my son offer to do a day's work?"

The joking hooshed after Uncle Alexander reloaded his long rifle and took aim. I held my ears. It felt like the kick of the gun jarred me just as hard as it did Uncle. A groan from the spectators told me he didn't succeed. This time the nail was only bent.

Oliver let out a happy squawk and clicked his heels together, just as chipper as could be.

"You lazy, no-good woodsy," kidded Will. "Ye always did manage to duck out of a job. Every time yer pa'd turn aroun' ye'd sneak off to some dang fishin' hole. I reckon ye'd be happy enough to have me gun backin' ye up when ye runned into Injuns out in the hills."

"That's fer darn shore, but I could do without yer name callin'. Heerd enough o' that back East."

"Like what?" They all wanted to know.

"Oh, Scotch-Irish riff-raff, tax-dodgin' rebels, ungrateful whiskey boys . . ."

"Ungrateful?" repeated Father in amazement. "Do they figger we're goin' ta thank them fer pushin' the brunt of the spirits tax on us? We're only a wee bit o' the population."

"Mebbe them high-handed Feds should leave us 'whiskey boys' alone."

"They been leavin' us alone fer years, up till now," Uncle Will pointed out. "I ain't seen any gov'ment troops out here fightin' Injuns, have you, Oliver?"

"Nay, but ye've got to remember, eastern folk have their own way of thinkin'—rather like viewin' a riverbank from a boat mid-stream. The scenery looks mighty different from the water than it does on shore. Some people believe the West is makin' a heap of money by slippin' whiskey through customs downriver into Spanish territory . . ."

"Pchww!" spat Uncle Will. "What a lot of mumbo jumbo. There ain't an honest man in the whole survey who's made one fip smugglin' whiskey down the Ohio. Now, if Congress'd give Mad Anthony Wayne some help to clear out the Injuns—mebbe the river could be opened up fer business."

"Well, ye got to know how the other side feels," argued the Freighter. "Back in Carlisle, fer instance, every other body I run into's sayin' the West has a voice in the legislature, if we'd stop our grumblin' we could appeal the whiskey excise."

There was a rumble of protests and Cousin Oliver wore a wry smile. It almost looked like he enjoyed egging-on his own kin.

"Did ye fergit to tell them our own 'voice in the legie-slayture' just happens to be the local tax collector!"

Everyone muttered dismay at the irony. Clearly, my father and uncles were agitated, but Oliver wasn't through.

"Git mad—all of ye, git hoppin' mad, but I been to this nation's capital an' there's one dead-serious bit o' news I think ye should hear. Ran into an old military man in a Phil'delphy tavern. He said it's the treasurer, Hamilton, ta watch out for. 'The Little Lion' he's called—wields a lot of power an' he's spoutin' off the view that the gov'ment won't fully 'stablish itself till the military is put to a test. So, the Feds may not care if Tom the Tinker keeps a few farmers from docily payin' the tax—an' mebbe they'll even let him get away with tar an' featherin' some excisemen, but any real outbreak of trouble an' ye can bet yer right arm they'll march an army out here for a show of strength."

No one believed him.

"Yer talkin' nonsense, Oliver. Why should this Hamilton feller want to fight a bunch of pore farmers who gave their own blood to wrench this country from the hand of the almighty British?"

"I'm only tellin' ye what I heerd."

"C'mon boys," interrupted Uncle Will, playing host. "Let's get back to more pleasant pursuits."

He set up a new target with a crude picture of a turkey painted on it. " 'Course, if there's anyone here who sees a likeness to John Neville, fire away!" Their jovial mood was restored and Oliver's warning was quickly forgotten.

All my uncles were crack shots. They took turns firing and proudly admired the detail of each other's weaponry. Each spent considerable time practicing to improve his accuracy and always toted along a gun to hunt game, fend off rattlers, or kill Injuns. Their long rifles were a part of themselves, like an extra appendage.

Just then, a couple of tough-looking strangers rode in on horseback. "Well, if it ain't the Mingo boys," declared Uncle Will. He picked up a whiskey jug and passed it around for all. The men must've ridden a good way for their horses were glistening with sweat. "What brings ye out here on a holiday?"

"Don' let us stop yer celebratin'. We're just out informin' the membership 'bout the military meetin' come Wednesday next..."

"How's yer leader, Davey Bradford?" asked Cousin Oliver in an exaggerated tone of politeness.

"Concarned as the next man 'bout unfair taxes..."

"Concarned be damned," heckled Oliver, "Forget about the whiskey issue for a minute. Do ye know what they're callin' yer 'Darlin' of the Survey' back East? The 'Idol of the Camp,' the 'George Washington of the West.'"

"I'm warnin' ye, Miller..."

Whatever the Mingo man was going to say got cut short when Cousin Oliver sprang over to shoo Lizzie and me off a stump where we were perched. He leaped on top and bellered out a challenge.

"I'm a whiskey-totin' freighter! I'm a coon-chasin' wonder. I'm a high-climbin' packer from the ol' Alleghenies! WHOOP! I's wet-nursed on whiskey 'fore I even oped me eyes! I's a derring-do fighter with a crackerjack aim an' I's lookin' fer Monongahela Rose. I's a cockamamie, dare-devil, die-hard of a man, an' I's lookin' fer Monongahela Rose. I's half tree toad an' half wild boar an' the rest o' me is rattler spit an' iron. I'm a rough-an'-tumble scrapper with a punch like white lightnin' who ken turn a woods into a pasture in one brawl. I can out-ride, out-shoot, out-drink, out-leap, out-brag, an' out-wit any man this side o' the Mississip from Pittsburgh to New Orleans, an' back agin to Phil'delphy. Come on, you dollups, you farmers, you dog-eared duffers

an' see how cagey I am to spar. I ain't had a fight in nigh on two hours an' I's restless as a cock without a hen."

He shifted his weight side to side atop his tree stump roost while his brothers shouted out their support.

"Whoopee! Awhoopee! Cockadoodledoo!"

"Stop yer crowin', Miller," hollered one of the Mingo boys, hopping off his mount. "Yore nothin' but a dead-beat, double-talkin', double-dealin', ditty-singin' dolt." He stooped over, flapping his arms like a chicken, adding, "Cheep, cheep, cheep!"

"Aha!" cried Oliver, "Ye've clucked afore the eggs're laid." With that, he dived onto his opponent, knocking him flat to the ground. The man recoiled instantly, found his footing, and clenched his hairy fists ready to swing. As Uncle stood up, he got booted in the ribs and fell backwards in a puddle.

It was a dreadful scene. Mother would be furious to see it and even more furious to find me watching. Part of me wanted to go, but a stronger side kept my feet planted firmly on the spot. I was fearful for Cousin Oliver and couldn't even look away.

"Ugh!" grunted the Mingo man. He snapped his foot in the air, except this time Uncle grabbed hold and wrassled him down. Soon, they were so covered with mud it was hard to tell one from the other. The grappling finally stopped as the challenger reached out, trying to throttle Oliver. It didn't work, for with one swift maneuver, Oliver pinned the man's arms behind his back and marched him over to a dead tree. He lifted the man up, hooked the back of his hunting shirt onto a broken-off limb, and left him dangling in mid-air like a spider on a long strand of web.

The roar of laughter grew as the thwarted challenger kicked, clawed and cursed at them from his helpless position. Even the other Mingo man was amused at the escapade.

"You bog-trottin' eye-sore; git away from me!"

"Calm down, man," Oliver crooned, "ye ain't lookin' so purdie yerself. I's only goin' ta thank ye for livinin' up our shootin' match this afternoon."

He grinned his easy-going smile and strolled off surrounded by his brothers. I was in a wide-eyed stupor until Father came over and led me away.

"What'll Mother say about this?" I wondered.

"If ye plan on stayin' through this evenin', don't bring it up," advised Father, keeping his gaze straight ahead.

I wasn't sure, but I think he meant we had a secret. Looking over my shoulder, I saw the Mingo man'd been set free. He gave us a resentful scowl before riding off with his friend.

XVII

THE FIDDLER'S TUNE

*Tom the Tinker started trouble
In the year of Ninety-four.
Seven cents on every gallon
Made the farmers dawgone sore.*

—"Yankee Tinker,"
Oliver Miller's Ballad

Cousin Oliver was nowhere to be found. All day long, he'd been sporting with my uncles or teasing the ladies and now when I needed him, he'd up and disappeared.

I left the heat of the clearing for the well-worn trail behind Uncle Will's cabin. If I remembered correctly, it wound through the hills before cutting over to Mansfield Run and the stillhouse. There was a calm about the woods at this hour. The shadows were long; it would be dark soon. Pausing a minute, I heard the peepers well into their noisy, nightly ritual. Another sound filtered through the trees as well. I listened a few seconds more, then dashed down the trail.

"Over here," came a call.

Peering down the bank of the run, I saw my cousin sitting on a whiskey keg, tuning his fiddle. It looked as if he'd given his face a couple of swipes down by the water and most of the mud had dried up and cracked off his clothing. I sat down at his feet and watched him plunk the strings and twist the wooden pegs.

"Are ye all right?" I asked.

"How's that? Oh, ye mean this," he said, patting his bald spot. He'd cut his head earlier in the brawl. "It's nothing," he scrutinized my earnest face adding, "Ye ain't frettin' 'bout wha' happened this afternoon, are ye?"

"I never saw a real fight before—never heerd ye talk like that."

"Fight?" He laughed his great laugh. "That 'tweren't no fight, Janie. That was jus' a couple o' grown men lettin' off some steam."

"But ye hung him up like the Portuguese did to me great-great grandfather . . ."

"Whoa, girlie!" Oliver laid his fiddle acrosst his lap and looked me dead in the eye. "Did ye see any bitin'?"

"No, but . . ."

"Any scratchin' or eye-gougin'?"

I stared at him, too shocked to reply.

"Well, there ye go," he said, taking my silence for a *no*. "We's only havin' a lil' friendly how-do. I hooked him up to the tree jus' to cool him off a bit. Now, if there'd been any real fightin', ye'd hae knowed it."

"Do ye have ta fight a lot—out on the road, I mean?"

"On the road, I's a whole diff'rent feller. Go fer days without seein' a soul or hearin' anythin' more comfortin' than the sound of horse bells. Most times, when I pull into a settlement after a thirty-mile haul, I find people are jus' as different as the horses I lead aroun' all day. Some folks're like me lead horse, Maggie—older, sure-footed, the type ye ken count on fer most anythin'. Some're fancy critters like me new spare animal, King George—smart, handsome, well-bred an' full o' spirit. Then there's Rupert—skittish, ornery, inexperienced. Have to keep 'im in the rear where me hind driver, Jake, ken keep an eye on him. I've met plenty o' Ruperts in my time—the kind ye wouldn't go the length of the door for. I try to avoid 'em," he added, catching my worried look.

"Now, don' get me wrong, I never was one to skip out on a friendly bout o' carousin'. When it comes right down to it, Pittsburgh's as fine a place as any for a good time. Every fall, that lil' tree-shaded village starts jumpin' with ferinners. Sometimes, it's like visitin' the inside of a hornet's nest."

" 'S that where ye heard 'bout King Louie gettin' axed?"

"Mebbe, mebbe," he replied. "I did run into some Frenchies down at the Whale an' Monkey Tavern, once. They talk in a buzz through their nose. It all sounded the same to me, but I reckon they feels the same way about our English kin who swallow up the words so ye cain't understand nothin' a-tall. Yessirree, Pittsburgh an' her rivers are a jump-off spot for the world. In one day's time ye ken hear the burr of a Scot, the twang of a Yankee, an' the gutteral cough of a German. An', there's always a couple o' Injuns walkin' aroun'. Why, I even saw Lew Wetzel[10] in town one time."

"Who's he?"

"He's a character, he is. Guess ye might say he's made a name for himself scoutin' Injuns." He had a devious look in his eye that made me think he knew a whole lot more than he was telling.

"Will ye take me there sometime?" I'd never seen Pittsburgh, although my parents once went to Coal Hill market across the river.

"Shore," he answered, giving me a cautious look. "Now, what's that yer hidin' behind yer back?"

---

[10] Lew Wetzel, a native of Lancaster County, Pennsylvania, was one of five sons of John and Mary Wetzel, who settled in Wheeling (in what was then Virginia) in 1772 . Years later, Lew and his brothers were captured by Indians. They eventually escaped and returned home, but his brief stint in captivity made Lew Wetzel a confirmed Indian hater and perhaps the most noted Indian fighter on the frontier during the Revolutionary period.

Though he never learned to read or write, he mastered the skills and craftiness of the Redmen. By the time he was twenty-one, his very presence in any community lifted the fears of an Indian attack. Once, after killing a prominent Indian, he was sentenced to be hanged, but frontier sentiment forced his release, whereupon he departed for New Orleans, dying there at the age of forty-four.

Wetzel County, West Virginia is named in honor of this frontiersman who lived by the code that the only good Indian is a dead Indian.

I was glad he noticed and couldn't bear to wait another instant. I presented him with the embroidered pillow and watched his reaction as he squeezed it in his great hands and gave the gold-stitched poem a careful inspection. "It's got real goose down stuffin'," I assured him.

"Now, ain't that fine," he praised. "No more seed bags or rock headrests for me. From now on, this'll be with me wherever I go."

"I wish I could go with ye—acrosst the mountains—travelin' all the time, meetin' all those strange people an' excitin' places . . ."

"Janie, I'll tell ye, it may sound ' 'xcitin',' but I's never more pleasured than when I's back here with me own flesh an' blood. I may act like a gruff ol' mule most of the time, but underneath I's jus' a simple farm boy with a heart big enough to love the last little tad that's got a drop o' Miller blood in 'im."

He grew quiet, almost shy after this rare expression of sentiment.

"I got somethin' fer you, too, Janie," he said, getting back to his fiddle. He tucked the instrument under his chin and scratched out a tune with the bow. I knew exactly what he'd play, listened for a while, then sang along.

"I got a gal an' you got none . . . Lil' Liza Jane . . ."

He'd always claimed this was my song and as often as he'd played it for me, I loved it better each time. As he ended the chorus with a catchy rhythm, I applauded him soundly.

"When ye hear that tonight, ye'll know I'm playin' it jus' for you." His eyes crinkled up in a fun-loving grin. "Come on. Yer ma'll be lookin' fer ye."

He threw back his head an' gave a deep laugh like he always did before relating a good one. Sometimes the best part of listening to his jokes was his own hearty enjoyment before the telling.

"Jus' remembered—this afternoon I told yer ma the Feds're goin' to start a new tax—on spinnin' wheels!" He bust out laughing in a huge guffaw. "That shore put a bee in yer ma's bonnet."

I wasn't sure I caught his meaning, but his good humor was infectious and I had to laugh along with him. As we meandered back through the trees to rejoin our relatives, I was certain that no one understood Cousin Oliver better than me.

"Pow, pow! yelled Ollie, running around a corner of the cabin. He was punching the air, chasing after his sister.

"I's a coon-chasin' fighter. I's a die-hard devil."

"Sara Miller! Where'd ye ever pick up talk like that?"

Mary boxed her daughter's ears and drew both children to her side. Resuming her chair beside Rachel, she stared out at all of James' kin assembled around the bonfire. It was out and out obvious who the culprit was who'd incited her youngsters to such wild behavior. Ever since the men'd come back from that useless gun contest, it was clear they were worked up over more than just target shooting or taxes. The whiskey'd been flowing freely and as the day wore on, bits and pieces of some blasphemous challenge floated around till it now spilled out of the mouth of babes.

"James's been avoidin' me all evenin'," she told Rachel. "Does he think I didn't know there was trouble when his nephew showed up this afternoon lookin' like a hog in a wallow."

"Now, now," soothed her sister-in-law, "They's jus' kickin' up their heels a bit."

Mary shifted the baby from one hip to another, wondering how many more times she could endure being called "Lovie." And speak of the devil, if Oliver wasn't sauntering over here this minute.

"Hallo ladies," he greeted, fiddle in hand. "Too bad you 'xpectant mamas'll have to sit out the dancin'."

His side-long glance made Mary cringe with embarrassment. He threw back his head and belted out a laugh.

"Oh, no!" thought Mary, bracing herself for another big windy.

"Ye know, Love, I heerd back East they's come up with a new tax."

"Did ye, now?" countered Rachel.

"Yep. Last month it was whiskey, this month it's butter churns."

"Git on with ye, Sonny!" She waved the joker away.

Mary wondered why Rachel encouraged the man so. He slapped his knee, getting the most out of his own joke, then positioned his fiddle and began a tune.

Instantly, the gathering grew lively. Mary watched the men stomp their feet. Off to one side, Jane and Lizzie jumped up, clapping. Soon, they linked elbows and started a dance, singing all the while:

Swappin' Song

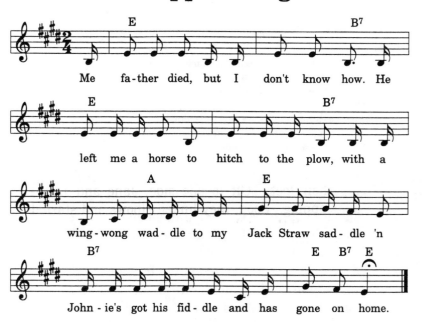

Me fa-ther died, but I don't know how. He

left me a horse to hitch to the plow, with a

wing-wong wad-dle to my Jack Straw sad-dle 'n

John-ie's got his fid-dle and has gone on home.

Verse 2:

I swapped me a horse 'n got me a cow
and in that trade I just learned how.
With a wing-wang waddle . . .

Verse 3:

I swapped me a cow 'n got me a calf
and in that trade I just lost half.
With a wing-wang waddle . . .

Verse 4:

I swapped me a calf 'n got me a pig
the pore little thing could never grow big.
With a wing-wang waddle . . .

Verse 5:

> I swapped me a pig 'n got me a hen
> to lay me an egg every now 'n then.
> With a wing-wang waddle . . .

Verse 6:

> I swapped me hen 'n got me a cat
> the pretty little thing by the chimney sat.
> With a wing-wang waddle . . .

Verse 7:

> I swapped me cat 'n got me a mouse
> his tail caught fire 'n burned down the house.
> With a wing-wang waddle . . .

Verse 8:

> I swapped me mouse 'n got me a mole
> the dad-burned thing went straight down its hole.
> With a wing-wang waddle . . .

The final verse was scarcely through before he started in again. "Hey Janie-babe." He scratched out a musical echo on his fiddle. "Hey, how ye doin' Janie-babe?" Again, the strings echoed his words, delighting the crowd. "Janie-babe has a boyfriend, Janie-babe has a boyfriend." The fiddle reiterated the phrase in a "nyah nyah" tune and Jane blushed right up to her hairline.

" 'S there anythin' else ye folks want to hear?"

"Lil' Liza Jane," someone called, setting everyone into a frantic search for a partner. Lizzie grabbed Tommy and Jane exuberently pulled her father into a four-handed reel. Mary drew her breath at the sight, for James was usually a restrained man, reluctant to public displays and dancing in particular. More and more of the family joined in till even Mother Miller was swinging left and right on Will's arm.

Oliver's fiddle sang out the melody at least three times— each time they changed partners and stepped faster than the last. The children clapped their hands to the lively beat pounded into the ground by dancing feet. Mary was hard-pressed to keep her own feet from wagging. Every once in a while one of the men'd stop singing and let out a hoot and every time Will danced his mother past Oliver, she'd yell, "Play it, Sonny!"

"This is a worldly song," Mary kept reminding herself. "This is a sinful, worldly song." It'd rest a lot easier with her if they'd put this kind of fervor into singing church hymns or even 'Scotland the Brave.'" James and Oliver knew perfectly well that, pregnant or no, she'd never be one to dance. Her family back in Cross Creek'd sworn an oath against it and to her way of thinking, it was just as sinful as working on Sunday.

"Cain't very well spoil everyone's frolic," she lectured herself, "not with my religious scruples. I'll jus' sit this one out an' we'll be leaving soon."

Absently she stroked Bet's coat and watched the flight of the lightening bugs in the early evening sky. The pup didn't know what to make of all this hoopla either, though she'd had herself quite a day, prancing among the cousins, ready to follow anyone who held a scrap of food.

By the fourth rendition of "Liza Jane," Oliver had the dancers moving through their slides and turns, swings and promenades at a vigorous clip. They collapsed for a breather and a sip of whiskey punch while their taskmaster launched into a tricky fiddle tune, "The Devil's Dream." His fingers tickled the strings and his bow zipped along so fast it looked like he'd take wing.

"Now ain't that peculiar," said Rachel. "Looks like he's got somethin' tied to the end of his fiddlestick."

Mary strained to see, but the music stopped and Will came forward to address the group. "Guess ye all heerd by now that Alexander held onto his winnin' record in the shootin' match earlier . . ."

"Don' fret, Will," interrupted the eldest brother, "I got a solid day's work all figgered out fer ye!"

"I'm shore." Will shook his head at the prospect, then turned back to the rest of his kin with a more serious expression. "Rachel an' I want ta thank all of ye for comin' out today an' 'specially Grandma an' all you ladies who had

a hand in stitchin' up that handsome quilt. It's been a Fourth of Joo-lie we'll never forget."

Rachel added her thanks and the proceedings were turned back to the fiddler.

"Reckon I got news of me own," said Oliver, taking one last sip of punch from a cow's horn. "My nephew Stubby did himself proud by winnin' the tommyhawk throw this afternoon."

There was mild applause for the boy. Mary could tell she wasn't the only one who thought him a nuisance at these family gatherings. She never would forget the time Stubby tied Jane and Sara to a tree and left them in the woods.

"Later on, young Alex beat out Stubby for first place in the boy's target shoot. Now, ain't that fine for a boy who jus' got his first squirrel shooter a week ago?"

Mary saw Will's eldest squirming proudly under the freighter's praise. "Hold it down, folks. That ain't the end of it. Alex wants to donate one of the prizes he won from Stubby to his own sister, Lizzie who, by the way, jus' happened to place third in the tommyhawk throw!"

There was a tremendous cheer as Oliver untied a blue silk ribbon from the bow of his fiddle and placed it in the hands of Will's tomboy daughter. Lizzie hollered for joy and flashed Alex a big grin.

"Oh, no!" Mary was horrified to think that Jane'd been right out in the middle of all that undignified carrying on. "Me daughter's cousins're 'bout as bad an influence as that unpredictable, whiskey-totin' freighter," she stewed. Mary couldn't help feeling grateful that Lizzie would be losing her hold on Jane when she moved away.

"Everyone, step closer now," directed Oliver. "Lizzie's goin' ta show ye a new step—it's the latest thing back in Bedford—called the *Irish Trot*. She'll be dancin' to a ditty I made up meself: *Yankee Tinker,* I call it."

Taking Jane as a partner, Lizzie began dipping and kicking through some startling, unlady-like dance and

Mary's worst fears were jumping before her eyes. As if that weren't enough, she was appalled at the words spewing out of Oliver's mouth to the tune of *Yankee Doodle*:

Verse: Tom the Tinker was a stinker.
        He shot holes in his neighbor's stills.
        It don't pay ta be law abidin'
        Grab yer gun an' join the fightin'.

Chorus: He don't want no whiskey tax,
        Not in Neville's handy—
        Got the farmer's riled an' vexed
        An' ready for a dandy.

Verse: Tom the Tinker started trouble
        In the year of Ninety-four.
        Seven cents on every gallon
        Made the farmers dawgone sore.

"That's the last straw," decided Mary, not waiting to hear another note. If she had her way, Oliver'd be out of her house for good, no matter that he was James' own nephew or how his grandmother treated him soft. She and her children would have nothing more to do with him. Grabbing the children, she pulled Jane out of her vulgar cavortings and faced her husband head-on. There wasn't an uncertain bone in her body now. Determination surged through her every pore.

"We'll be goin' now, James," she said in an icy hoosh.

XVIII

THE MILVILLE HARVEST

*I felt my blood boil at seeing Neville along to pilot
the sheriff to my very door.*

—William Miller,
as quoted by Hugh Henry Brackenridge

"**M**others!" I exclaimed to Bet, in disgust. "Yore lucky yores ain't aroun' an' Olivia's lucky hers'll have nothin' ta do with her. Come on."

The pup followed me over to a tree where I knotted a rope around the trunk in firm jerky tugs. The rough actions suited my urge to scream and throw things.

"Mother says ye can't come. Mother says ye'll spook the workin' critters up where the men are reapin'. Mother says, Mother says . . ." I got so sick of hearing Sarie use those words.

Looking down into Bet's questioning eyes, my mood softened. "Ye wouldn't do any harm, would ye girl?" I bent over to stroke the velvety fur on the tips of her ears and muzzle, then gently tied the rope around her neck.

My mother'd been making things miserable for over a week now. With the explanation that her "time was gettin' near," she'd thrown a lot of extra chores my way. The truth of the matter was, she'd been trying her best to keep me busy and away from Cousin Oliver. Ever since the Fourth of July doings up at *Milville*, when she dragged me out of the dancing and insisted on leaving early, she'd been having one of her "difficult dispositions." That's what Father called it. I wouldn't be going to Lizzie's at all if it weren't for Grandma wanting me to deliver this rye-straw mare she'd made.

Bet gave my face a friendly lick. I bopped her lightly on the nose. Tucking the mare under one arm, I picked up the dinner pails and headed up the trace. It was hot—sticky hot—even in the shade. My grip on the pails was clammy and beads of perspiration popped out on my skin as I panted my way uphill. Linsey-woolsey felt unbearably scratchy this day, but "Mother said" I had to wear my mob cap, apron, and of course my wool socks and moccasins. Why did she have to be so strict when Aunt Rachel let Lizzie run barefoot all summer? Aunt Rachel'd make me a much better mother. She was fun-loving and maybe— maybe somehow—she'd let Bet and me slip off to Kentuck with them this fall.

I came to my favorite spot along Mansfield Run where the water trickled over smooth flat stones and spread itself thinly across thick, black mud. Kicking off my footwear and tossing aside my apron and cap, I waded into the run. The cool, gooshy ooze slithered between my toes and I felt like spending the entire day right on the spot. Now, what would "Mother say" about that? I continued my mud walk at a leisurely pace until sunlight streaked through the trees overhead. Father and the reapers would be wanting their noon meal. I was about to don my clothing, then thought better of it and hid the whole bundle behind a bush. It was too hot and Mother'd never find out if I came back for them before going home.

My feet were deliciously bare as I finished the trek to *Milville*. I remembered all the fun of my last visit. Lizzie'd been so happy about her hair bow and who'd of guessed that bossy old Alex'd stick up for her and win it back from Stubby? There'd be plenty of fun today, too. There always was up at *Milville*. Of course there wouldn't be foot races or contests, but Lizzie and me'd get in a good talk and maybe Cousin Oliver'd have time to play his fiddle, come noon. I'd never forget how surprised he was to get that pillow. He'd taken special care of it, which wasn't his usual way with the bulk of his belongings.

The men were hard at work as I reached the field. Their backs gleamed a toasty brown from all the hours spent in the unrelenting sun. Sickles slashed through hay. Occasionally, someone'd stop to wipe his brow or take a draught of cool water or shot of whiskey, but then it was back to work.

I recognized the large-framed man on the near side of the field as Big Henry; he often worked for Father. Slow of speech and deliberate in his movements, his strength was such that, over the years, he'd snapped a score of pitch-fork handles in two. Big Henry liked to do his hootie owl imitation for us kids. He'd give a slow, "W-o-o-o-m-p, W-o-o-m," then: "boom, boom!"—he'd thump his fists on his great chest.

"Did ye know Big Henry's missin' half his fingers?" asked Lizzie, sneaking up behind me, Injun style.

"What?"

"Look closely sometime; he's only got 'bout five fingers, all counted, on both hands. Cousin Oliver says Big Henry got drunk once an' laid out all night in the dead of winter. He froze up so bad that two or three of his fingers had to be cut off each hand."

I cringed, then craned my neck for a closer look at the big man who was bent over piling sheaves. Suddenly, he sprang back, giving a throaty shriek. Even from where I stood, I could hear the ominous click of a rattlesnake winding through the hay. Big Henry hefted a club in the air and pounded that rattler silly, then he stuck the point of his sickle through the head and hoisted the snake high enough for all to see. It was a common occurrence this time of year—I'd seen it plenty of times. I'd seen worse, too, when a person or critter'd die a slow, hideous death from a poison bite.

"Lizzie, yore right! He *is* missin' fingers." I got the creeps watching the big, stub-fisted man fling the killt rattler against a stump.

Father'd come over for the dinner pails and my kinfolk were right behind him.

"Hey Janie-babe!" Cousin Oliver was grinning his wide smile. "How ye doin', Janie-babe?" He used that sing-songy voice like the night he'd teased me with his fiddling at the bonfire. If it'd been anyone else, I would've felt shy, but Oliver could get away with teasing. I reckon he could get away with anything. That's why Mother didn't like him.

"What ye got there?" asked Uncle Will.

"Grandma sent this along." I set the rye-straw mare in his hands. "She says ye best keep on reapin' so's ye ken send it on to Elder Kiddoo."

"Did she, now?" smiled Uncle. "Seems to me, you were the one who got stuck with the mare last year, Jamie."

"That's right," Father confessed, "an' I'll tell ye, it wasn't fun bein' the brunt of me neighbors' jokes the whole winter long."

"Well, that ain't goin' ta happen to me," promised Uncle Will. "With men like Big Henry helpin', I'll be done in no time an' I'll pass that ol' mare along quicker 'an ye ken say 'Jack Ketch!' "

"Or, Tom the Tinker!" kidded Oliver.

"Hoosh up, ye joker."

"With men like Sonny in the work party, ye'll have to serve double the whiskey." The men laughed at Cousin Oliver. I figured he had to take just as much teasing as he passed out himself.

"Come along, ladies," said Uncle Will with a genteel nod, "Ye heerd enough of this rough, field-hand talk. I 'xpect Rachel'll want ta see this." As he picked up the straw mare, we followed him back to the house.

"Mama, Mama. Tommy's outside shootin' horny toads out of his sling shot," tattled Lizzie.

"Well, fetch 'im in here. Now what's all this, Will?" She sized up the rye-straw mare with mock disdain. "Ye ain't plannin' on makin' us laughin' stocks, are ye?" Rachel banished the scruffy figure to a corner and brushed bits of straw from the table she was setting.

"Not a-tall," vowed Will. He stretched his arms overhead, easing the crick in his back. "With the bee I've got workin, we'll pull the harvest in today an' I'll drop the mare off at Kiddoo's on my way to Mingo."

"Best news I heerd all day. Now, everyone sit down." She lifted a heavy skillet in one plump, freckled arm and doled out generous portions. Her billowing pregnancy couldn't suppress the bustle in her gait. "What's the matter Janie? Sit down—fore yer johnnycakes git cold."

"I . . . I never had a meal at the grown-ups' table," I stammered, "not ever. At home, we're not allowed."

"Woosht! Ye got ta eat, don't ye, chit? Hurry up, now— afore Tommy nabs yer vittles."

From across the table, Will admired his wife. She'd always been a pretty thing. Her red hair and blue eyes were stamped on every youngster in their healthy brood. She exuded vitality. Even today, when there was scarcely a breath of air to be had inside the sweltering cabin, she was taking things in stride. Why, most women'd be crankier than an unmilked cow under the circumstances, but there was Rachel—joking about his farming repute, when the truth of it was, his personal repute'd been misconstrued for some time. Not long ago, the neighbors thought he'd made a bad match when he wed the daughter of a poor drifting squatter, but the neighbors' opinions were off about other matters as well. Marrying Rachel was the smartest thing he'd ever done and he knew it. Her sweet disposition kept the family going and she took to his Kentucky plans right off without a sorry word. She always made the best of things and, sure as one foot followed the other, he loved her for it.

Loud knocking interrupted his thoughts. Rachel lifted
the latch and swung the door open to reveal a tall, serious
gentleman in fancy military garb.

"William Miller?" There was an imperial air about the
newcomer. He ignored Rachel's greeting.

"Aye," Will acknowledged, rising instantly from his chair.

"I'm Major David Lenox."

"Lord hae mercy! It's the sheriff," gasped Rachel.

"What business have ye here?" Will motioned his wife
aside and wasn't sure he wanted to hear the answer.

"I'm here in my official capacity as U.S. marshal, to serve
you with a writ for non-compliance with the federal law
that requires all stills to be registered."

"Speak English, man. What does this mean ta me?" Will
clenched his fists and gritted his teeth. His muscles went
taut, facing the moment he'd always known was inevitable.

"The writ officially cites William Miller to appear in
United States Court in Philadelphia to answer charges and
to pay a fine of two-hundred-and-fifty dollars."

Not waiting to hear any more, Jane and Lizzie flew out
the door to carry the news to the men in the field. As the
girls ran off, Will was stunned to see Gen. John Neville—
the Tax Inspector of the Fourth Survey, himself—on
horseback in the lane.

"Shall I read the document aloud?" queried Lenox.
Receiving no reply, he unfolded a paper and began, "Be it
known that one William Miller, citizen of Allegheny County,
Commonwealth of Pennsylvania, shall set aside all manner
of business and excuses . . ."

Will did not hear the man's words. He felt his blood boil
at seeing Neville along to pilot the sheriff to his very door.
There'd been a time when Neville was against the excise as
much as anybody. When old Graham, the excise man, was
catched and had his hair cut off, Neville said they ought to
cut the ears off the rascal as well. And when the distillers
were sued some years ago for fines, he talked as much as

anybody against it, but he wanted to keep in the state assembly then. Once he got a chance for a federal post, he took it. Will'd always been for Neville in his elections and it put him mad to see the man coming to ruin him.

" . . . to appear in his proper person before the judge of the District Court of the United States at Philadelphia upon August 12, 1794."

"Make haste, major," called Neville from his mount.

The officer refolded the document and held it out, but William did not accept it.

Just then, Will looked up to see his work party running toward them from across the field. Lenox panicked when he saw the crowd. The writ floated to the ground as he sped to his horse and set off. Neville's presence triggered an emotional eruption among the men, whose blood was already racing from liquor in the July heat. They grabbed whatever was handy—a club, a gun, a hay-fork—and rushed the officers, trying to head them off in the lane.

"Ye outrageous ol' fogy!"

"Kill the bloody bluenose!"

But the farmers were too late. They found the lane in a cloud of dust. Neville'd beaten out their footrace. Without hesitation, Big Henry fired a shot at the escaping officers, causing them to rein in their mounts and shout a warning:

"Desist!" commanded Lenox. "Desist, lest ye all be arrested for insurrection and assault on a U.S. marshal . . ."

"That's right," seconded Neville, "How dare ye?"

William reached the scene just as several more shots went off toward the horsemen, who wisely chose to retreat. A chorus of oaths and threats followed them as they disappeared from view. The men were left in an enraged, chaotic state as they gathered around William.

"What exactly did they want?" James asked.

"They wanted two-hundred and fifty dollars," seethed Will, vehemently. "They wanted me to go to federal court in

Phil'delphy—'twill keep me from going to Kentuck this fall after I've sold my plantation an' am gettin' ready."

Will turned in exasperation to look back at his house. A bit of white stuck up from the dirt by the doorway. The writ lay exactly where Lenox had dropped it. "They want ta ruin me," he said in a devastated whisper. Walking toward the cabin, Will ground the paper into the dirt with his boot heel.

There was a queer silence from the throng that'd been so boisterous only moments ago.

"There'll be no more work this day," James announced. "Ye'd all best go home."

Reluctantly, the men broke up. When the Miller brothers were alone, William confronted James: "Do ye still believe in the good will of our man, John Neville, Jamie? Do ye think our 'blood connections' made one tad o' difference to 'im this day? Do ye? Do ye?" He clutched the throat of his brother's shirt and shook him wildly, venting his wrath.

"Easy, Will, easy."

"All right, sit on the fence if ye must." He abruptly loosed his grasp. "Now I want ta know—who's goin' ta ride with me tonight? Who's comin' along with me for the militia meetin' down in Mingo?"

James stared at his brother unflinchingly.

"Damn ye," cursed Will, flabbergasted by James' detestable self-control.

"I'll ride with ye," offered Oliver. "I've nothin' better ta do."

"So," he said, allowing the disturbing events of the day to sink into his skull, "That's the way it'll be."

He walked off alone.

XIX

THE VIGIL

*Surely the churning of milk bringeth forth butter,
and the wringing of the nose bringeth forth blood:
so the forcing of wrath bringeth forth strife.*

—Proverbs 30:33

Grandma spent the night in her chair—rocking, waiting, rocking. The rocking pacified her worries some, but did little to stir the oppressive humidity. Outside, the crickets were noisier than usual. "Must be a rain comin'; we shore could use that," she thought, dropping into a light sleep.

A gentle morning breeze lifted away the heat in the house. Grandma allowed herself to wake slowly, lingering a while to enjoy the fleeting coolness.

Was that a mourning dove's coo? Her eyes rolled open and she shrugged off the doleful sound, not wanting to think what it could mean.

Then Janie, clad in a thin linen shift, burst into the room asking, "Where's Cousin Oliver?"

"Asleep in the barn, I imagine."

"He's not; I checked. He hasn't slept there a-tall an' Maggie's not in her stall."

She knew her grand-daughter was right, but didn't want to alarm her. "Sonny always takes off unexpected, Janie; that's his way . . ."

"But Grandma, ye didn't see it yesterday. Somethin' awful's happened; I know it."

The old woman had never seen Jane so worked up. She'd been shooed off to bed in all the confusion last night and James'd been so tight-lipped it was hard to tell exactly what had happened. Taking the girl in her arms, she let her tell the whole story in a gush of stammered words and half-choked sobs.

" . . . an' Uncle Will got so m-mad he started sh-shakin' Father. That's when Cousin Oliver decided to ride out to some m-meetin'; an' I know he's in trouble. He don' mean ta be, Grandma, but he's such a lively man—trouble jus' has a way o' catchin' up with 'im. He needs me an' we've got ta find 'im!"

"Don't be silly, Jane," her mother scolded. Mary'd been listening from the stairs for some time. "Get dressed an' back down here to help feed Sarie, then I want ye to march out to the woods an' fetch back the clothin' ye left out there yesterday."

Obediently, Jane slipped from her grandma's grasp and hurried upstairs. Mary didn't say a word, but Grandma could feel the friction rising between them. She pounded away at some corn with a hand pestle and irritably wondered how a young, slip-of-a-thing like Janie could peg Oliver to the letter, while her daughter in-law had no understanding of the dear boy.

When James came in, Mary fussed over him, serving his breakfast of porridge and chickory brew. "Lord be praised ye come home when ye did, James. Oliver an' Will are shore ta get mixed up in evil doin's at Mingo. I'm so proud ye stayed clear of it."

Grandma could see her son's nerves knotting up, but he remained quiet. She and James had heard this speech of Mary's at least three times since he'd gotten in last evening.

"An' it's a good thing, too . . . I heerd Reverend McMillan's decided to deny communion tokens to anyone who breaks the excise . . ."

"Mary!"

Jamie's frustrated cry cut the girl's banter in midsentence. Looking hurt, she picked up the baby, who'd begun to whimper. Jamie ran his hands through his hair, struggling to regain his composure.

Suddenly, Lizzie arrived. "Uncle James, Aunt Mary!" She stood in the doorway looking as frantic as Janie had earlier. "Mama wants to know if ye got any news of Pa. He didn't come home yet an' we's all wonderin' . . ." She broke off, unable to put her fears into words.

"Nay girl, we heerd nothin'. Oliver's not back either. Now if ye'll all excuse me, I've got work to do."

"But, James, ye didn't finish . . ."

"I've had all I keer to."

Jiggling the crying babe in her arms, Mary watched him go. His double meaning hadn't escaped her.

Grandma watched them both, thinking how sickly her daughter-in-law looked. "Don' worry, Lizzie. The meetin' prob'ly ran long an' the boys decided ta wait for daylight afore startin' back. Now, run on home an' help yer ma."

The red-headed tom-boy was gone as quickly as she'd arrived and Grandma turned around to a sea of wee questioning faces. "By crackies, what a sorry lot!" she exclaimed. "Why don' ye take the young-uns down to the run, Janie, an' I'll be along directly with the wash?"

Once the house emptied, Grandma quieted the baby and seated Mary in her rocker. "Ye look peaked, Mary. Mebbe ye should. . ."

"I don't understand him!"

"Who? Jamie? Why, he's jus' confused, child. He wants ta do what's right fer you an' the children, but he doesn't want ta see Will ruined either. There's no cut an' dry solution."

"But I've had nothin' but praise for his decision."

"Too much praise, ta my way o' thinkin'."

Mary was baffled by the remark. So, Grandma laid the babe in his cradle and drew up a chair. It was unusual for Mary to confide in her and she truly wanted to help. "I ken only tell ye what Mother Tidball always tol' me—that a man is like a sailin' boat—ye got ta give him some headway, if ye 'xpects to guide 'im a-tall."

"Mother Miller, I do try ta bite my tongue, but lately James's been edgy, either hidin' Oliver's mischief from me or speakin' cross like jus' now. He hurts me so an' he's never got a word of apology."

"It ain't easy fer a man to confess his mistakes to his wife."

"Mistakes!" The girl was too upset to catch the old woman's meaning.

"The biggest mistake I see aroun' here is the coddlin' of that over-grown grandson o' yores. Ever since he's come home, Oliver's spread trouble faster than a cankerous sore. He's at the heart of me problems with James—an' the children too! I 'xpects he's never studied the words of Proverbs: He that troubleth his own house shall inherit the wind!"

The emotional outburst made Grandma give up her well-intended counsel; the girl was beyond reason. "That's a good one for you to remember, Mary. 'Course I always go by Matthew, meself: Judge not, that ye be not judged."

On her way down to join the children another verse of Proverbs came to mind: Speak not in the ears of a fool, for he will despise the wisdom of thy words. Bible rhetoric spun through her head as she set her wash tub on an old stump by the run. Soaping up a pile of soiled aprons and work shirts, she plunged them into cold water and scrubbed fiercely. She thought the extra vigor would squelch her worries, but there was no solace to be found this morning; her mind wouldn't rest.

Dumping out the rinse water, she watched the suds lock into the current and drift down Catfish Run. It was as though her own life were racing downstream and she couldn't break the flow. She could only adjust to her surroundings as she'd always been obliged to do. Ever since she and her husband traipsed up this watershed from the Monongahela, there'd been adjusting—adjusting to the lack of womanly company, adjusting to the needs of ten hungry young mouths—adjusting to the loss of her man.

"My dear Oliver, rest his soul!"

Thank goodness he didn't live to see his sons get embroiled in this bugaboo. It occurred to her that he'd probably react just like Will and want to find some new stretch of untamed wilderness. The purply veins that protruded from her bony, time-worn hands made her wonder if she could take it. Probably not. No, another move would be the end of her.

The children's playful babble drew her attention upstream. Sarie and Ollie waded out to "Fort Pitt"—the little strip of land where the two runs joined. They splattered about in a noisy game of Injuns, completely oblivious of their sister's silent vigil.

Poor Janie. She'd never seen anything like this before— her own kin and neighbors riled into an angry, gun-shooting mob. She didn't know what to make of it and to be quite honest, Grandma didn't know either.

The moping girl who sat dabbling her feet in the run bore little resemblance to the spunky lass who'd set off for a golden day at *Milville,* but then yesterday was never meant to be another July Fourth. Things were just getting out of control. In the sour aftermath of events, Janie'd taken it upon herself to keep the youngsters from getting underfoot

of their over-wrought elders. Such a little peacemaker—
Jamie's eldest. Grandma called the child over, but didn't
have the heart to chide her idleness.

"Dwellin' on thin's don't help."

"But . . ."

"I know. Yer worried about yer Cousin Oliver an' Will,
but they's grown boys now an' ornery as they be, there's one
thin' they learned from their ol' Ma—somethin' I've tried to
teach you, too—that every tub's got ta stand on its own
bottom."

"What's that s'pose ta mean?"

"It means ye got ta face whatever happens to ye, Janie.
Ye got ta seek the Lord's help an' find the strength to stand
alone in this life, if need be."

She drew the girl close, burying the neatly braided head
in her arms. There was a sound on the road. She looked up
and saw something stirring out of the corner of her eye. It
was a man on horseback and, curiously, he was leading a
riderless horse behind. Her first twinge of dread broke into
a violent surge of pain as she recognized the horseman and
saw the body he had slumped over his saddle.

"Grandma, what's wrong? Yore hurtin' me!"

Instinctively, the panic-stricken woman'd tightened her
grip on Janie. She wished with all her heart that the pore
girl would never have to see what stood before her now.

"Sweet, merciful Jesus: tell me it's not so; tell me I'm
dreamin'!" Janie pulled loose, whirled around and let out a
scream. There'd be no hiding things from her now—no way
to keep her from seeing that familiar bald head or the blood
seeping down the side of Will's horse.

"He's hurt bad, Ma. We got the bullet out, but he's lost a
lot of blood."

Will's words set Grandma in motion. Her take-charge
reasoning surfaced above the shock. In the seconds that
followed, she managed to alert Mary and, with Will's help,
they got Oliver up to her bed on the second floor. He was

unconscious and barely breathing—his middle a terrible, bloody mess. Jane was sent off to fetch and boil water while Mary found some linen scraps and began to staunch the flow.

"It don't look good. It don't look good," Grandma muttered, removing her apron to rip it up for bandages. If only she had her grandfather's doctoring services now. "Curse this infernal backwoods—no doctors—no proper medicine—no shred of respect for the preciousness of life." They administered to him as best they could, but she could feel her own strength giving way with every drop of blood that Sonny lost.

Looking helpless, Will left the room. Grandma followed her bedraggled son downstairs. He read her shattered expression correctly and began an explanation.

"We got to Mingo late last night. The meetin' was jus' breakin' up. Some men left, others stayed on to hear how that dog Neville brought the sheriff to me door—how he threatened to arrest us an' called us insurrectionists. It got plenty of them riled, an' Holcroft said we ought to capture Lenox an' bring him back to Mingo Church. . ."

"Capture a U.S. marshal? He musta been loopie!"

"That's what I thought, Ma. Me an' Oliver an' some of the men that worked up at my place—we were afraid that after the shootin' yesterday, Neville'd be issuing arrest warrants agin us. Ye know what that'd mean—a trial in Phil'delphy an' months lost on our farms. We went along to confront Neville—to get 'im to give up his warrants an' 'is commission. We didn't aim to do any shootin'. Of the thirty men who went, only fifteen had guns an' only six of them worked. It's all my fault, Ma. Oliver never cared 'bout ridin' out ta Bower Hill." He raged at himself, totally distraught.

"Don't blame yerself, Will, but what in God's name happened when ye got there?"

"We found the general had just got up. After some words, he fired first. It was from the windows. A horn was blowing in the house at the time of the firing. It was then I seed he hit Oliver."

The old woman went numb as she listened to the rest of Will's ugly tale. She hastened upstairs to relieve Mary as Will, still in shock, left for Alexander's farm to carry the tragic news to Sonny's parents.

"The bleedin's slowed some. I think I'll make up a poultice. 'Twill draw out the infection." Mary fled the room with a hand cupped over her mouth, looking deathly pale.

"Tell me he'll be all right, Lord," prayed the old woman.

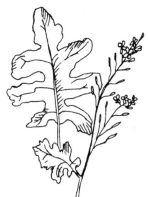

Mary returned, acting more herself and carrying an assortment of herb cures. She cleansed the wound with sliced burdock greens, then bruised some plantain leaves, steeped them in boiling water and applied them as a poultice.

"I'm sorry for gettin' sick jus' now." She spooned hot tea down Oliver's throat. "My mother always made this creek willow brew to ease pain an' cut fever. It may help." The girl turned away from the pitiful sight on the bed. "Mother Miller, I've spoken porely of Oliver—even today, but ye got to believe, I never meant for this to happen."

"Hoosh girl, I know ye'd never be one ta shout 'I tol' ye'— not under these circumstances. Why, it may be yore own know-how on doctorin' plants that'll pull Sonny through. I'm grateful to ye fer that. Ye have a good heart, Mary, she told her earnestly, "Ye jus need ta let it show more."

When James got in, he made a bee-line to his brother's bed. Seconds later, he was downstairs demanding answers. "Who done this?"

Grandma and Mary didn't look up from their task of chopping yarrow root. They were making an ointment to numb the pain around the wound.

"It was Neville shot Oliver," Will stated.

"The blitherin' scum! An' I thought . . . go on."

The tears streaming down Grandma's cheeks ran unchecked, for her hands were occupied with mortar and pestle. "He said Neville musta been waitin' for them—'cause the mansion was bolted up—all 'xcept for the front door gapin' wide open."

"Why was that?"

"Will was afraid there might've been a swivel or a big gun there."

"Good God! I canna believe it!"

"Believe it, Jamie, for very few words were spoken afore yer nephew fell shot." She threw down her pestle, adding goose grease to the mixture. "Next thing Will knew, a horn was blowin' inside the mansion. Musta been some kind of signal, fer the Negroes started firin' from out their cabins on the men's backs. Several more were shot afore they got off as well as they could,"

"Fired on their backs?" James was incredulous. "What was Neville thinkin'?"

"There was no thinkin' involved," Grandma stated simply, "Those men had no more chance than a grasshopper loose in a chicken house."

They'd finished the root salve and carried it up to their patient. James spent the rest of the evening pacing the floor beside Oliver's bed. Finally, he came down to brood by the fire, but Grandma thought he did more gaping at his gun on the hearth mantel than he did at the flames.

Will returned before dawn with Alexander and Martha Jane. Grandma hurried out to escort them to Oliver's second-floor bedside. She didn't like what she saw. Her son appeared to be ready for a good three day's ride—his shot pouch and saddlebag were fully packed and his gun was primed and glinting in the sun.

"How's Sonny?" he asked before she could voice an objection.

"We've checked the bleedin', but the infection's spreadin' an' he's feverish . . . . Jus' what do ye think yer up to, Willie?"

Before Will could answer, Alexander and Martha Jane were already racing toward the door. "The men're gatherin' at Couch's Fort today. I'm ridin' over to speak with Thomas an' John afore . . ."

"Lord, no!" she cried, "Don't go back to Neville's house. One more pull o' that dog's tail, boy, an' ye'll be whistlin' 'whoda-thunk-it.'"

"I didn't say I's goin' ta Bower Hill. I said we were meetin' at Couch's Fort—then we'll decide what ta do."

"Think of what happened to yer nephew."

"That's 'xactly what I am thinkin' 'bout."

His determined expression turned to one of wonder an' Grandma soon learned the cause. Jamie emerged from the house with Mary at his heels. He had his rifle clutched in one hand.

"Think of what yer doin', James! Think of our children!"

"That's all I've done is think," he replied, not slowing his pace. "Now it's time to act."

Mary hurried around trying to face him. She was flustered, but found her Bible tongue quick enough, "It's an honor for a man to cease from strife, but every fool will be meddlin'."

"Stop it, Mary!" He grabbed her shoulders and faced her head on. "I ken barely stand me own torment without ye addin' yores."

Mary sobbed uncontrollably. "If ye insist on leavin'— I'll . . . I'll have ta leave, too. I'll go back to me family in Cross Creek." Her eyes were lit with fear as she pleaded desperately with her husband. Clearly, she was scairt to the core.

"Now yer talkin' nonsense," he retorted. "Yer a Miller now—so get a grip on yerself an' start actin' like one. Our children need ye," his voice softened some. "My nephew's lyin' up there—mebbe on his death bed—an' he needs ye, too. So bear-up woman, an' let me do what I must."

He and Alexander made their way to the barn, leaving Mary feeling whoozy—a feather could've knocked her down. By the time Grandma got a steady arm around the girl, Jamie'd reappeared, leading Ol' Dan. Without another word, the three brothers mounted up and rode off.

"God go with 'em."

"They say misfortune happens in threes," said Mary in a small, dazed voice. "First there was trouble at William's the day the writ was served; then Oliver got shot . . . What could . . ."

"Trouble in threes? That's a big windy," scoffed Grandma. She'd thought of the old superstition herself, but didn't want to lend it credence.

"I thought I'd try a new poultice when we change Oliver's dressing this mornin'. Some folks say flax seed an' cornmeal works wonders."

"Now yer talkin'!" Grandma was encouraged by Mary's change in temperament.

"An' could ye speak with Jane, Mother Miller? Ye have such a way with her an' I'm afraid she's takin' this whole business with Oliver porely. She's been at his side for hours—last I seen, she was proppin' his head with that pillow she made. Maybe ye could get her to come down an' help make up some sage tea."

Grandma couldn't believe her ears. Either Jamie's words'd made an impression on Mary or the girl'd come to realize that working was preferable to worrying.

Once inside, they heard Sonny moaning upstairs. There were several loud thuds and Janie was squealing. Suddenly the wounded freighter shoved past his mother and appeared at the top of the stairs. He stood there in his breeks, his hair askew and his chest a bound-up maze of bloody bandages.

"Ma, Ma!" he implored Martha Jane, "Don' let Pa whup me—I's only out fishin' with Cap'n Jack . . ."

"Lord hae mercy, he's delirious—thinks he's a boy again back at Friend's Cove!" The fire of fever-craziness was burning in his eyes.

Janie ran down past her cousin and stood behind her mother. "I tried to keep 'im down, Mama, but he wouldn't stay."

"Giddup, Maggie, we got ta run this whiskey to Carlisle an' find Sweet Rosie. Giddup! Halloo, Cap'n Jack . . ." He rambled on some more, teetered on the rail, then came down a step or two and started singing, "Oh, I got a gal an' ye got none. Lil' Liza Jane . . ."

"Oh no! He's bleedin' anew." Mary started up the stairs, but hesitated when Sonny continued his wild jabbering.

"Stop!" he shouted, pointing a finger at his in-law. "Ye money-lovin' cur . . . Don' shoot . . . Don't! We jus' want ta talk . . . No! Oh God, Jamie, I'm killt. Where are ye Willie? I'm dyin' . . ." As he sagged into Martha Jane's arms, Grandma and Mary rushed to help.

"Good Lord, he's torn himself ta pieces agin." Mary ministered to the glistening red bandages. "He's burnin' up with fever. Janie! Pick me some camomile flowers an' catnip leaves from the garden."

"Yes, Mama."

"Ye know what it looks like?"

"Yes."

"Well hurry then. We'll brew up a tea ta help 'im sleep." The girl disappeared.

"Love, Lovie . . ." Oliver's head seemed to clear and he began to recognize them. "Where's my pa . . . an' Jamie an' Will? Not off ta Neville's, are they?"

Mary nodded, trying to get a grip on the man.

"No, no!" shouted Oliver, breaking her hold. "Don' let 'em go—it's a bloody business. Neville's sure to report it . . . Washington'll send in the troops. I tol' 'em, I tol' 'em. Don' they see what happened to me?" He stretched out an imploring hand to Grandma, then his head slumped into his mother's lap. Together, the women half-dragged, half-pushed him up the stairs.

"Mebbe the old pastor'll stop 'em. Reverend Clark, Reverend Clark!"

"Back ta bed with ye, Sonny. That's where ye belong. Mary, start a fire an' get some fresh bandages. He's got the life-blood flowin' out of him."

Down below, they heard Janie calling, "Mama? Mama, I've got what ye wanted . . ."

XX

FORT COUCH MUSTER

Turn back, O man, foreswear thy foolish ways.

—Old 124th

"Well, would ye look at that," said Will, shading his eyes in the direction of the old fort.

"Must be a good five hundred farmers here," Alexander figured.

They walked their horses up the North Branch of McLaughlin Run and joined the group. Ever since the 1770s, Nathan Couch's Fort had stood on the South Trail leading up to the Washington and Pittsburgh Road. It struck Will as peculiar that the old log-and-daub palisade, originally designed to protect the settlers from Injuns, was now a meeting place for men who found it necessary to seek justice against their own government.

The news of Will's summons had traveled swiftly among the settlements dotting the Monongahela Valley. Will recognized militiamen from as far away as Brownsville, and Washington and Greene counties, but the bulk of the gathering was from the Mingo area. Some men had come angered by events of the previous attack. Others, like David Bradford, were eager to use the power of the mob for their own political schemes. Many, like Alexander, Will and James, had come unsure of what course to take, but hopeful that Neville's resignation would put an end to the whole matter.

"Let's hire an assassin to go an' pick off the ol' moneybags," remarked a tough-looking woodsy, who'd tied back his wild mange of hair with a red bandana. Will, who had never seen the man before, was greatly relieved when cooler heads prevailed.

Newly assembled, their first item of business was to select a committee to have general direction over the expedition. John Holcroft, Benjamin Parkinson, and Will were chosen— their main duty being to designate an officer to have immediate authority over the men. Will suggested Holcroft, but he refused to undertake the responsibility again. Holcroft nominated Parkinson, who was the president of the Mingo Society. But Parkinson also declined, saying he hadn't had enough military experience.

The committee then unanimously agreed to offer the command to Maj. James McFarlane, who had done excellent service in the revolution and was the ranking officer of the gathering. McFarlane accepted reluctantly.

Just then, there was an unexpected interruption by Reverend John Clark, who had made his way down the trail from Bethel Meetinghouse which stood on the hill above the fortress.

The pastor had gone in and out among these people for years. He shared his preaching duties between the congregations of Mingo and Bethel and was well-known and revered by all. Today, Will thought he looked even more lanky and spindly than ever in his black suit with the silver buckled breeches. Hat in hand he stood, the long white hair combed back into a queue. He would not give up this bit of old-fashioned dignity even after thirteen years on this rugged frontier. He stood there like an ancient prophet— the light of divine wisdom burning in his eyes. His seventy-six years were evident in his stooped shoulders and bloodless cheeks, but they did not diminish the intense emotion he possessed as he stretched out one hand and began his plea.

"I come to raise my feeble voice against this foolishness. My holy office, my concern for your spiritual welfare, my duty an' conscience—all compel me to warn you against your hostile purpose. I also come as your friend," he urged. "Brethren, understand that. Believe that, please."

A Sabbath stillness fell over the throng as they heard this devout man who stopped them in their tracks, as Elijah did Ahab long ago. He looked about the crowd as if to catch the eye of members of his own flock, then got to the gist of his speech:

"You are in a rebellious way and rebellion is as the sin of witchcraft. You are leaving here with the intent of shedding blood."

"Wasn't us who shed first blood. Remember ye that!" It was the same character in the red scarf who'd wanted to assassinate Neville. Will reckoned there was a considerable element of reckless back-woodsies who were out for a good fight and figured there'd be no neutrals by the time they reached Neville's plantation.

The Reverend calmed the muttering crowd and went on, "I know ye feel grievously wronged by the government an' ye feel ye have an honest quarrel against General Neville an' his excisemen. But, if ye attempt to solve your problems by way o' the gun, ye not only break the laws of your mother country, ye also break God's holy commandment, 'Thou shalt not kill!' "

A wave of murmurs swept over the crowd. The men moved like shiftless horses under the scorching sun. Before anyone could offer a reply, the minister continued quickly, Consider this, my friends: No wrong can be righted by the doing of greater wrong. Your act is one of war, disguise it as ye may. Ye're talking war against the United States, war against Washington—the very man ye were all proud to call *General-in-Chief* not twenty years ago. Ye fought against British tyranny then an created this great land—so ye could find peaceful ways of making an' changing the laws. Ye canna throw that away. Truly not!"

He paced a bit, seemingly groping for the right words to strike a chord of reason. "I don't believe ye've thought this

whole thing out. Suppose ye drive Neville out of his house
and banish him from these lands. Will it end there? Alas,
no! Like King David of old, ye may be driven into exile,
weeping and lamenting your errors as ye go. Suppose ye
destroy Neville's house. What then? Do ye think a boulder
set rolling down a steep mountain will stop before it's run
its course? Nay. It'll crush an' destroy everything in its
path—so beware—lest your own houses be left desolate
unto you. Do ye think the inspector will not resist you?
Don't be deceived! He is a man of blood and spirit like
yourselves, a man of war since his youth. He has armed
himself and his servants—ye can be sure—like the ancient
days of Abraham when he went against the kings of Sodom.
If ye don't turn back, this day will not be without bloodshed.
Return to your homes before it's too late! Remember God's
word . . ."

The esteemed minister flung his hat to the ground and
outstretched both arms appealingly to the people. His eyes
slowly scanned the sea of up-turned faces and paused on
Major McFarlane, who stood uncertainly by his mount.

"They that take the sword shall perish by the sword," he
concluded passionately. "God forbid that ye should throw
your lives away on such a quarrel. Your leaders are self-
deceived. They are deceiving you. Remember your solemn
duty to your country. Remember the oaths of allegiance ye
proudly swore in the patriotic days that tried men's souls
during the struggle for independence. Remember your
wives and children who may this day be widows and
fatherless."

He paused a second, reading the worry on their leader's
face and seized the opportunity. "You, James McFarlane,
am I not to marry you to Miss Mary Patterson on the
morrow? This should be a time of beginning, man, not a
cause for sorrow. How can I reconcile that bonny young
lass when she finds herself betrothed to a bullet-ridden

corpse? Can ye march off so valiantly to your death an'
think so little of your love?"

McFarlane stepped back involuntarily at the minister's
personal plea. He was a grand sight in his blue camblet
coat, leather overalls, and black-cocked hat. A military
cutlass hung from a broad belt strapped across his
shoulders.

"Reverend Clark, me Mary knows she's weddin' a military
man an' I canna back away from what I see as me duty.
These men aren't being led inta battle; we're going as a
show of force against this tax business. That's well within
our rights as United States citizens an' we've seen what
little regard Gen. John Neville has fer those rights. Jus'
ask Alexander Miller how many rights were upheld fer his
son, Oliver—or the five other men who were wounded at
Bower Hill."

"It's hard to see rights clearly through a fog of grapeshot,"
counseled the pastor. "Don't dance with death, major, she's
a lighter foot than ye—than all of ye," he added with a
sweep of his arm.

"Reverend, we thank ye fer yore lovin' concern fer us all.
Truly, ye believe all ye've said an' have spoken fer our own
good as ye see it. We reverence ye as a man an' honor ye as
a minister, but this is a secular matter an' we must trust
our own experience an' judgment."

"It's up to us to take a stand. We're bein' used, can't ye
see? It's a plot by the big distillers an' by those schemers in
the capital to stomp out free competition among us
independents. We have no money to pay the tax. How can
we when they're taxin' the main cash crop we've got? So,
there it is—we have a right ta our say and a say here in the
West, not in Phil'delphy!"

"And after that say—can ye steel yourselves to losing your
plantations when the federal troops are called in to
respond? Can I find enough ground in Bethel Churchyard

to bury each an' every one of ye when ye're hung for treason? For it's treason ye're talking, plain and simple."

His accusatory finger swept over all and stopped when he spied the Miller brothers. "And you, William, are ye marching for revenge when less than a fortnight ago ye told me how eager ye were ta move off and be clear of any confrontations?"

"I'm sorry, Reverend," Will answered, uneasily. "I wish the world I had yore holy eyes ta see through, but I've only got these two o' me own. Yesterday, I seed Sonny's youth bleedin' outta him an' it made me feel so very old. I'm not goin' along ta do any killin', but I've got ta have justice. By God, I'll stand in a hail of musket fire an' shout out me grievances, but Reverend, I'll be heard!"

"Aye, aye," shouted his comrades.

Reverend Clark could see the argument slipping away from him, but hooshed them all with a glance. "So, it's come down to this, has it? Ye've backed Neville into a corner an' expect 'im ta jump at your commands. Well don't be surprised when he acts out of desperation like any other threatened animal. Don't tempt God, don't ever do that."

"Oh my friends, hear me. I speak out of love for you and yours. You have never had cause to doubt my love. I would lay down my life for you, if I might bind your assent with my blood. Out of this love, I plead with ye. I warn ye! Hear me brethren, hear me! Turn ye, turn ye, for why will ye die, O house of Israel?"

The patriarch ceased, dropped his arms, and bowed his head in silent prayer. The men were still, each pondering the pastor's eloquent message. Next, there was a shuffling as they looked at each other, uncertain whether or not to proceed. One man threw down his rifle and joined the Reverend in prayer. Several others did likewise.

Seeing this, McFarlane mounted up and hastily cried, "Attention! Forward!" before any more men could be swayed. The rag-tag detail began to move slowly down the dusty road.

A few gathered around the pastor to assure him they would go home. Others passed by grasping his hand and seeking his blessing, but there was nary a man present who didn't remove his cap out of respect for the good minister.

"I'd like to take yore advice," one passerby confessed, "but how ken I sneak home now—like some naughty school-child?"

"This is pride," quoted Reverend Clark. "Sinful pride. And pride goeth before destruction . . ."

The old man was spent and appeared lightheaded. The three Miller brothers eyed each other once more before Will grabbed his reins and fell in behind the motley company. The last thing he saw at Couch's Fort that day was Jamie and Alexander leading the weary pastor uphill to Bethel Meetinghouse.

XXI

TRAGEDY AT BOWER HILL

Maybe it'd all been a nightmare and by morning,
he'd wake up and think only of this waterway,
flowing downstream to the Monongahela as it had a century
ago and would a century hence.
Human pain should be piddily in comparison but, somehow,
it didn't feel that way now.

—Thoughts of William Miller,
along Catfish Run

Thus, the die was cast. The midnight antics of Tom the Tinker, the overheated reactions of some incited field hands, and the unfortunate bloodshed during the first visit to Neville's had all come to a head. The populace had organized itself into a full-fledged backwoods army.

Marching afoot or on horseback—the mood of the militiamen was varied. Some laughed and joked, making loud threats. Others moved silently, as if troubled by a heavy conscience. Clearly, their reasons for joining forces were as diverse as their weaponry of rifles, clubs, pitchforks, and old Revolutionary muskets.

Bower Hill lay four miles off, as the crow flies, but the winding hills of Washington County made the trek much longer. Here and there, the virgin forest shading the road broke into half-finished clearings encircled with rough-hewn worn fences. Amid the tree stumps were potato patches or fields of Injun corn and, occasionally, a farmer hard at work.

"Join us, join us!" was the cry.

Where the springs or clear brooks appeared were also the settlers' cabins. Women carrying babes waved sadly from doorways. Ruddy children ran to join the passing cavalcade for part of the way. Their enthusiasm gave momentum to the party, and who could begrudge their cheery exuberance when they were looking at more people than any of them had seen in a lifetime? The children called out their excitement amid shouldered make-believe rifles, caring little for the marchers' cause.

"We shore picked a scorcher fer this showdown," declared Will, mopping his brow. He'd caught up with his friend, Benjamin Parkinson. "Do ye s'pose Neville's had time ta call in the Fort Pitt garrison?"

"Could be, Miller. That Neville's a wise ol' coon an not an easy one ta catch nappin'."

The procession continued on and on, finally stopping at the edge of the woods near Bower Hill. Here, they allowed time for the stragglers to catch up and regroup into a solid force.

At the end of a narrow plateau stood the finest mansion in all the western country. It was an imposing wooden structure, a story-and-a-half in height with wide halls and spacious verandas on two sides. Most of its materials had been transported from England and the East at considerable cost. Everyone knew about General Neville's fine china, carpets, and looking glasses.

The men emerged from the woods and climbed along the ridge bearing their own flag containing six broad stripes. Nearing the yard, William and the other leaders realized their movements had come as no surprise: The place was an armed fortress.

The entryway to the house was flanked on one side by a long row of slave quarters. On the other side was a barn, a distillery, and other farm buildings. All were manned. Uniformed soldiers appeared on the verandas. From a gabled window below the roof's peak, a woman waving a white cloth was visible.

It was plain to see that General Neville had summoned troops from the U.S. garrison at Fort Pitt—where his brother-in-law, Major Kirkpatrick, and his son-in-law, Major Craig, were ready to assist.

McFarlane ordered three men of good standing to approach the house under a flag of truce to demand the inspector's commission and all his official papers. The men were met outside by Kirkpatrick. Their conversation was brief.

Will leaned on his rifle along with Ben Parkinson and the rest of the troops, anxiously awaiting the results. If circumstances had been different, he might've admired the breathtaking view down the steep slopes to the valley of Chartiers Creek. Or, he might've noticed the open look-way cut through the forest to the opposite hillside, *Woodville*, the home of the inspector's son, Col. Presley Neville. (The opening made it possible for the two families to signal each other from their uppermost windows.)

Word came back that Neville was not at home. McFarlane sent a second message to demand that six persons be permitted to search for the inspector's papers and take them. This was refused, prompting a third truce flag party which requested that the women and children withdraw. They left soonafter, probably for *Woodville*, and the attack began.

The militiamen fought Injun-style, hiding behind stumps, logs, and any other thing that rose above ground. Some aimed their rifles, providing cover while others zig-zagged forward, a few at a time. Once exposed, they kept themselves in a crouch, trying to make the smallest target possible against the steady barrage of gunfire that rattled off from the armed slaves. The real danger came from the soldiers at the main house, whose firing was more selective.

"I've got no stomach fer this," groaned Parkinson, crawling up beside Will. He ducked behind a tree just as a shot seared the bark beside his head.

"I've tangled with Injuns in me time, but this beats all."

"Aye, an' would ye look at McFarlane," nodded Will. " 'E must think he can't be hit by the way he's dancin' through the middle of it."

Both men squinted their eyes over their gunsights and scanned the buildings intently as the major motioned a whole line forward. They darted ahead trying to get within range. The thick logs of the outbuildings and closed shutters of the house made it hard for the farmers to find a target. Nevertheless, the crack of their rifles echoed down the valley and sporadic volleys were traded on both sides.

"They say there's a thin line atween courage an' foolhardiness," mused Parkinson as he rushed to re-load his weapon.

"God help 'im—I'd say McFarlane's fool'ardy, if I didn't know 'bout all his military awards."

The major finally had all his men positioned and ordered the whole line to open fire on the house. The heavy shooting left the yard choked with bluish smoke that drifted through the early evening air to the ravine below.

"What's that?" shouted Holcroft, pointing toward the house.

"A white flag is wavin' from the gallery window," agreed McFarlane, peering out from behind a fence. "Thank God we can cut this wretched business short. Cease fire! Cease fire!" he commanded.

The order was heard nearby, but the shooting continued on the flanks. Impatiently, McFarlane stepped out from hiding and waved his rifle, repeating the order: "Cease fire!"

Will wasn't sure he'd seen a white flag. He wasn't sure whether Kirkpatrick and his men took McFarlane's appearance as a signal for attack or whether the white flag had been used as a cowardly trick to gain advantage. At any rate, the rifles barked from the house and a wounded James McFarlane dropped to the ground. It all happened so fast, there was no time to think. A disbelieving cry rose from the ranks as they pelted the house in a vengeful rage. The garrison and cabins gave full reply till the earth rumbled beneath Will's feet and his elusive targets became a blur.

John Holcroft sprang ahead and dragged McFarlane's body back behind the shelter of the trees. Will ran to the spot—no matter that bullets flew in his path. He knelt down, pulled a flask from his shirt, and drew it to the major's lips.

"Too late," declared Holcroft, supporting their leader in his arms. " 'E's in God's hands now." He laid McFarlane down as gently as if he were a babe as the men stared grief-stricken at his blood-spattered form.

"McFarlane is killt! McFarlane is killt!" The news spread rapidly down the lines. "Spitefully killt under the ruse of a white flag . . ."

"Burn the cowards! Burn 'em all out."

The enraged men were totally beyond their leader's control as they charged the outbuildings with fiery torches. Soon, the Negro cabins were afire, causing the servants to flee toward the main house. The wind spirited flames to the barn, stable, and distillery. Then, the mansion itself began to smoke and blister. Long blazing fingers reached up around the rim of the roof. The whole countryside was alerted to the sorry business by thick, black billows of smoke that poofed high above the house. It wasn't long before the soldiers came gagging and sputtering out through the main door. They threw down their weapons as the militiamen rushed to surround and escort them down to the grove. Holcroft detained the leaders and ordered that the garrison soldiers be released on the nearby road to Pittsburgh.

Meanwhile, the house was being plundered. The wine cellar was ravaged and barrels of whiskey were rolled out in the open. Will saw the liquor broken into and freely imbibed. He also noticed that the red-scarved woodsy and his cronies bashed in several whiskey barrels and rolled them into the fire. Seconds later, the barrels exploded in a gigantic sheet of blue flames.

"The place is doomed," Will pronounced, shielding his eyes from the intense heat and bright light.

"Aye, there'll be no dousin' o' Neville's mansion now," agreed Parkinson. "Asides, these boys are in no mood ta save it."

Ben and Will looked around despairingly at their men who'd arrived only a short while ago with such hopeful intentions. Now, they lolled about—no better than a drunken, destructive mob.

"We'd best try an' cool a few tempers here afore that woodsy gets any ideas of crossin' the Chartiers an' burnin' *Woodville.*"

"No doubt o' that, Miller. I've had me share o' trouble fer one day—fer a whole lifetime, come ta think of it."

"Who ye got there?" asked Will, addressing David Hamilton, a fellow Mingo officer. Hamilton had his musket poked square in the back of a prisoner.

"It's Major Kirkpatrick, hisself, if ye please. 'E practic'ly sneaked away with the garrison boys afore I picked 'im out. Holcroft wants the men ta take 'im back to Mingo to answer some questions."

"Men?" scoffed Kirkpatrick, "All I see is a tipsy pack o' God-damn whiskey boys."

"Spare us the self-righteous clack, major; move along."[11] Hamilton gave a jab with his musket and the two set off down the ridge.

---

[11] "Kirkpatrick, after being carried some distance under guard was taken by David Hamilton behind him on horseback; when, thinking himself to be protected, he began to answer those who came up occasionally with indignant language, when Hamilton said to him, 'You see I am endeavoring to save you at the risk of my own safety, and yet you are making it still more dangerous for me.' On this, he was silent; and being carried some distance further by Hamilton, he was advised to make his escape, which he did." — *Incidents of the Insurrection*, Hugh Henry Breckinridge

The events that followed were to become a hazy blur in Will's mind. He remembered drifting among the drunken revelers, trying to persuade as many farmers as he could to go home. He and Ben assisted the wounded and managed to help the slaves keep their smokehouse from burning. The Negroes were determined to save it since it housed their bacon.

One thing stuck out from the rest: the sight of an old horse being led in and draped with the lifeless form of James McFarlane. The death of their leader threw a gloomy shadow over everyone. The Mingo men who retreated alongside the corpse were soon joined by other farmers who'd also seen enough.

As they descended the ridge, Will gazed back at the remains of Bower Hill. Against the inky night sky, it looked like a giant open hearth that'd smoldered down to a few embers in the wee hours of the morning.

Will rode along in a state of non-feeling. He couldn't think of what further trouble might lie beyond this day. He couldn't think of how the Reverend's prediction had come true. McFarlane's death had left him numb.

Rumors had Neville escaping in a dress with the women and children, and Kirkpatrick as firing the fatal shot at McFarlane, but Will didn't hear. He barely noticed his peers turning down their respective lanes, one by one, until at last he was alone.

It was Catfish Run that finally roused him from his stupor. The water churned along noisily, splashing constantly—no matter how painful or joyous the events of any particular day. The hoot of a night owl and the ever-crying peepers cast their unvarying sounds through the darkness. One could glean either grief or bliss from their tones, Will suspected, depending on one's mood. He wished the ugliness of this day could be forever hid in the pitch black cover of night. Maybe it'd all been a nightmare and by morning he'd wake up and think only of this waterway, flowing downstream to the Monongahela as it had a century ago and would a century hence. Human pain should be piddily in comparison, but somehow it didn't feel that way now.

As he approached *Mansfield,* he noticed the tapers in the windows were still lighted. Dismounting, he walked around to the front of the house and found Jamie and Alexander standing in the doorway. They looked so forlorn that Will regretted playing a part in their torment. He wanted to comfort his brothers, put their minds at ease and tell him how he respected their peaceful intent.

"They was right," thought Will. "They an' the Reverend were right all along. If I hadn't been so bull-headed, I would've believed 'em."

He faced them calmly and without bitterness. "Today, we've seen Bower Hill burnt ta the ground an' Jamie McFarlane killt. Ye did right, Jamie and Alex, ta follow the Reverend."

It wasn't an easy admission for Will to make, but they took no relish in it. James just stood there whittling a stick with the blade of his hunting knife.

Were their movements a ploy against idleness, or was it something else?

"We prayed fer ye, Will," spoke Alexander. "We prayed ye'd come home alive . . . 'cause we lost Oliver. I lost my son this evenin'."

XXII

THE WAKE

Weep not for him who is dead,
Nor bemoan him;
But weep bitterly for him who goes away,
For he shall return no more
to see his native land.

—Jeremiah 22:10

"So what's yer will, Ma, a plot in Bethel Cemetery or the woods above Boyer's Farm?"

Some years ago Grandpa'd been buried on a wooded slope halfway between *Mansfield* and Bethel Church. It was the local burial ground before the meetinghouse was built. Nary a Sabbath'd gone by since, that Grandma hadn't walked that lonely stretch of hillside on the way home from services.

"I 'xpects 'is grandfather would appreciate some company, though Lord knows, I wish it was me bein' buried 'stead o' Sonny. I always s'posed I'd be the next one laid ta rest aside yer pa."

"Don' talk that way, Ma," objected Father. "Ye canna 'xpect all your young-uns to outlive ye."

"Well, that certainly was my intent when I brought ye inta this world an' wet-nursed ye from pups."

Grandma always said that old men go to their deaths, but in this case death caught the family all of a sudden. My poor cousin didn't even have a decent set of clothes for his bury-hole.

"There's an old suit of his grandfather's up in that chest in the attic," Grandma recalled, preparing to climb the stairs.

Right away, Mother and Aunt Rachel blocked her path, leading her back to the corner pallet by the fire. They tried to calm her with assurances that they would see to all the bathing and dressing of Cousin Oliver's corpse. She didn't argue, though I thought it cruel of my elders to keep Grandma idle at this time. She wasn't needed, they said. It'd be too disturbing for her and Martha Jane, they said. Grandma'd always found comfort in work, however unpleasant, but she sat down shakily and I could almost see the sorrow washing over her.

My deserted brother gave a cry, so I set his cradle in motion. The innocent eyes of Sarie and Ollie peered in at Grandma from the door. They were curious about the goings-on and didn't know what to make of it. The old woman pulled them both into her weary arms. We all listened as the soft murmurs of the women working upstairs were punctuated outside by the steady thud of iron upon wood of the men building a coffin.

The shock of this loss numbed me to the core. The only task I'd been able to accomplish was early this morning when I fetched-in the water the women needed to bathe the corpse. Since then I'd sunk into a corner beside Grandma, my arms clasped around Bet, my eyes fixed on some unseen spot. The familiar faces around me were transformed into strangers in the slow moving dream that had become this never-ending day.

"Ma, I've had word through a militia friend that the Wallaces won't arrive till well after the funeral."

"Aye, Will," Grandma nodded meekly, "I expected as much ... oh me youngest, me youngest," she muttered and rocked.

I knew Grandma missed my aunt Mary, who'd married into the Wallace family way off in Cross Creek, near Ohio

Territory. All my other aunts and uncles lived within a day's walk and their children were well-known to me, but there were Wallace cousins that I scarcely knew.

The neighbors trickled in as the day wore on. Edna Sweet, the Dinsmores, Peter Croco, his wife, and gawking boys, eight of Grandma's ten children and their families—they set the table with pots of stew, vegetables, or puddings and paid their respects. The men settled in for a good talk while their wives plied the young-uns away from Aunt Martha Jane and Grandma, looking hard at them to see how they were "bearing up." The bulk of the mourners arrived at dusk, having come straight from Major McFarlane's burial down in Mingo.

Grandma drifted about lighting tapers, allowing her untasted cup of tea to be replaced. Children trudged in and out, their faces smeared with fruit pie. Their mothers batted away flies from the growing spread of vittles and coaxed the grieving family members to have a bite. I turned a cold shoulder on the supper Lizzie offered and continued my agonizing stupor. I remembered the countless times Grandma'd set out, basket on arm, to one plantation or another for just such a gathering. Even at the end of a long winter when food was scarce, she'd always managed to squeeze out a buttermilk pie or basket of oat cakes for a neighbor's wake.

The short gown I wore clung to my sweaty frame and my breathing caught in the pain across my chest. Not talking, not eating, I felt like a ghost meandering my way out of all their doting clutches.

"Ye've made my mistake. Death comes as a terrifyin' blow when ye let someone become so precious in yer life." Grandma'd followed me outside. "It's my own fault," she said more to herself. "I shoulda taken a stick to that boy more often. I shoulda treated him like the others 'stead o' excusin' 'is willful ways an' devious pranks."

"But, Grandma ..."

"It's hard to step on the child whose easy laughter stirs up so much joy in my ol' heart. An' once they's growed, there's no turnin' thin's around. But I could've sided squarely with yer mother on the excise mess," she fretted. "Sonny might be alive today if I'd spoken out agin Will an' really put me foot down."

It didn't matter now. I didn't care two hoots about old Tom the Tinker anymore. I felt removed from it all, as if Grandma's family and friends were intruders in our own house—as if there were some other self sitting here considering the bits of conversation that escaped the gathering.

"I heerd David Bradford wants ev'ry farmer in the Western Survey to meet at Braddock's Field an' march on Pittsburgh."

"Where will it end?"

"I hope me James'll have no part of it."

"Well, my husband has no int'rest in the movement agin the government," Mrs. Billy Fife announced proudly.

"Well la-di-da-dah! Where's yore sense o' civic duty, woman? Where's yore patriotic spirit?" I recognized Jeannie Smith talking. "Robert ain't int'rested in an uprisin' either, but I'm fer doin' thin's an' I tell ye, when that meetin' day dawns—I'll clean his gun, fill 'is pouch with balls, make 'im a new pair o' moccasins, prepare three days rations—whatever it takes—an' I'll say, 'Robert, go an' do what ye can. Talk with yer friends, persuade yore neighbors ta go home an' stop this madness with Bradford an' 'is schemes."

"Hoosh woman, did ye fergit how this family jus' lost their own son on just such a mission o' 'reason?' "

"That's all right," Mother interrupted, siding with her friend. "Jeannie's got a right to speak her mind. 'Sides, I admire 'er pluck an' the trust she has in her husband's good judgment." My mother sounded like a different person, I thought, surprised that she and not Grandma should be the strong one hosting this vigil.

"That Oliver," one man sighed, " 'E shore stuffed a lot o' livin' into 'is thirty-three years. 'E packed quite a whallop with some o' those yarns he'd spin. I remember how one time he got me an' that ol' buzzard Eli ta gigglin' like schoolboys—he doubled the whiskey in the weddin' punch at his own brother's shiveree, then he made sure every last body had a pot an' pan to clang. Why, I musta blushed clean up to me scalplocks the day he . . ."

"That's enough Walter. We're all well aware of the boy's shortcomin's. I only pray that the good Lord . . ."

"The Good Lord'll receive 'im as a high-spirited man an' a source o' joy to many," interceded Mother, quelling the first mutterings against Cousin Oliver. "I 'xpects I best warn ye, there'll be fiddle music at the services tomorrow."

"Ye don' say!"

"The devil's instrument!"

"Praise him with lute an' harp. Praise him with strings an' pipes," quoted Mother. "Grandmother Miller felt Oliver would've wanted it that way."

"Bless her heart," declared Edna Sweet, "that woman's always been right there fer me, 'specially since Benjamin passed."

"Aye," agreed another, "an' there's none of us here should fergit all the fair trades Oliver made fer us acrosst the mountains."

"Hogwash!" Grandma uttered aloud, pushing herself up on her feet. "I've heerd all I want to 'bout 'how Sonny was' an' 'what Sonny did.' A body'd think he'd been gone a whole score o' years, ta hear ye all talk."

As for me, any minute now I expected to see Cousin Oliver leading his pack team up the lane with Maggie's bells jangling. I remembered the other night when I thought I heard the solitary sound of his fiddle lingering in the air, like twilight on the hills.

Grandma marched toward the doorstep, past her neighbors and kin. "Don' go in there Ma," Father urged, "the room's like a furnace an' the taint's overpowerin'."

"I want ta be with my grandson," she replied, ignoring his advice. I grabbed her hand and together we entered a room lit with dozens of candles. They cast a wavering shadow over the walls and across the oblong poplar box that'd been propped up on two chairs. Stepping closer, Grandma moaned when she saw the figure inside. I opened my fingers a crack and peered out at the body that used to be my favorite cousin. He wouldn't like being laid out so neat. Mother'd taken a haw comb to his mangy hank of hair and slicked it back smooth as a whisper. His beard'd never been so tidy, but most unusual of all—he'd never laid so still.

"Oliver started roamin' afore he could walk. Ever since 'e was a tike Ollie's size, he was a real ball-o-fire; used ta be scairt of that ol' red rooster peckin' the backside o' his pants. He ran away so much, I's always afeared he'd get nabbed by Injuns or fergit 'is way home." She laid a loving hand on her grandson's brow. "When 'e got some years on 'im, the stay-at-home chores never appealed—he'd rather haul the grain to mill instead or run some pots to the smithy . . . Well, the Lord's taken our rovin' freighter fer his own. He's gathered up his cheery soul and vigor and left behind a well-groomed, stony-faced body."

She smiled bitterly at the kind touches added to the coffin—one of Rachel's tiny stitched kerchiefs in a pocket, my embroidered pillow tucked under his head, and of course, the fiddle resting by his side. Grandma hugged the instrument to herself as the wind kicked up and a light rain started to fall. Talk below lulled to a hush through the wee hours of the morning till all that was left was her boys keeping watch outside.

"This rain'll shore cut the heat."

"First one all month. I's startin' ta feel as parched as Mary's pore truck patch."

"It's a blessin', it is. A good rain'll get the water level up so the river's fit fer travel. I don' wanta rush that new babe o' Rachel's, but it'd shore set my mind at ease ta get a head-start on our Kentuck move."

"They's still goin' to Kentuck, Grandma." I bit my lip and couldn't halt the tears.

"I thought Oliver's death might change Will's mind" She sank into her rocker-chair, hurting at the very idea. "Course he's got other thin's to consider," she scolded herself. "There'll be no last-minute reprieve, Janie—no miraculous cure fer keepin' the family together. They aren't movin' acrosst the Monongahela, or even out to Cross Creek. They's goin' to Kentuck . . . Why, they might as well jump into Oliver's bury hole tomorrow for all we'll ever see of 'em again."

Next morning, there were a few blessed waking moments when all memory failed. But the truth came flooding over me all too soon when I caught a final glimpse of Cousin Oliver's face before Father shut the coffin lid forever and hammered it tight with iron pegs. I followed the coffin downstairs and watched the men load it on a wagon. My aunts pushed a trencher of mush at Grandma, brushing down the folds of her old meeting dress and fussing with her hair, but she broke free of them to join the pastor and his family, just arrived. She had no words, just squeezed their hands and let Father lift her into the saddle atop Dolly. It was Mother who did the talking and organizing. She was the one who made the final arrangements.

"Mrs. Reverend an' I shore are sorry ta be here on a 'casion such as this," apologized Dido. She laid a hand on Grandma's and recalled how happy they'd been at their last meeting—the quilting bee.

"Two funerals in as many days," someone mumbled in dismay. "It's an ill omen, it is."

"I won't be goin' to the funeral," I told Mother firmly. All I could think of was escaping. I wanted to run off with Bet and be alone out by my chestnut tree. Mother and Dido traded looks and the Negress motioned the family on. With a flip of the lash, Cousin Alex set the wagon moving and the funeral procession began. Grandma's five sons surrounded the coffin—Alexander, John, Will, Thomas, and Father. I couldn't help thinking that soon there'd be just four. Her daughters were there, too, all except the youngest. Word had come in this morning that Aunt Mary was too close to giving birth to make the trip from Cross Creek. They'd have to wait a few weeks.

"I didn't even know she was expectin'," Grandma'd said, ruing the miles that kept the blessed news from her.

The band of mourners began their trek along Catfish Run, leaving Dido and me behind.

"It's all too sad," I told her. "It's too awfully sad to see Cousin Oliver lowered into a hole in the ground forever."

"Well chile, that depends on how you look at it," reflected Dido. "My mam always said it was a joyous thing to meet yore maker. I'll bet Oliver's smilin' down at us right now from the glory land."

"Do ye think so?"

"I know it in my heart, Janie, an' he might like to see you's there to say good-bye." She led me by the hand and I was powerless to resist. True to her beliefs, she began a joyous song and her angelic voice filled the valley. Nothing came out when I opened my mouth to join her, but Dido held her head high as if she could see the 'glory land' she'd described and the music poured out of her, sweeter than all the honey in Uncle Thomas' hives.

Wondrous Love

Andante, freely

1. What won-drous love is this___
2. To God and to the lamb___
3. When we're from sor- row free___

Oh my soul___ oh my soul? What
I will sing___ I will sing. To
We'll sing on___ We'll sing on. When

won-drous love is this? Oh- my soul.
God and to the lamb I - will sing.
we're from sor- row free We'll sing on.

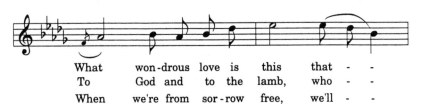

What won-drous love is this that - -
To God and to the lamb, who - -
When we're from sor-row free, we'll - -

guards the   Lord   of bliss?   To___
is   the   great   I   am   And___
rise and   joyous   be.   And___

send such per - fect   peace___   To my soul___   to my
Christ the son of   man___   I will sing___   I will
through e - ter - ni - ty___   We'll sing on___ we'll sing

soul.   To___   send such per - fect peace
sing.   And___   Christ the son of man
on.   And___   through e - ter - ni - ty

to___   my   soul.
I___   will   sing.
we'll   sing   on.

We reached the hill above Boyer's farm and Reverend Clark began to preach. Beside the sandstone slab that marked Grandpa's grave was a deep gaping hole, freshly dug. I didn't hear much of the Reverend's words as I watched the men lower Cousin Oliver's remains into the black earth. Was there any sight more sobering?

"Surely, every man stands as a mere breath ... his days are as an evening shadow." The frail pastor looked poorly, his voice quivering more than usual—probably the result of the double duty he'd seen these last chaotic days.

"After all these years of ministering to my flock, I've noticed the difference faith makes in people's approach to life. There are those who believe in a vengeful God. They are so afraid of passing to a hereafter of hell and brimstone that they never really exist. They have breathed rather than lived. There are many of us who've fashioned a simple life for ourselves—working, watching our children grow, and following Christ's loving example.

Then there are still others—a rare few perhaps, with a questionable talent for finding 'adventure' in life. Such people are seldom seen at meeting and therefore, easily led astray. They seek the risk, the thrill of worldly ways rather than the path of spiritual rebirth which awaits the faithful in heaven. Often they meet their end suddenly—like a bolt of lightening striking against a half-grown tree. Such a man was Oliver Miller. He was cut down in the summer of his life. I am uncertain about the facts surrounding his violent death, just as I am uncertain as to the state of his soul."

I was indignant. How could he question my cousin's fate? This was too much to bear. Cousin Oliver had his own kind of faith. Grandma said he had a keen eye for the beauty of this old earth and a kind hand for helpless critters. Every time he'd wander off beyond these lonely hills, he'd come back full of what he'd learned from his 'adventures.' Some might say he had a flair for excitement—that he did things on a lark right up to the day of his death, but he tasted fully of this life and served God in his own way.

"Talking with Oliver's kin today, I find a single thread running through all their remembrances. They speak of his mirth, his music, and his mischief—though always in a kindly sort of way."

"And so we hold him in prayer before a merciful and compassionate God. Consider Oliver's example well, for we know naught when the last shadow falls. Glean all you can out of each and every day, but remember the Lord's word that, 'even so in Christ shall all be made alive.' For in the time of our living is the making of our death." He shut the Bible tightly and offered a final prayer:

A light from the household is gone.
A voice that we loved is still.
A place is vacant at our hearth
Which time can never fill.

Grandma handed Oliver's fiddle to the preacher's adopted son and prayed silently as he began a hymn. The familiar music touched my heart and soothed away some of the pastor's doubts. It filled the hillside and vibrated in my memory long after the final string had stilled. The kinfolk filed past the grave. Black clods—representing the "dust to dust"—fell from their fingers in hollow, pelting thuds.

Grandma turned white when a mourning dove began to coo. "Death's music," she called it—having heard it at the passing of her parents, her sister, her husband . . . her grandson. A shudder ran through her under Uncle Will's strong grasp. She stretched out a hand toward the bury hole and fell forward into blackness.

XXIII

THE FAREWELL

The songbirds leave us at the summer's close.
Only the empty nests are left behind.
And the piping of the quail among the sheaves.

-"The Harvest Moon,"
Henry Wadsworth Longfellow

The tips of the sumac bushes were singed with scarlet and the maple leaves showed yellow near the veins. A late September frost had brought other hints of autumn as well. The gum trees flecked with red, a string of wild ducks in the sky—everything was changing all around me. At least my chestnut tree looked the same. It would be as stubborn as the old oaks about giving in to nature.

I climbed up to my hidey place. My thoughts wandered with my gaze acrosst the wooded valley bottoms. It didn't feel safe when you loved someone who died. It felt like something basic was missing—a split shingle roof or a warm chimney stone—something you'd always counted on was gone. Pretty soon, Grandma'd be gone, too. It was hard to believe. She hadn't been the same since her collapse at Cousin Oliver's funeral. She'd taken to her bed and didn't seem to know me. All the waiting on her, the reading, the talking, the singing were for naught. When she did look my way, her eyes went through me—lost in some world I couldn't touch. She hadn't spoken a word in more than a month until today. In a few muffled phrases, she'd shaken up the whole family with her notion to move out to Cross Creek and live with Aunt Mary. I felt deserted, betrayed, and ran out to my secret spot—the one sure thing that wouldn't be leaving me.

Before long, I spied Lizzie running down the path toward *Mansfield.* I didn't call out, but soon after, she reappeared with Bet, and darn if that pup didn't give me away.

"Janie, come down," she hollered. "Yer ma tol' me how ye've been mopin' aroun'; now come down afore I drag ye down."

She waited a bit, then started up the tree. I twined my arms and legs firmly around a limb and wouldn't look at her.

"Come on, Janie," she said, easing up on her threat. "I've got somethin' fer ye—somethin' I made meself."

She jumped to the ground and continued her coaxing, but I wouldn't be moved. I couldn't face her. She was leaving me too, just like Grandma and Cousin Oliver.

"Well, if ye won't come down, I'll just leave yer present here by the tree. Don't s'pose ye heerd, but I got a new brother. Pa named 'im Oliver. Ain't that nice? 'The Lord giveth an' the Lord taketh away,' Ma says. I know ye'll like 'im Janie, when ye see 'im."

I doubted that. It hurt too much getting attached to people who were leaving. Besides, no one could replace Cousin Oliver.

I waited till Lizzie was gone, then shinnied down the tree and looked around. Tucked in a curve of the roots was a corncob doll. She was dressed in creamy husk and had red wooly curls. I picked her up and leaned back against the chestnut tree, trying to avoid Bet's slobbering licks.

"Yech!" I protested, wiping my mouth, but the pup was determined to have her happy way. She nudged me under the elbows till I was forced to pat her, then when she'd stolen enough strokes, she circled around three times and flopped down contentedly. Bet made loving look so simple. I curled down beside her and fell asleep thinking how I'd suffered a lifetime in the change of one season. Summer'd swept by in a whirlwind, leaving only empty days ahead.

When I wakened, the woods had that golden look of early evening. Bet also heard the shuffling of leaves and bounded away. I wasn't too pleased to see her return with Father.

"Mind if I sit down?" he asked.

He didn't scold or even look mad and, after all, I did duck out on my chores. We just sat there quiet-like for the longest time. "I found somethin' o' yores," he said at last. "It was lodged 'tween some rocks down in the run." He held out a tiny ear of red corn. It put me mad to see it.

"That ol' Injun said red corn'd bring good luck. Well, I ain't seen any . . . so I throwed it away." My face flushed and my lip trembled.

"I see," replied Father, pondering a bit. " 'Course, I reckon that depends on what kind of good luck yer talking about." He looked down at me seriously. His eyes were full of understanding and he hugged me close.

"I know yer hurtin', Janie. We all are, but one thin's fer certain—ye shore have been good luck to me. I never thought a girl-child could be me right arm, but ye are . . . I'm so proud of the way yer gettin' closer to yer ma. It's made her very happy."

It was true. There'd been a new bond between Mother and me ever since she tried so hard to save Cousin Oliver. She even stuck up for him at the wake.

"Nobody knows better than me how ye've helped out since yer new brother was born. Why, ye took on a growed woman's chores an' it ain't been easy with both yer mother an' Grandma down . . ."

"Grandma won't even talk to me," I cried.

"Don' be too hard on her, girl. In her own way, she's hurtin' jus' like you."

"But she talked to Aunt Mary—even gave her that fig jar and said she wants to leave."

"Slow down now, let's not go callin' a rose a skunk cabbage." He knew I didn't understand.

"I mean, mebbe we've all come ta takin' Grandma fer granted. She's been doin' thin's fer us as long as I can remember. Why, one winter when I's jus' a biddy fellow, we were snowed in fer months. There was nary a ground squirrel or possum ta be had, but somehow or 'nother, yer Grandma finiggled it so's she had enough maple sugar to make me birthday sugar-jack. To this day, I don' know how she did it!"

"She let me an' Sarie go mudwalkin' once, but she's different now."

"That may be, but Grandma's spent her whole life lookin' after us an' she's all wore out. It's time fer us to take care of her an' start givin' back some of what she gave."

I hadn't thought of it that way. Leave it to my father to make sense out of so many mixed up things.

"Guess we never really understand dyin' or growin' old till it takes hold of someone we love. But it's part of life, Janie, an' we've got ta face it, like it or no."

"Face it," I mused, "that's what Grandma told me the d-day Cousin Oliver w-was shot. She said ye got ta seek the Lord's help an' find the strength ta face up to whatever happens in this life."

"Yer Grandma is a very wise ol' woman."

"Jus' like you," I told him in earnest.

"Aho! So I'm an old woman, am I?" He gave a hearty laugh, twisting my meaning. "Hold it right there," he said, noticing the faint glimmer on my lips. "I know Grandma an' Oliver both'd be glad ta see that."

He picked up the corncob doll and gave her a look-see. "Where'd ye get this?"

"Lizzie made 'er."

"I should've known. She looks jus' like Lizzie."

He was right. Funny, I hadn't seen the resemblance myself. The woolen hair was dyed red and the eyes were bits of indigo blue cloth. She even had a pouch like the one Lizzie wore belted around her waist.

"That's a right nice gift," Father admired.

I had to agree, though I felt guilty for not thanking my cousin or even speaking with her.

"Tonight, yer witnessin' a special event," Father declared, changing the subject.

Dusk was now long gone. I only realized it when he pointed out the big old moon that loomed above the trees. It was pleasing to the eye and bright enough to light the forest.

"There's only one night all year long when the moon hangs this close to the earth. It's called the Hunter's Moon."

I was struck with wonder, but it was more than just the moon. It was something Cousin Oliver said once. Now, what was it?

"Uncle Thomas has a work bee out tonight. I's s'posed ta go over an' help 'im harvest by moonlight, but I figger it's jus' as important fer me ta be with me good luck girl."

He made me feel so much better. I picked up the red ear, as well as my doll, and halfway down the trail in the bluish half-light, it came to me. Cousin Oliver said that by the time of the Hunter's Moon, he'd be gone.

Early October, 1794

One morning about a week later, Lizzie made her usual boisterous entry into our log house. But today was different. She looked strange. I hadn't seen her so excited since July Fourth, when Cousin Alex won back her silk ribbon. She wore it now—that and about everything else she owned.

"Lizzie! What all've ye got on?"

"One shawl, one short gown, two pair of drawers, three aprons," she counted, pulling out the layers of clothing at her neckline, "my everyday skirt, my meetin' skirt, an' look . . ." She hiked up her hem. "No bare feet today!"

It was mighty peculiar to see Lizzie's feet covered with anything—much less two pair of wool socks and a set of newly stitched moccasins. She had her shoes knotted at the laces and slung around her neck.

"Pa says we got ta wear ev'rything so's the wagon won't overload." She hesitated, reading my sad expression. "Ye know we're goin' today, Jane?"

I nodded.

"Did ye find yer doll?"

Again, I nodded.

"Well, run quick an' fetch 'er. I've got someone ye got ta meet."

I obeyed and followed her outside half-heartedly. Buck and Bright stood ready in their shiny metal shoes and heavy wooden yoke. Swirls of steam billowed from their nostrils in the chill October air. I could see my own breath, too, and pulled my shawl up around my shoulders.

The oxen were hitched to a wagon piled high with all their worldly belongings—tools, bundles, a rocker chair, the base of Aunt Rachel's spinning wheel, two apple saplings, even a basket full of chickens. Kegs of salt, powder, and whiskey were strapped to the sides and a big rain barrel was hooked to the back. Two heavily packed horses were tied single file behind the wagon. They pawed the ground, eager to be off. Alex, Tommy, and Aunt Rachel brought up the rear, making quite a procession.

"Over here," Lizzie called, shooing me along. "Janie Miller, I'd like ye ta meet yer new cousin, Oliver."

With that, she pulled back the blanket flap and there in Aunt Rachel's arms was the funniest looking young-un I'd ever seen. He wasn't serious at all like my own new brother, James. This Oliver had a fuzzy mat of soft red hair and lively blue eyes like his sister, but there was something curious about those eyes and pouty little mouth.

" 'E's got the Miller mischief in 'im, he does," said Aunt Rachel, taking the very words out of my mouth. Just like his namesake, I thought. I was truly sorry for begrudging this babe his name. Clearly, he deserved it.

"Did ye hear 'bout this 'vote of submission' the gover'ment wants us all to take?" Father asked.

"*You* all ta take," Uncle corrected, but Father rambled on as if he hadn't heard.

"We're s'posed ta sign a promise sayin' we'll obey the laws of the U.S. an' support the excise tax. Well, I don' like it. If I sign my name to that, it's like admittin' guilt ta somethin' I had no part in."

"You know that an' I know that, but are ye so shore ye can convince the federal troops when they arrive? Protect yerself an' sign, James. Ye know ye'll have to admit ye went to Couch's Fort an' Braddock's Field."

"But those weren't violent meetin's," Father pointed out. "An' thanks to men like Brackenridge an' Gallatin, the march on Pittsburgh from Braddock's Field was peaceful."

"That may be, but you're the one who's left to face the questions—you an' other men like yerself. The leaders in this mess are gone. Last I heerd, Neville an' Davey Bradford both fled downriver—the scoundrels! An' look at me, Jamie. I voted for peace months ago when my militia took a tally, but I could never acknowledge that an' go home safely. I've had to deny it ev'ry day since an' do whatever my company insisted upon. But soon, I'll be clear of it, too. So sign, Jamie; don' open yerself up fer any trouble. Ye've no idee a what ye'll be accused—an' my name shore ain't goin' ta help ye none."

'Political converse' didn't interest me anymore. I had no ear for grown-up talk—not since Cousin Oliver. . . . Bet and Lizzie and I stole away to the barn.

"Thanks fer the doll, Lizzie. She's the most beautiful one I ever seed—even better than those fancy dolls with china faces that Grandma tol' me 'bout. B-but I jus' wish there's some way that I could be with ye in Kentuck . . ."

"There is," Lizzie claimed. "I figgered it all out."

My heart strings were tugging as she dug into her pouch and drew out another corncob doll. It was dressed like mine, but had dark braided hair, blue cloth eyes, and a tiny whittled bucket on one arm.

"That's me!" I cried, delighted with the likeness.

"Shore is," she proudly confirmed. "I've been thinkin' 'bout today for a long time, Jane, an' I wanted to fix thin's between us. I thought if you kep' a doll like me an' I took a doll like you, it'd be like we's together, even though we ain't. Do ye see what I mean?"

"It's a wonderful idee, Lizzie, thank ye." The tears slipped down my cheeks, but I managed a smile.

"Don' let Alex see that, ye know what a tease he is 'bout girls bein' crybabies."

She dabbed at my eyes with one of her aprons. I tried very hard to be brave. "Oh," I remembered, "These are fer you."

I handed her a poke of chestnuts that I'd picked out at my hidey spot tree. We flung our arms about each other and hugged our look-alike dolls, then set off as a twosome, content to have one last secret to share.

Just then, Mother appeared from the house, leading Grandma. Ever so slowly they crossed the yard to the waiting wagon.

"Will saved ye a right cozy spot, Mother Miller," Aunt Rachel assured her.

She spoke as if to a child. I'd heard how older people sometimes had a second childhood, but I had trouble accepting it in my own Grandma, especially when she'd always been so active. Grandma clutched Father's hand and Mother's too, then she had a hug for each of us children. Her small black Bible never left her hand through the whole round of embraces. When it came my turn, she looked at me with recognition and there was a bit of the old flutter in her eyebrows.

"It'll be all right. It'll be all right," she whispered.

I only wished she'd keep her arms about me so I'd know it was so, but it had to end. Uncle Will lifted Grandma up into the wagon and pushed her few possessions under the seat.

"I shore am grateful to ye fer takin' Mother out ta Cross Creek."

"We're glad ta have 'er with us, Jamie. 'Sides, this way we'll get a chance to visit the kinfolk there an' we'll avoid Pittsburgh altogether."

They talked on and on about water levels and picking up the Ohio River further west, and such. Neither man was usually so talkative, but today they both sensed the seriousness of the occasion and grasped at any bit of conversation as if to put off the leaving.

"I've wrapped up yer fig jar, Mother Miller. This way it'll arrive safe an' sound for Mary, down in Cross Creek. You be shore ta say hello to my side of the family out there an' . . . oh! I almost fergot—yer Tidball tea set."

Grandma clutched her Bible and her heirloom. The tea set was the only thing she had left from her Grandfather Brownhill, the king's surgeon, but she pushed it back towards Mother. "You keep it, dear," she said, absently.

She was off in her dreamworld again, staring at the log house and watching Lady Tidball preening her feathers by the run.

"What's this?" Uncle Will asked, as Father handed him one last bundle.

"It's Oliver's fiddle. Ma didn't see fit to bury it with 'im— guess she's just to practical for that. So, you an' Sonny being kindred spirits an' all—we want you to have it."

"But, I ain't got Sonny's ear for music." He looked doubtful.

"That's all right. I've got a hunch yer newest boy may have a knack fer it."

Uncle Will was at a loss for words. As Aunt Rachel packed the instrument in with her farewell quilt, he checked over the wagon one more time, and the final moment came.

"I'll try an' send word when we get downriver ta Louisville," Uncle Will promised. "I know the family here at *Mansfield's* in good hands an' ye'll do the right thing when the time comes." He lashed his whip beside Bright's ear and the creakety wagon began to roll.

"Good-bye!"

"Good-bye!"

"Remember me, Jane, when you look at yer doll 'cause I'll be thinkin' of ye."

"Watch out fer Injuns an' don' let Alex boss ye."

"Don' worry, I can whup 'em all," she boasted. "I'll be back one day. Good-bye, Janie!"

Her hand slipped out of mine. She put the dark-haired doll in her pouch, picked up the wheel to Aunt Rachel's spinner, and followed her family down the lane.

I stood there desolately until the wagon disappeared. The tears ran freely, for I no longer cared what Cousin Alex might think. I knew in my heart that I'd never see Lizzie again. That was the truth—the plain truth, as Reverend Clark would say.

When I turned around, Sarie was waiting for me. She sensed my hurt and brought out her husk doll that Grandma made last spring. From the woebegone look on her face, I knew what she was afraid to ask. I couldn't decide whether Sarie looked older to me or whether playing dolls just didn't seem so babyish today.

"Don' cry, Janie."

She held out her pudgy hand and together we found a quiet spot. We played by the waters of Catfish Run and, somewhere off in the big butts, a mourning dove cooed. The doleful sound suited me fine, for my loss was great. "Cling to the little things," Grandma used to say. A song, a doll, a black and white dog, a red ear of corn, a loving sister, nurturing parents—these things were left me.

And now, like the soft brown ink in my father's Bible, the bitterness I felt in that October of 1794 has faded. I look back kindly on my girlhood in the Pennsylvenny backwoods. Most of the people who lived in the log house are gone now. They wed or died or moved away, but many an evening by the fire their memories haunt me like the ghost of Tom the Tinker.

The jingle of a bell, the honk of a nasty goose, a copper-bottomed still, the face of an old doll, or a line from the Good Book—everyone knows Aunt Jane can work up a tale over any little thing.

POSTLOGUE

To Our Readers,

The character, Janie, was a real live person. We think of her as a curious young girl in the days of Tom the Tinker, but as life would have it, the child grew up. She witnessed several generations of events around her family home on Catfish Run and recorded them in her diary. Through her efforts and the memories of Miller kin alive today, true family stories such as the hanging of Great Grandfather Brownhill and the romance of Elizabeth and Thomas Tidball have been told right up to today.

James Miller's Bible, the whiskey still, the old stone house—these are things still in existence. In fact, Grandma didn't know it, but when she gave her youngest daughter her prized fig jar, she started a family tradition. The jar is still in the family and passed from mother to youngest daughter.

The other characters were also real: Dido, Indian Peter, John Holcroft (the Tinker), James and Mary Miller—all were alive during the summer of the Whiskey Rebellion. Many characters were easy to write about because so much was known about them from existing wills, ledgers, and old documents, etc. If the data was sketchy about an individual, the authors tried to depict the character as true to the times as possible.

We thought you might enjoy knowing more about what happened to these people after the turbulent summer of '94.

HUGH HENRY BRACKENRIDGE—Mr. Brackenridge was educated at the College of New Jersey, under Dr. John Witherspoon. He was a licensed preacher and became a chaplain during the Revolutionary War. At the end of the war, he studied law and opened a practice in Pittsburgh in 1781. One of the city's most prominent early citizens, he was accomplished as a classical scholar, an able lawyer, and a man of keen wit and great eccentricity.

Brackenridge was instrumental in chartering the Pittsburgh Academy and in planning the formation of Allegheny County in 1788. Drawn into the events of the Whiskey Rebellion at the request of Neville's son, Colonel Presley Neville, Brackenridge attended a meeting following the attack on Bower Hill. He played the role of negotiator and peacemaker between the angry farmers and the government.

He successfully persuaded the militiamen gathered at Braddock's Field to march peacefully through Pittsburgh as a show of strength and order. He also suggested that the people of Pittsburgh should offer them food and drink; thence the burning and destruction of the town was avoided.

For many years Brackenridge was head of the bar in Western Pennsylvania. Later, he became a justice on the Supreme Court of Pennsylvania. He wrote a book, MODERN CHIVALRY, and many poems.

WILLIAM MILLER—Hugh Henry Brackenridge provided considerable insight into the position of William Miller and his family during the Whiskey Rebellion. On August 28, 1794, both men attended a meeting in Frederickstown to discuss the recent violence at Bower Hill. Returning home, Brackenridge encountered Miller and later recorded their meeting in his book, INCIDENTS OF THE INSURRECTION IN THE WESTERN PARTS OF PENNSYLVANIA IN THE YEAR 1794.

Brackenridge describes the dilemma of William Miller as follows:

> In our company that night . . . was one of the name (William) Miller. When he first joined us I was suspicious of him knowing he had been a principle in the two attacks upon the house of the inspector and commanding a company upon Peter's Creek in a settlement through which we had to pass. I did not know but he might have been dispatched with orders to arrest me as I went through. I communicated this to some of the other members in the company and we took care to ride fast enough not to put it in his power to be much ahead of us. He lodged with us where we halted a few hours and slept on the planks at the house of a German.
>
> In the morning when we set out, which was early, on our way, I kept close by him and fell into conversation. He had been in the American service during the war with Great Britain, had been employed chiefly in the western country in the war with the Indians . . . had distinguished himself for fidelity, acclivity, and bravery on every occasion. I led him to talk of his services and he gave the history of a variety of incidents.

Brackenridge then asked William about the day Neville accompanied the sheriff to his farm, Milville.

"The federal sheriff," said Miller, "was reading the writ and General Neville was on horseback in the lane . . . when he called to the sheriff to make haste. I looked up and saw a party of men running across the field as it were to head off the sheriff. He set off with General Neville and when they got to the head of the lane, the farmers fired upon them."

"Do you think," asked Brackenridge, "they fired with balls and meant to hit them?"

> I believe they meant to hit them, they pursued them and would have killed them." Miller continued, "That night at Mingo it was concluded that we would go on to Neville's and take him and the marshal. I felt myself mad with passion. I thought . . . $250 fine would ruin me and to have to go to federal court in Philadelphia would keep me from going to Kentucky this fall after I had sold my plantation and was getting ready. I felt my blood boil at seeing Neville along to pilot the Sheriff to my very door. He (Neville) had been against the excise as much as anybody. When old Graham the excise man was catched and had his hair cut off, I heard General Neville say they ought to have cut the ears off the old rascal and when the distillers were sued some years ago for fines, he talked as much as anybody against it. But he wanted to keep in the assembly then.
>
> But when he got an office himself (Inspector of the Fourth Survey) he took it. I was always for Neville in his elections—and it put me mad to see him coming to ruin me.

During the same meeting, Brackenridge also records William's remarks about the first attack on Neville's home:

> There were about thirty men—with fifteen guns—six only in order. They found the general just got up. After some words he fired first. It was from

the windows. A horn was blowing in the house at the time of the firing. The door was open, but we did not rush in for fear of a swivel or big gun there.

The Negroes fired out of their cabins upon our backs and shot several and we got off as well as we could.

"Well what now?" asked Brackenridge, "are you for war?"

"No," replied William, "I voted for peace, but if I was to acknowledge that I need never go home. I will have to deny it and I will have to do whatever my company insists upon me doing now. But I expect to get away soon and be clear of it."

"As we came up to the house," recalls Brackenridge, "three pretty children presented themselves on the outside of the fence that enclosed the cabin and one of them said putting his fingers between the rails, 'Daddy, I have got a little brother.' (The woman had been brought to bed in his absence.) I was sensibly affected with the reflection that possibly that daddy might come to be hanged and that brother fatherless before it could be known that he ever had one."

On October 10, 1794, William Miller sold the last section of his land, over 76 acres, to Thomas Kiddoo. Before the arrival of federal troops in the fall, William carried out his plan to take Rachel, Lizzie, and her brothers down the Ohio River.

According to the Barton research, TRACKING WILLIAM MILLER, Lizzie and her family traveled by flatboat down the Ohio River to Limestone (now Mayville), Kentucky, then overland some 15 miles to settle on Fleming Creek.

The trip from Pittsburgh to Limestone took about two weeks. Travelers at the time were on the look-out for Indians. Indians were known to force white captives to appear on the riverbank and call for help to passing flatboaters. The successful campaign against the Indians by Anthony Wayne, culminating in the August 1794 Battle of Fallen Timbers, put an end to most of these Indian attacks on voyagers. Undoubtedly, William Miller and his family were cautious.

Records of the Fleming County Census and the 1828 Revolutionary War Pension Application find William Miller owning over 500 acres of land, much of which he sold for a nominal fee to his eleven children. For example, Lizzie married Thomas Hulse and in 1827 they purchased 60 acres of land from her parents.

The early 1800s marked a time of great spiritual revival across the frontier state of Kentucky. There were "camp meeting" services and dramatic increases in church membership. The Millers, staunch Presbyterians, eventually became members of the new Christian Church.

By September, 1833 various couples comprising the Miller family sold their land in Fleming County and moved to Indiana. The move was most likely caused by a severe cholera epidemic that swept through Kentucky in June and July of 1833. Flemingsburg— just seven miles from the Millers' farms—was very hard hit. One out of ten residents were killed by the disease.

The Millers relocated to Traders Point, Marion County (13 miles NW of Indianapolis). According to his 1835 pension application, William and Rachel moved to Marion County, Indiana, "because his children had moved" to that state. William and Rachel spent their final years in Indiana.

JAMES MILLER - James was the youngest son of Oliver Miller, Sr. He succeeded his father to the plantation and also held the office of Justice of the Peace. After territorial disputes between Virginia and Pennsylvania were settled, James Miller took out a warrant for their tract on September 26, 1786. A patent was granted him for 424 acres, 39 perches on March 23, 1797 under the name of Mansfield. He continued to operate the farm and the family still.

James was one of the last men in the area to submit to paying the excise on whiskey and to register his still. After the unrest during the summer of 1794, many farmers were required to sign an oath of allegiance in order to regain their citizenship. Miller signed his oath on November 15, 1794. A copy of this rare document of the Whiskey Rebellion is on display at the Oliver Miller Homestead in South Park, Pennsylvania.

An account book dated 1815 shows that James continued to operate his still and sell whiskey, but he was widening his sales to include meat, hay, oak planks, etc.

One of the few Millers to live through all phases of the house at Mansfield, James added a stone section to the wooden structure in 1808. By 1830 the house was entirely of stone. He died on March 4, 1844, at the age of eighty-one and was buried in Bethel Cemetery. Dr. George Marshall, the pastor at that time, records that, "He was long an honest, sincere, and upright member of Bethel Church."

JANE MILLER - Janie carried out her idea of writing down her grandmother's stories. She was well known for her diary and long remembered as the family "storyteller."

She married a widower, John Work, who had a daughter by his first wife. In 1837, they moved to the Lebanon Church area (presently part of West Mifflin near the Allegheny County Airport). Janie lived to be ninety-four years old. She and her husband are buried at Bethel Church Cemetery.

MARY TIDBALL MILLER - There are differing accounts of Grandma's final years. Surviving Miller relatives state that she was buried beside her husband, Oliver, on a neighbor's farm which was the original burial place designated by Bethel Church (presently on a hillside near the entrance to South Park).

It is possible that she lived out her later years with her daughter, Mary Miller Wallace, in Cross Creek. Records at the Cross Creek Cemetery indicate that she was buried in 1813 at an advanced age. Grandma began a family tradition when she gave her fig jar to her youngest daughter, Mary Miller Wallace. The earthenware crock that had been her wedding gift from relatives in County Antrim, Ireland, is still passed through the youngest daughter of each generation. Mary Wallace gave it to her youngest daughter, Rebecca Wallace Barton, who gave it to her daughter, Florence Barton McCortle.

OLIVER MILLER III—Janie's brother, Ollie, eventually inherited the homestead at Mansfield. He lived there many years with his wife, Mary Wilson Miller. He died in 1864 and Mary continued to live at the homestead until her death in 1898 at the age of ninety-five.

REVEREND JOHN CLARK—was born in 1718 in New Jersey. He graduated from Princeton and served churches in New Jersey, Maryland, and Pennsylvania. Clark first visited Western Pennsylvania in 1781 and in the following year, he moved from Maryland to a tract of land which he called "Plain Truth" (now a part of Coverdale and where Bethel Park Senior High School stands). With him were his wife, Margaret, his adopted son, William Jones, and two black slaves, Dido and Dave. Reverend Clark was sixty-five when he became the first pastor of Bethel and Lebanon Presbyterian Churches. He was described as wearing eighteenth-century small clothes with buckles and a stock. He was the only minister in the region to wear a white wig, or peruke, which he tied in a queue.

When five hundred men gathered at Fort Couch on the morning of July 17, 1794, to organize an attack on Gen. John Neville's estate at Bower Hill, the seventy-six year old pastor came down from Bethel Meetinghouse and tried to reason with them—many of the farmers were members of his own congregation. They intended to demand Neville's resignation as tax collector of the area. Clark told them he understood their anger over the unfair tax, but counseled that the use of force would only bring in federal troops and more trouble. The men marched on Bower Hill, however, and as predicted, a battle resulted that left the leader of the farmers, Maj. James McFarlane, killed. The angry insurgents then burned the home and farm buildings of Gen. John Neville.

Reverend Clark's will provided that upon the death of his wife, Margaret; his plantation "Plain Truth" would be sold to Jefferson College to provide funds for poor and pious young men to study for the ministry. He also specified that Dido be set free. He died in 1797 at the age of seventy-nine and is buried in Bethel Cemetery. His epitaph reads:

> In yonder church I spent my breath
> And now lie slumbering here in death
> These lips shall rise and then declare
> Amen to truths they published there.

DIDO—Dido and Dave were black slaves brought with the Clarks from Maryland in 1781. Dido is mentioned in the "Western Missionary Magazine" of 1803 as a pious colored woman with uncommon vocal powers whose voice could be heard above the combined voices of the congregation during the revival of 1787. Upon the death of Margaret Clark (1808), Dido was freed as the will of Reverend Clark specified:

> It is also my will that my Molata slave Dido be set free, and that she receive one feather bed, one coverlet, one quilt, two blankets, one pair of sheets and pillow cases, one shift, a spinning wheel and pot, three volumes of Davis's Sermons, Doddridge's RISE AND PROGRESS OF RELIGION IN THE SOUL, ten pewter plates, three pewter basons and a small soup dish, eight spoons, one milk cow and one ewe.

She lived her later years in the area of Chartiers Valley. The records of Reverend John McMillan show that she made her living by quilting and making feather ticks.

The historical collections of Washington and Jefferson College indicate that a "Mr. John Holmes presented a claim against the education fund of this college for the support of Dido Munts." Since Reverend Clark had bequeathed a major portion of his estate to Jefferson College, in 1838, the college committee reached an agreement with Mr. Holmes to give Dido one year's support for $110.00. In the following year there is a motion "to remove Dido Munts to the poorhouse" where it is believed she died soonafter.

The male slave, Dave, was mentioned on an inventory when Reverend Clark died, but no other information about him has been found.

DAVID BRADFORD—Born in Maryland in 1760, David Bradford emigrated to Washington, Pa. and became an attorney in 1782. Later he was appointed deputy-general for Washington County and in 1792, he was elected to the state legislature.

A prime figure in the Whiskey Rebellion, Bradford is described as boisterous, rash, and impulsive. And yet, he possessed a kind of eloquence well-suited to influencing angry farmers. He retained the good will of the people of Washington, though later he was considered lacking in stability and judgment. He used drastic means to oppose the whiskey tax, such as aiding in a plot to seize mail sent between Pittsburgh and Philadelphia. The stolen mail contained references to persons and events dealing with the burning of Bower Hill.

In THE WHISKEY REBELS, Leland Baldwin states, "the man must have gone mad with delusions of grandeur . . . he had visions of himself as the Washington of the West, laying the foundation of a new nation." Bradford resolved that by involving the entire western country in the opposition, he could discourage extreme federal punishment. Thus he ordered a call for a militia muster of the Fourth Survey on August 1, 1794. Between five thousand and eight thousand men arrived at Braddock's Field. Bradford assumed the office of major-general and dressed in full martial uniform. Riding a splendid horse, he issued orders to the militia groups as they arrived. Plans to march on Pittsburgh (then a small log cabin settlement of 376 people) faded overnight, due in part to the calm reasoning of Hugh Henry Brackenridge, a Pittsburgh attorney."

After the Braddock's Field assembly, President Washington ordered fifteen thousand troops into the area. Bradford fled his fine home in Washington, Pa. a few days before the federal troops arrived in November. He traveled by flatboat into Spanish territory where he obtained a Spanish land grant near Natchez. Pardoned in 1799, he returned to Pennsylvania only once in 1801 to dispose of his property.

JOHN HOLCROFT—came to Western Pennsylvania from Fairfield County, Connecticut prior to 1786. He lived East of Gastonville in a log house that stood near the present stone dwelling along Finleyville and Elrama Roads. Married twice, he had ten children by each wife.

A leader of the Mingo Militia, Holcroft was one of the chief characters in the Whiskey Rebellion. Using the name of "Tom the Tinker," he and some of his followers posted warnings on trees, fences, or barns of farmers who were ready to pay the federal tax on whiskey. They were warned to desist from paying this tax or else their still and buildings would be "tinkered with." In several cases, such as William Cochran and James Kiddoo, these threats were carried out.

Holcroft was the leader of the first group of farmers who went to Bower Hill. The visit resulted in the wounding and eventual death of James and William Miller's nephew, Oliver Miller. John Holcroft also participated in the attack on Bower Hill two days later with the large group of farmers who burned the estate to the ground.

When the federal troops came to Western Pennsylvania in the fall of 1794, Holcroft had fled the area. He returned to his home in January 1795, after the trouble had quieted down. He died in 1818 and is buried in Mingo Cemetery.

GENERAL JOHN NEVILLE—was an aristocratic Virginian born in 1731, the son of George Neville, who had been kidnapped from England as a lad, and Ann Burroughs, a cousin of Lord Fairfax. He first entered Western Pennsylvania as a soldier in Braddock's expedition during Lord Dunbar's War and moved into Chartiers Valley seven miles from Pittsburgh in 1775. That same year, he occupied Fort Pitt along with one hundred Virginian militiamen and commanded there until 1777. Later he was taken prisoner at Charleston, but was exchanged in time to be present at the siege of Yorktown. By the end of the Revolutionary War he had obtained the rank of brigadier general.

Upon his return home, Neville was elected to the Constitutional Convention and voted for acceptance of the constitution. He amassed a considerable fortune having held or sold close to ten thousand acres of land. Bower Hill, his home overlooking Chartiers Creek, was one of the finest plantations in the western country.

He was chosen a member of the supreme executive council of Pennsylvania and was elected to the state legislature where he voted against the proposed whiskey tax. When Neville became the inspector of revenue in 1794, his neighbors noticed a change in his views on the excise tax. He opened a tax office in his home and at other locations throughout the region.

On July 15, 1794, when he accompanied the U.S. marshal to the farm of William Miller to serve a tax delinquency summons, real trouble began. Miller, angered by the fact that that he had supported Neville in his elections, refused to receive the summons and the officials were chased off the premises by a group of field workers.

The incident prompted John Holcroft to lead forty other farmers to Bower Hill. The men had come for various reasons, but all were united in their anger against Neville. The tax inspector ordered them to "stand off". He had armed his slaves and commanded them to fire. This resulted in a shot that struck Oliver Miller. Several other farmers were also wounded.

The bloodshed aroused farmers from several counties to meet at Fort Couch on July 17. They marched on to Bower Hill which Neville had fortified with a unit of soldiers from Pittsburgh. The farmers demanded Neville's resignation, but his son-in-law, Major Kirkpatrick informed them that he was not at home. (Baldwin states that Neville concealed himself in a nearby thicket and probably watched the entire conflict. Historian Noah Thompson records that Neville left that day with the women and children, disguised as a woman himself.)

The farmers then demanded that a committee be allowed to enter the house and search for Neville's official papers. When this was denied, the fighting began that led to the death of the farmer's leader, Major James McFarlane. The insurgents were enraged and set fire to the outer buildings. Soon the main house caught fire and all that was left was the smokehouse.

A few days later, Neville and the U.S. marshal, David Lenox, set off down river on a boat manned with soldiers. In Wheeling, the soldiers returned to Pittsburgh and the two men went on to Marietta alone. There they acquired two guides who led them East by way of Clarksburg, Virginia. They reached Philadelphia on August 8.

Neville returned to Western Pennsylvania when events had calmed down. He died on Montour's Island in 1803. There were a number of accounts written for and against Neville's role in the Whiskey Rebellion. One of his strongest literary defenders was his relative Neville B. Craig who wrote THE HISTORY OF PITTSBURGH. Other historical writers such as James Carnahan and Judge Lobingier were more sympathetic with the plight of the farmers.

MAJOR JAMES MCFARLANE—According to Noah Thompson, James McFarlane was "one of the most popular men in the community (Washington County)." He and his brother Andrew had served in the war under General Washington and were among the first early settlers of the area.

As the ranking officer, McFarlane was chosen to lead the group of five hundred farmers to the home of the tax collector, General John Neville, on Bower Hill. He accepted reluctantly, hoping to use his influence to keep the men under control and avoid unnecessary bloodshed. Fighting broke out after Neville refused to resign his commission. Under a flag of truce there was a lull in the firing. McFarlane stepped from behind a tree and was shot. His death enraged the farmers who burned the barn and other buildings. The insurgents carried the body of their beloved leader back to the McFarlane home in Elrama on the Monongahela River. He was buried at Mingo Creek Cemetery by the old Mingo

Meetinghouse. The funeral assemblage was very large and the service was conducted by Reverend John Clark. His epitaph reads:

> Here lies the body of Major James McFarlane of Washington County, Pennsylvania, who departed this life the 17th of July, 1794, aged 43 years. He served during the war with undaunted courage—in defense of American Independence, against the lawless and despotic encroachments of Great Britain. He fell at last by the hands of an unprincipled villain, in the support of what he supposed to be the rights of his country, much lamented by a numerous and respected circle of acquaintances.

RESULTS OF THE WHISKEY REBELLION

President George Washington proclaimed February 19, 1795, a special day of thanksgiving for "the seasonable controul which has been given to a spirit of disorder in the suppression of the late insurrection." The story of the Whiskey Rebellion came to an end. After the exciting events of 1794, life for Jane Miller, her family and friends moved along on a more even keel.

Over the next few years, the Federalist administration succeeded in subduing the Indians. Mad Anthony Wayne defeated the Indians at the Battle of Fallen Timbers in Ohio Territory and Britain signed the Jay Treaty, agreeing to give up its Northwest posts to the United States. Gradually, the frontier people were convinced that the government was strong enough to protect them. And at last, when Spain agreed to open navigation and trade on the Mississippi River, the settlers were no longer totally dependent on Eastern trade.

By 1800, the power of Hamilton, Adams, and the Federalist Party gave way in the election of Thomas Jefferson, a Democratic-Republican. The change in administration resulted in the repeal of the hated excise tax.

Money, the medium of exchange in the East (and a rarity in the West), was gradually brought into the area by those same soldiers who had been sent to quell the uprising. Government outlays of cash for military supplies and payroll came into the local people's hand as well.

The soldiers who originally came to Western Pennsylvania at Washington's order, later began to advertise the potential of the area. Many of them returned with their families and bought farmland. Immigrants of all kinds came to find jobs in boat building, glass making, and other industries. The opening of the rivers attracted travelers to Pittsburgh, the Western economy was stimulated, and the town established itself as the "Gateway to the West".

Farmers who had depended heavily on rye whiskey as a cash crop, now found a ready market for many farm products. Hay and straw became the principle money crop of farmers for miles around Pittsburgh. It was used in public and private stables, in packaging glass at the new factories, and by numerous businesses that delivered wares by horse.

The bitterly divided opinions of the settlers during the rebellion affected the churches as well. A period of decline was followed by a great awakening and religious revival which spread rapidly throughout the country in the early eighteen hundreds. A realization of the evils of alcohol lead to the rise of the temperance movement which caused many churches, including Bethel, to take a stand against intoxicating liquor. So eventually the old Miller still ceased its whiskey making and served the remainder of its years as a rain barrel at the side of the old stone house.

EXISTING HISTORICAL ITEMS

Will of Oliver Miller, Sr., February 3, 1782, probated March 12, 1782
Ledger of Oliver Miller, Sr. 1750-1754
Inventory of Oliver Miller, Sr.'s Belongings, 1782
Oliver Miller Sr. Land Title, July 1, 1775
Oath of Allegiance signed by James Miller, November 8, 1794
James Miller Account Book, 1815
Miller Family Bible
Fig Jar of Mary Tidball Miller
Miller Family Whiskey Still
Military Service Pension Applications of William Miller

HISTORICAL SITES TO VISIT

Oliver Miller Homestead—old stone house on site of Oliver Miller's original log house in Allegheny County's South Park, Pa.

Presley Neville House—home of John Neville's son

David Bradford House—home of the Washington County leader of the Whiskey Rebellion, Washington, Pa.

Log House—Upper St. Clair, Pa.

Bethel Presbyterian Church Historical Room—artifacts, pictures, documents, and records dating back to the mid 1700s.

Bethel Church Cemetery—gravesites of Revolutionary War soldiers, early settlers such as James Miller, the Fifes, Gilfillans, etc. (brochure available)

Mingo Presbyterian Church and Cemetery—gravesites of Major James McFarlane, John Holcroft, the David Hamilton family

HISTORICAL LOCATIONS TO OBSERVE

Mingo Falls—remnants of rock ledge where a young boy hid during the federal soldiers' roundup of whiskey rebels in November, 1794 (along Pa. route 88, just below Mingo Church on left side)

Gilfillan Farm Trail—opposite South Hills Village Shopping Center, Pa. route 19, Upper St. Clair, Pa.

SUGGESTED READING

Allen, Hervey: (trilogy) TOWARD THE MORNING, BEDFORD VILLAGE, THE FOREST AND THE FORT, Farrar and Rinehart, Inc., New York, 1948.

Baldwin, Leland: THE DELECTABLE COUNTRY, Lee Furman, New York, 1939.

Grey, Zane: THE SPIRIT OF THE BORDER, Al Burt Co. (Pocket Edition) 1942.

McCook, H.C.: THE LATIMERS, A Tale of the Western Insurrection, George W. Jacobs and Co., Philadelphia, 1898.

Russell, Andrew Lyle: THE FREIGHTER, Roxburgh Publishing Co., Boston, 1915.

Smith, Helene: THE GREAT WHISKEY REBELLION, REBELS WITH A CAUSE, MacDonald/Sward Publishing Co., Greensburg, Pa., 1994.

Turnbull, Agnes Sligh: THE DAY MUST DAWN, THE ROLLING YEARS, The McMillan Co., New York, 1942.

Wiley, Richard T.: SIM GREENE AND TOM THE TINKER' MEN, Gibson Press, Pittsburgh, 1943.

Day, Reed B.:THE WHISKEY INSURRECTION, Closson Press, Apollo, Pa., 1992.

CHILDREN'S NOVELS ON WESTERN PENNSYLVANIA HISTORY

Fritz, Jean: THE CABIN FACES WEST, Coward McCann, 1958.

Fritz, Jean: BRADY, Coward McCann, 1970

Smith, Helen and Swetnam, George: HANNA'S TOWN, 1973.

Eckert, Allen W.: BLUE JACKET, 1967.

BIBLIOGRAPHY

Baldwin, Leland: THE DELECTABLE COUNTRY, Lee Furman, New York, 1939.

Baldwin, Leland: PITTSBURGH, THE STORY OF A CITY, Pittsburgh, 1937.

Baldwin, Leland: WHISKEY REBELS, Pittsburgh, 1939.

Barton, Ann and William: TRACKING WILLIAM MILLER, presentation to the Oliver Miller Homestead Associates in Bethel Park, Pa., March 10, 1991.

Bennett, Daniel: LIFE AND WORK OF REV. JOHN McMILLAN, D.D., Daniel Bennett, Bridgeville, Pa., 1935.

Boyd, Crimrine: A HISTORY OF WASHINGTON COUNTY, PENN-SYLVANIA, WITH HISTORICAL SKETCHES OF MANY OF ITS PIONEERS AND PROMINENT MEN, Philadelphia, 1882.

Brackenridge, H.H.: HISTORY OF THE WESTERN INSURRECTION IN WESTERN PENNSYLVANIA, W.S. Haven, Pittsburgh, 1859.

Buck, Solon J. and Elizabeth A.: THE PLANTING OF CIVILIZATION IN WESTERN PENNSYLVANIA, University of Pittsburgh Press, 1939.

Connor, Anna T.: CORNCRAFT, A.S. Barnes, SanDiego, 1980.

Corbett, Doris S. and Wright, J.E.: PIONEER LIFE, University of Pittsburgh Press, 1968.

Dahlinger, Charles W.: PITTSBURGH, A SKETCH OF ITS EARLY SOCIAL LIFE, B.P. Putnam and Sons, New York and London, The Knickerbocker Press, 1916.

Degelman, William C.: HISTORICAL NARRATIVE OF BETHEL PRESBYTERIAN CHURCH 1776-1936, 1936.

Dinsmore, John Walker: THE SCOTCH-IRISH IN AMERICA, Chicago, 1906.

Doddridge, Joseph: NOTES ON THE SETTLEMENT AND INDIAN WARS, republished by John H. Ritenour and William T. Lindsey, Pittsburgh, 1912.

Eagleson, Hodge McIlvain: RIGHT HERE IN SQUIRREL HILL, The Jackson Church Press, 1953.

Earle: STAGECOACH AND TAVERN DAYS, McMillan, New York, 1938.

Fletcher, Stevenson Whitcome: PENNSYLVANIA AGRICULTURE AND COUNTRY LIFE, 1640-1840, Pennsylvania Historical and Museum Commission, Commonwealth of Pennsylvania, 1950-1971.

Forrest, Earle R.: HISTORY OF WASHINGTON COUNTY, S.J. Clarke Publishing Company, Chicago, 1926.

Guthrie, D.W.: JOHN McMILLAN THE APOSTLE OF PRESBYTERIANISM IN THE WEST, University of Pittsburgh Press, 1952.

Hanna, Charles: SCOTCH IRISH IN AMERICA, G.P. Putnam, New York and London, The Knickerbocker Press, 1902.

HISTORY OF ALLEGHENY COUNTY, L.H. Everts, 1876.

HISTORY OF THE PRESBYTERY OF WASHINGTON, James B. Rodgers Printing Co., Philadelphia, 1889.

MacArtney, Clarence E.: NOT FAR FROM PITTSBURGH, 1936.

MacArtney. Clarence E.: RIGHT HERE IN PITTSBURGH, 1937.

MacArtney, Clarence E.: WHERE THE RIVERS MEET, 1946.

Lathrop: EARLY AMERICAN INNS AND TAVERNS, Tudor Publishing Co.

Lorant, Stephan: PITTSBURGH, THE STORY OF AN AMERICAN CITY, Doubleday & Co., Inc., Garden City, New York, 1964.

Love, Gilbert: GO-GUIDE, The Pittsburgh Press, 1976.

Preston, Walter W.: HISTORY OF HARFORD COUNTY MARYLAND, 1608 to the War of 1812, Press of Sun Book Office, Baltimore, 1901.

Sloane, Eric: BOOK OF EARLY AMERICANA, Doubleday.

Sloane, Eric: A MUSEUM OF EARLY AMERICAN TOOLS, Ballantine, New York, 1964.

Sloane, Eric: OUR VANISHING LANDSCAPE, W. Funk, New York, 1955.

Smith, Joseph: OLD REDSTONE, Lippincott, Grambo & Co., Philadelphia, 1854.

Taylor, J.P.: CONDENSED HISTORY OF THE WHISKEY INSUR-RECTION, Historical Magazine of Monongahela's Old Homecoming Week, 1908.

Tunis, Edwin: COLONIAL CRAFTSMEN, World Publishing Co., 1957.

Van Voorhis: THE OLD AND NEW MONONGAHELA, Pittsburgh, 1893.

White, Alvin D.: THE HISTORY OF CROSSCREEK PRESBYTERIAN CHURCH, McClain Printing Co., 1969.

Wolfe, Preston: HISTORY OF THE WOLFE FAMILY AND ALLIED BRANCHES, 1939.